The Zeal of the Convert

Also by Burke Wilkinson

NOVELS

The Adventures of Geoffrey Mildmay
  Proceed at Will
  Run, Mongoose
  Last Clear Chance
Night of the Short Knives

NAVY STORIES

By Sea and by Stealth

BIOGRAPHIES FOR ALL AGES

The Helmet of Navarre
Cardinal in Armor
Young Louis XIV
Francis in All His Glory

ANTHOLOGIES

Cry Spy!
Cry Sabotage!

Burke Wilkinson

The
Zeal
of the
Convert

Robert B. Luce Co., Inc.   Washington—New York

Copyright © 1976 by Burke Wilkinson

Library of Congress Catalog Number 76–3922

ISBN 0–88331–086–4

Contents

v

vi

Foreword

The life of Erskine Childers is like a song known only in snatches. People say, "Oh, didn't he write *The Riddle of the Sands?*" Or, "Wasn't he the Englishman they shot for being more Irish than the Irish?" Or, again, some may remember that, skilled yachtsman that he was, he ran guns from Belgium to Ireland—guns that were later used in the Easter Rebellion.

Like Lawrence of Arabia, Childers was a man around whom legends gather and myths cling. Like Lawrence, too, he possessed the adventurous heart and the gift of words. Charm and courage were Childers' in large degree, as they were Lawrence's. And both seem to have possessed an element of self-humiliation, an intuitive conviction that suffering is somehow good for the soul.

The mystery of Erskine Childers was compounded by Winston Churchill. When, as a member of the Irish Republican Army fighting a lost cause, Childers was taken prisoner by forces of the Free State in November of 1922, Mr. Churchill said, "I have seen with satisfaction that the mischief-making, murderous renegade, Erskine Childers, has been captured."

Prejudging the prisoner, in effect urging his execution with a high-handed disregard for due process, the British Cabinet Minister went on to call Childers "this strange being actuated by a deadly and malignant hatred of the land of his birth."

"Such as he is may all who hate us be," Mr. Churchill concluded with a snarl and a flourish.

Erskine Childers was indeed British-born. But Churchill knew very well that Childers' mother was as Irish as his own mother was American. And he knew, too, that Childers, as Parliamentary Civil Servant, as the author of the prophetic spy novel, *The Riddle of the Sands,* as mounted gunner in the Boer War and Royal Naval Officer in World War I, had rendered the Empire distinguished service. Churchill's statement is simply an extreme example of how the Irish problem, in its days of ultimate strain and agony, reduced men of chivalry to words and deeds that did them little credit.

Seven years later, Mr. Churchill, conscious as ever of the tides of history, modified his harsh judgment, In *Aftermath* (1929) he wrote, "another man of distinction, ability and courage fell a victim. Erskine Childers, who had shown daring and ardour against the Germans in the Cuxhaven Raid, had espoused the Irish cause with even more than Irish irreconcilability." By then peace had come to Ireland at last, and Churchill could afford to be more generous spirited to a fallen foe.

What did turn Erskine Childers, Establishment figure of some fame and great promise, into gun-runner and revolutionary? For what abiding purpose did he become rebel-on-the-run, and end his life as martyr, facing a Free State firing squad across the courtyard of a Dublin barracks?

This biography, based on independent research and containing much new material, seeks to resolve that mystery.

One source that has recently become available are the Irish State Papers, held secret until March of 1976. In particular, the Cabinet minutes of the Free State's Provisional Government during November of 1922, with their supporting documentation, shed a cold new light on Childers' death.

As in the life of Lawrence, there are elements of heroism, of sacrifice and bitter irony, in the Childers story that impart a universality transcending revolt in the desert or insurrection in green fields.

1.   The Boston Connection

It was the first visit of a British military unit to the United States since Yorktown 120 years before. It was the first time that such a unit had come to Boston since that blustery March day in 1776 when General Howe and his troops sailed down the harbor in sullen evacuation.

The Honourable Artillery Company of London came at the invitation of the Ancient and Honorable Artillery Company of Massachusetts to repay a visit of the latter in 1896 when "they did make a pilgrimage to London to visit the parent organization from which it sprang." Parent and offspring were the oldest military organizations in their respective countries.

The Dominion liner *Mayflower* sailed from Liverpool on September 23, 1903. King Edward VII, the Colonel of the Company, sent a bon voyage message predicting "a most gratifying reception in the United States." As the *Mayflower* slipped her moorings, every ship in the Mersey saluted her.

Erskine Childers—small, neat, clipped of mustache and speech—lined the rail with the other gentlemen rankers of the Honourable Artillery Company.

The thirty-one year old Englishman was something of a celebrity, for *The Riddle of the Sands,* with its full cargo of adventure and suspense along the German coast, had come out earlier in the year and was already a bestseller.

Childers and his comrades-in arms had spent a year of harsh campaigning in the South African War. They had played their part in the pursuit of Christian de Wet, the celebrated guerrilla leader, leaving ten of their number on the African veldt and under the stubborn hills called *kopjes* by the Boer.

Now they were in the mood for fun.

The nine days at sea had a pattern of their own. Each morning the Company cleaned and inspected arms. There were squad drills and sword exercises. The first night out the Company gave a concert for the other passengers. Private G. St. J. Lobb rendered "I'm a Jonah Man," billed as a humorous song. Private E.A. Fisher brought down the main saloon with "Yo, Ho, Little Girls," and Lieutenant Colonel the Earl of Denbigh and Desmond, C.V.O., the commanding officer sang "Love's Coronation," with "Alouette" as an encore.

(Lord Denbigh's Edwardian credentials were impeccable. He was a former Royal Artillery officer who had seen service in Egypt and India. He had also been aide-de-camp to the Lord Lieutenant of Ireland and was currently Lord-in-Waiting to the King and represented the Irish Office in the House of Lords.)

Sunday the Rev. Dr. Leighton Parks held divine service in the saloon, and delivered a well-received address on "The Miracle of the Anglo-Saxon Race." Last night out came the climax: a fancy dress ball with handsome Lord Denbigh as Father Neptune and the comely Lady Denbigh as Britannia.

It was all the perfect embodiment of those piping days of Edwardian peace.

A delegation of "Ancients" was waiting to board the *Mayflower* below Boston Light. As she came up the harbor "every ship large or small joined in the reception with display of bunting. . .with screech of siren or toot of whistle." By Order of the Secretary of War, Fort Warren spoke with a 21-gun national salute. Not to be outdone, the Secretary of the Navy sent the cruiser *Chicago,* and Vice Admiral Douglas of the Royal Navy ordered H.M.S. *Retribution* down from Halifax. Both were in holiday array of flags and signal pennants.

As the *Mayflower,* also fully beflagged, neared her Charlestown dock, the officers and men of the HAC, 173 all told, were drawn up on deck in full uniform. From the top of the Bunker Hill Monument the Stars and Stripes and the British national ensign waved in fraternal welcome.

Mary Alden Osgood watched the great parade from one of the Beacon Street houses. She was a young woman in her midtwenties with auburn hair, a broad fair brow and a most charming smile. Crippled in early youth, she had endured and overcome great pain. At thirteen an operation had restored the use of her legs in some degree. She had learned to walk again, to laugh and to live a near-normal life. Her friends called her Molly.

It was the greatest parade since the Grand Army of the Republic, everyone said. Every militia unit within range came to greet the HAC and to march with them. There was in fact a confusion of uniforms. Even the two wings of the Ancient and Honorable Artillery Company were turned out in a manner that the Company's own official report admitted was "kaleidoscopic."

Then the HAC swung into view. First came the infantry in tight-fitting scarlet coats and bearskins, then the artillery, blue-coated and wearing jaunty busbies. All frogs and facings were of silver, indicating volunteer status, but the way they marched, in the characteristic British quickstep, was beyond all doubt professional.

"The Englishmen walked as if on dress parade, the Americans as if on business bent," one Boston newspaper noted.

Now Battery A of the Company was passing the house where Molly watched. There was not all that much to differentiate the marchers, for each was cocky of step and unwavering of glance. But for as long as he was in view, Molly's eyes followed the dapper figure, the perfectly cradled sabre and the

3

total, swinging assurance of Gunner Erskine Childers.

That night, blissfully unaware that his time of freedom was fast running out, Erskine Childers along with his HAC comrades enjoyed an evening of vaudeville acts staged in their honor at Faneuil Hall. Star turns were Act 4, featuring Mr. Al Leach and the Three Rosebuds (from the "Girls Will Be Girls Company"), followed by the incomparable Mr. Raymond Hitchcock.

Later, at Company headquarters in the Prince of Wales Suite of the Revere House, there was considerable revelry. This was made possible in good part by "The Ten of Us," some of the more sporting of the Ancient and Honorable Hosts. Each put up $1000 for the entertainment of their English guests. One survivor mentioned 24-hour-girl-and-drink service. Anyone who has ever taken part in a British military "bash" will know that there was also considerable cheerful breakage, wrestling and brawling.

The next night a group of the HAC visitors had been asked to dine with Mr. Sumner Pearmain, a popular stockbroker and banker. Mr. Pearmain, whose many English friends included H.G. Wells and Sir Frederick Pollock, had received word from an English lady that Erskine Childers was one of the Company, and so he was among those invited.

Childers, a little the worse for the previous evening's wear, wrote a polite note to Mr. Pearmain saying he hoped that the latter would excuse him from dining, as he had lost his evening clothes and had a considerable black eye. A hand-delivered note from Mr. Pearmain brought the reply: "Come anyway." Mr. Pearmain had also invited his niece, Margaret Osgood Warren, and her husband Fiske Warren, already of Single Tax fame. At the last minute "Gretchen" Warren, as she was known, became ill and begged her younger sister, Molly Osgood, to go in her place.

Molly went and, as fate would have it, sat next to Erskine Childers at dinner. By the end of the evening, according to a family chronicler, both knew that "they would never be part-ed."

4

Margaret Osgood Warren and her daughter—a portrait by John Singer Sargent

Monday night, October 5, was the Great Banquet for the HAC in Symphony Hall, with 1033 gentlemen guests. The ladies were allowed in after dinner for the speeches, "in balconies not required by the band."

Gov. John L. Bates and Mayor Patrick Collins were among the speakers, as were the venerable Sen. George Frisbie Hoar and former Navy Secretary John D. Long. The Hon. George Lyman, Collector of the Port of Boston, responded to the Toast to the President and Lord Denbigh, in resonant form, to the toast to the HAC. One highlight of the evening was the regimental fire as "made" by the Company—a series of hisses led by Lord Denbigh in a long right-to-left gesture and culminating in an explosive cheer:

"ssss . . . ssss . . . ssss . . . ssss . . . ssss . . . buh-LOOM!!"

Erskine Childers hissed vigorously along with the rest, but by now his mind was on other matters. Soon there were wonderful drives with Molly in a 1903 Winton touring car, and trips to Harvard, Massachusetts, where the Warrens had a house.

Neither seems to have had any doubt but that fate had brought them together. All past experience took on new meaning in light of an ecstatic present and a future they would soon share.

Some weeks after his comrades of the HAC sailed home from their triumphant visit, Erskine Childers proposed to Molly in a canoe on Bare Hill Pond at Harvard, and was joyously accepted.

The promising Mr. Childers—the not-yet-very-complicated Mr. Childers, sailing man and Establishment figure—was marrying one of the most unusual women of her time. She was tiny, but under the fair brow and beneath the charming smile was a will of tempered steel.

The skating accident that cost Molly Osgood the use of her legs happened when she was three. Both hips were injured, with tubercular abscesses developing in cruel succession. For ten years she was literally a basket case, for she was

6

carried everywhere in her specially constructed basket, which also served as her bed.

Her father, Dr. Hamilton Osgood, a practicing physician with a scholarly turn of mind, was her strong support. When she was still very little, she confessed to him that "more than anything she wanted to be like other people." Very gently he explained that "she could do it only by taking her thoughts away from herself and putting all her mind on interesting things and on the friends around her."

When the pain grew too great, she would ask her nurse for her toy umbrella and it would not be removed until she could smile again. When she was seven, she told her father that she did not think she could go on. Dr. Osgood said, "Now we can really begin." He had long had an interest in hypnosis, and would later publish a book on the subject. He taught Molly how mind and will could triumph over affliction and how she must learn to "let the pain flow over her."

Dr. Osgood, short, bald, with the broad Osgood forehead and a pointed beard, was very fond of his brother-in-law, Sumner Pearmain. They were in fact more like brothers than most brothers are. They were properly Bostonian in their clubs and country houses, their ties to Harvard and to England. They also shared a trait that was a little unusual for men of their background: they liked the Irish rebels who fled to America or came there in the Irish nationalist cause, and they opened their fine houses to them.

Dr. Osgood saw to it that Molly was included in everything possible. Lying in her basket, listening to the soft-spoken, volatile Irishmen who trooped through, she heard and absorbed a lot.

John Boyle O'Reilly was everybody's favorite Irishman, including Molly's. He was born in County Meath and at fourteen joined the Fenian Movement. In 1863 he enlisted in the 10th Hussars, his purpose being that of "furthering the revolutionary cause and learning the arts of war for future use." Arrested three years later on five capital charges, including

7

the formenting of mutiny, he was condemned to death. Ultimately the sentence was commuted to twenty years' penal survitude and he was transported to Western Australia. Escaping to sea in a small boat, he was picked up by the whaling bark *Gazelle* out of New Bedford. Six months later he arrived in America. The first thing he did was apply for United States citizenship.

He came to own and edit *The Pilot*, the voice of the Catholic-Irish in America. His novel, *Moondyne*, told of his hardships in an Australian chain gang, under a thin veneer of fiction. Poems poured from his pen. He was said to rank "next to Whittier, Longfellow and Holmes in the popular heart of New England and America."

He had a "great shock of black hair," William Hovey tells us, "a clipped beard equally black...erect, soldierly bearing." His fierceness was belied by his eye, for "a kindlier, truer, merrier eye no man ever had."

Confined to her own small basket prison, Molly could sympathize with O'Reilly, enduring solitary confinement in the stifling iron cells of Dartmoor and Pentonville. Chained as it were to her bed, she could identify with O'Reilly, led in chains through London to his convict ship.

The magic name "Parnell" also became familiar as talk of Ireland's hopes for freedom flowed around her.

Like a dangerous bacillus in the blood stream, Molly's hostility to British imperialism would be dormant in her intellect from crippled childhood to active maturity.

In 1890—the year O'Reilly died—she had the operation that gave her some mobility. She was thirteen at the time. Three years later a second operation made it possible for her to have children. The courage and self-discipline which she had developed lasted all her life. She almost never used the pronoun "I", and had no self-pity.

Her bold, firm handwriting, as analyzed by an expert, tells us a lot: "She went toward people she cared about, never holding back. She was highly intelligent, quite stubborn, not

8

proud, not easily influenced by others, deeply spiritual, modest and not very intuitive." Something she wrote, in a rare moment of self-appraisal, is revealing, too: "For unknown reasons, two gifts were given me as I crossed this strange place the world—a love of giving and a hunger and thirst after righteousness."

Now all that reaching out, all that caring, all that love of giving would be concentrated on one person.

The wedding took place at Trinity Church on January 6, 1904. It was the coldest January in years. Nantucket was ice-bound, and at Orange, Massachusetts, the temperature was 50° below. Japan and Russia were on the brink of war. Owen Wister's *The Virginian* had just opened on the New York stage to rave reviews. Lily Langtry was visiting Langtry, Texas. The day before, President Roosevelt nominated Mr. Taft to be Secretary of War.

Tall palms were massed in the chancel of the church, and there were two vases of Ascension lilies on the Communion Table. Everyone was in his proper place—with Bishop Lawrence of Massachusetts officiating, Wallace Goodrich at the organ, and a throng of Boston's best in the pews. The celebrated Dr. William Rainsford had come from New York to assist the Bishop. Dulcibella Childers was maid of honor—and almost everybody knew that her brother had named the yacht in his famous novel for her.

The best man was Robert Barton of County Wicklow, double first cousin of the groom. There were Coolidges, Blakes, Kidders among the twelve ushers, three Rainsfords, Roger Merriman and Beverly Rantoul.

Dr. Osgood looked happy and handsome. Everyone was talking about his wedding present to the happy couple: the sturdy gaff-rigged ketch called *Asgard*.

Everything was white—Molly's satin wedding dress, her bouquet of lilies of the valley, the pleated skirts and chiffon hats of the four bridesmaids.

The only splash of color in the great vaulted church was

9

Dr. Rainsford's crimson hood. No one at the time thought this bit of ecclesiastical scarlet was in any way unusual, but some would cite it later as a portent of tragedy.

How Erskine and Molly Childers joined forces in Ireland's cause. . .how Erskine with his gift of eloquence and his convert's zeal plunged into the cause. . .how he went beyond *her* with the sadder, lonelier passion of the martyr. . . such is our story, a story whose groundwork was laid and whose dim outlines could already be seen in Boston that fall and winter, as 1903 shivered into 1904.

2.   A House Called Glan

Erskine Childers was born in London on June 25, 1870. He was the second son of Robert Caesar Childers and Anna Henrietta Barton Childers who lived at 58 Mount Street, just south of Grosvenor Square.

The Childers family had all the correct ruling-class attributes and connections, including a cousin, Hugh Culling Eardley Childers who, in due course, would be Secretary of War, first Lord of the Admiralty, Chancellor of the Exchequer and, finally, Home Secretary, in various Gladstone Cabinets.

Robert Caesar and Anna Childers were quite remarkable people—more so than their proper connections and conventional West End address might imply. Robert Caesar as a very young man had been a civil servant in Ceylon, where he acquired a consuming interest in the Pali language and the sacred texts of the Buddhists. When his health broke down in 1864, he returned to England. He devoted the rest of his short life to the translation of Pali documents and to the preparation of his great pioneering work, a two-volume dictionary of the language. Childers died of consumption and exhaustion at the age of thirty-eight.

The entry about him in the *Dictionary of National Biography* contains an extraordinary tribute: "To an unusually powerful memory and indomitable energy Childers united enthusiasm in the cause of research, a passionate patience, rare even in new and promising fields." These traits young Erskine would inherit in marked degree.

Anna Henrietta, born Barton, was a member of an Anglo-Irish family which had farmed in Country Wicklow for nearly three centuries. Her brother Charles Barton was married to Robert Caesar Childers' sister Agnes. The Bartons lived in Glendalough House near the little village of Annamoe.

By all reports Anna Henrietta was a woman of great spirit and beauty. Nursing her husband in his long last illness, she contracted tuberculosis and died in 1883, leaving two sons, Henry and Erskine, and three daughters—Dulcibella (called Dulcie), Constance and Sybil. Erskine was twelve at the time.

Family ties with the Bartons in Wicklow had always been close, and the Childers children had often visited there. The five small Bartons, double first cousins of the Childers brood, were more or less their match in age. Now Charles Barton and his wife Agnes generously asked the five orphans to come to live at Glendalough House. Soon they settled in as part of a typical "Ascendancy" family.

Ascendancy families spoke a pure English, with little or no trace of the soft Irish brogue. They were Protestant, owned most of the land, sent their children to English schools. The native Irish regarded them with an odd mixture of deference and dislike, not totally unmingled with affection.

This ambivalent relationship had its origins far back in the misty time when the first wave of foreign invaders washed over Ireland. Beginning in the 9th century, Viking marauders began to raid the Irish coasts and came back to colonize them. With his victory at Clontarf in 1014, Brian Boru, the High King of Ireland, broke the Viking hold at last.

Next came Norman-English adventurers, encouraged by that energetic Plantagenet king, Henry II. They were led by the great Earl of Pembroke known to history simply as Strongbow. Landing in Wexford in 1169, he soon put the brave but disorganized Irish chieftains to rout.

12

Strongbow's Norman-English knights were rapidly absorbed into Irish life, the mixture of two hardy races proving salutary to both. Although nominally in vassalage to the English Crown, these Hiberno-Norman dynasties—De Lacy and Fitzgerald, Butler and Burke among them—produced a succession of near-independent overlords.

English onslaughts, usually in response to Irish attempts at rebellion, filled succeeding centuries. They culminated in the brutally-efficient Cromwellian conquest (1649–53). Catholic Irish were massacred by the thousands, and some ten million acres of Catholic lands sequestered. Many of the survivors were driven into the sparse and rocky country west of the Shannon. Some were retained to work the land for their new masters.

So the Protestant Ascendancy was born. Both political power and fertile lands would belong to the victors for more than two centuries.

There was, for a time, a clockwork Irish Parliament in Dublin, wound to serve Protestant interests. During the reigns of William and Mary, of Queen Anne and the first two Georges, the Parliament enacted a series of Penal Laws which consolidated the impoverishment and degradation of the Catholic Irish. No Catholic could vote or sit in Parliament. No public office was open to him, nor was the bar or the bench. Catholic archbishops and bishops were banished and a bounty of £50 placed on the head of any caught trying to slip back into the country. Subtle cruelty in a horse-loving country was the law prohibiting a Catholic from owning a horse worth more than £5. Worse still, a Protestant could buy any Catholic-owned horse that caught his fancy by paying that same low-ceiling sum.

The Penal Laws were so complex, so loaded in favor of the Protestant Ascendancy, that much of the one-fifth of the land still remaining in Catholic hands went the way of the rest.

After the ill-starred rebellion of 1798, the Irish Parliament was abolished. From then on, by the Act of Union, the United Kingdom of Great Britain and Ireland was ruled by the Mother of Parliaments in Whitehall. Beautiful Georgian Dublin, once the stage-set to a lively world of noblemen, scholars and artisans, went into long eclipse. . . .

The 19th century brought some amelioration to the serfdom of the Catholics. Daniel O'Connell, the Great Emancipator, was able—by his resonant leadership and well-organized Catholic Association—to obtain for his followers the right to vote, hold office and sit in Parliament (1829). But the failure of the potato crop in the late 1840's, and the failure of the British to demonstrate any great urgency in helping the starving Irish, brought more disaster. A million Irish died and a million emigrated. The total Catholic population was halved thereby. The survivors became the first generation of a grimmer race that was, increasingly, in the mood to seek redress for ancient wrong by all constitutional means and, failing them, by violence.

Like so many of the landed gentry of the Ascendancy, the Bartons were convinced Unionists. That is to say, they fervently believed that Ireland should stay under British rule. The winds of change that were blowing in Catholic Ireland—the growing wish for Home Rule and freedom, and the secret brotherhoods that were forming to achieve these ends—were much talked-about by the grown-up Bartons and the rest of the Wicklow gentry. But their way of life, still serene and safe, was scarcely touched at all.

To the young Childers, the Bartons were kind and welcoming. In due course they built a pleasant addition along the southern side of Glendalough House to make room for the five orphans.

The village of Annamoe is little changed to this day. It is hardly more than a wide place in the Dublin-Glendalough road—and one of the very few hamlets in all Ireland that has no public house. Just south of the village, the wide road narrows to negotiate a fine old bridge with four stone arches.

14

Under the arches, the Avonmore river goes caroming down its pleasant valley to the sea.

Behind the stone gateposts of Glendalough House the long drive runs along home fields of hay and barley. In the fields, clumps of pine, straight as musket barrels, stand guard. The drive is agreeably lined with beech and yew and hoary oak. The farther fields tilt upward toward a steep back-drop of mountain.

The house itself, which the family calls Glan, sits hand-somely on a green promontory above the fields. It has a stone facade, mullioned but unmistakably Victorian, and, behind, an L-shaped range of buildings with parts going back to the 17th century. A hill known as the Scard rises sharply behind Glan—wilder, more desolate than you would expect just thirty miles south of Dublin.

It was a wonderful place to be young in. The small Bartons and Childers had 1500 acres of farmland to roam, as well as water gardens, alleys of tall cypress, mysterious wood-lands and the wild Wicklow hills. Lough Dan, drained by the Avonmore, and the twin lakes at Glendalough held white trout for the catching. Below Wicklow Head and along the Silver Strand were sand and pebble beaches where the family picnicked. (Sometimes, when the wind was right and the Irish Sea in turmoil, the crash and suck of the waves could be heard at Glan, a good eight miles inland.)

Young Erskine took full advantage of the wonders of Glan and its countryside. As Desmond Ryan wrote, "the magic of Ireland surrounds his boyhood." He roved far afield along the coast and back into the wild hills. In these years he developed his gifts for solitude and concentration, and also a growing interest in the Irish people. Each Barton and Childers child, at a suitable age, adopted some local family or individual as a special project, visiting them regularly with presents and good cheer.

Since Charles Barton was High Sheriff of the county as well as popular squire, the family entertained a good deal.

They always dressed for dinner, and when there were guests the full white-tie ritual was in order.

Sometimes young Robert Barton, ten years Erskine's junior, accompanied his older cousin on his rambles. Their affection grew into a lifelong bond—in which their mutual awareness of Ireland's need to be free was a strong strand.

Robert Barton, who died in 1975, lived all his life at Glan. An authentic hero of the Troubles, he served in an early Irish Cabinet and was the last surviving signatory of the 1921 Treaty which brought the Free State into being.

Robert Barton remembered well what his cousin was like as a boy. Childers had a dislike, almost a fear, of violence. At the same time he had a healthy wish to excel in all manly outdoor skills. He learned to shoot, to ride and sail and climb. He never did become a first-class horseman, but pluck and determination made him adequate. A born sailor, he turned into an even better one, testing himself in gale and storm.

It was at Glan that Childers developed reading tastes that would last a lifetime. Alexandre Dumas and James Fenimore Cooper were among his favorites. (Nearly forty years later Frank O'Connor noted with surprise that Childers, on the run now, and with a price on his head, was still reading *Twenty Years After* and *Deerslayer* with unabated pleasure.)

In a more serious way Childers was fond of Ralph Waldo Emerson. Certain passages from Emerson's essay on *Self-Reliance* would become his abiding star:

"Trust thyself: every heart vibrates to that iron string. . .Whoso would be a man must be a non-conformist.

"I am ashamed to think how easily we capitulate to badges and names, to large societies and dead institutions."

(From his earliest days Childers himself was a privileged member of a large society. In due course he received honors and awards from it. But capitulation to its rules and shibboleths was never to be his lot.)

16

In the same essay comes another sentence that made its indelible mark on the young Childers:

"It is easy in the world to live after the world's opinion; it is easy in solitude to live after our own; but the great man is he who in the midst of the crowd keeps with perfect sweetness the independence of solitude. . . ."

Then we have the most famous of all the Emersonian dicta, one that Childers absorbed and retained for life:

"A foolish consistency is the hobgoblin of little minds, adored by little statesmen and philosophers and divines. With consistency a great soul has simply nothing to do."

Emerson goes on to give his own Rule of Wisdom for avoiding such consistency:

"Never to rely on your memory alone. . .but bring the past for judgment into the thousand-eyed present, and live ever in a new day."

Shortly thereafter, still on the sin of consistency, Emerson makes an analogy that Childers the sailing man could readily understand: "a hundred tacks, seen from a sufficient distance" becomes not a zig-zag course but an "average tendency."

To these passages from the Emerson essay Childers would constantly return. They were charts that helped him plot his own perilous and seemingly-inconsistent course.

Herman Melville was another navigation aid to which he often turned. An especial favorite was the passage in *Moby Dick* when Bilkington sets sail from New Bedford on an icy winter night. To Bilkington the port is his ship's "direct jeopardy". The whaling bark must therefore "seek all the lashed sea's landlessness again for refuge's sake rushing into peril, her only friend her bitterest foe."

So also would Childers live his own life—like Bilkington's bark, like the petrel that seeks out the caverns and windy hollows of the sea.

Another of Childers' enthusiasms was Tennyson's *Ulysses*. The line "Come, my friends, 'tis not too late to seek a newer world" held special appeal for him. Writing to Dulcie during his college years, he confesses that "these lines always send a strange thrill through me and are half-responsible for any longing I ever have to desert civilization and

'. . . .wander far away
On from island unto island, to the gateways of the day.'

"So," the letter goes on, "if I ever disappear suddenly for a year or two you will know what sent me!"

When his Uncle Charles Barton died in 1885, the serious and self-contained Erskine—rather than his light-hearted older brother Henry—became the trusted deputy to his widowed Aunt Agnes. Together they held the clan together, even though Erskine was away a good part of the time during his school and college years. This partnership could not always have been easy, for Aunt Agnes, with her fierce Childers blood, was the most reactionary member of the family. She was so unbending in her Protestant faith that the Catholic postman was not allowed to come up the drive. When in later years the thorny question of Home Rule was discussed at dinner—mostly by Erskine and his cousin Robert—Aunt Agnes often stormed out of the room in anger or tears in face of their increasingly liberal views.

Erskine entered Haileybury in the fall of 1883. It was a good, solid English public school, a typical training ground for servants of Empire. There, in the green Hertfordshire countryside, future soldiers, churchmen, civil servants learned the ground rules. Young Childers was by no means unaware that he would be expected to play his part. As one of his schoolmates said of him, "his steady resolve to devote his life to the service of his country (England) was not learned from the hills of Wicklow, but from his years at Haileybury."

Despite the fact that he was small for his age and had developed a sciatic limp, Erskine made the Rugby XV as a

18

three-quarter or running back. He does not appear to have acquired much of a reputation as a scholar, perhaps because he admittedly spent a good deal of time "sailing strange craft on the local river Lea." But he did pick up the lively and revealing nickname of "Perk."

Many years later, after Childers' seeming defection and the bitter tragedy of his execution, Haileybury reclaimed him as its own. The school historian's tribute in the *Haileyburian* (April, 1935) was Number Two in a series of *"Great Haileyburians"*. There is quite a full account of his youth and then an interesting comment on his Boer War service: "He had left Haileybury a Tory and an Imperialist but the South African War had taught him something of the spiritual force that lies behind the rebellions of small nations." This, as we shall see, was more part of the Childers legend than the strict truth.

The article goes on to summarize his World War I service, "including a year as navigating officer of a squadron of small 40 foot torpedo-carrying hydroplanes on the Belgian coast."

In describing the dramatic last weeks of Childers' life, the article quotes evidence of how "serene and contented and fulfilled" he was on the eve of his execution. It also equates him with the mythical hero of Kipling's "If." Then comes the surprising and courageous conclusion at a time when Childers was still thought of by many as rebel and renegade, traitor even: "The school can take pride in having realized its ideal in the person of one of its own products. In an inscrutable way, Haileybury is fulfilled in Childers."

Glan—the Victorian facade, built in 1846

Side view of Glan, built in 1750

3.   Deeper into Wicklow

Some miles deeper into the county of Wicklow a gaunt
Georgian house called Avondale sits four-square among silver
firs. From a hill crest it commands the same Avonmore river
—wider now—that flows past the Barton lands and Glan. In
it, during those years when the young Childers and Bartons
were growing up at Glan, there lived another Ascendancy
squire who was one of the most remarkable men of his time.
His name was Charles Stewart Parnell. In the late 1870's and
all through the 1880's he was away from Avondale a good deal
of the time. As a member of the British Parliament, first for
Meath and then during most of his spectacular career for
Cork City, he became the undisputed leader of the Home Rule
block in the House of Commons.

Parnell moulded his 82-odd followers—squires, Fenians,
Land Leaguers, journalists, soldiers of fortune, lawyers—into
a battering ram with which to assault British opposition to
any form of freedom for Ireland. They voted as a man whatever he told them to vote. He developed techniques of obstruc-
tion and filibuster to such a degree of efficiency that he and
his one-plank delegation held the balance of power for almost
a decade. He was called the Uncrowned King of Ireland, but
for all practical political purposes he was the Uncrowned
King of England as well.

When he backed the Conservatives—as he did in 1885—

Gladstone's Liberal Government fell. When, shortly there-after, Gladstone showed increasing support of Home Rule, Parnell shifted again. In the ensuing General Election the Liberal-Home Rule combination was swept back into power, and Lord Salisbury's Conservatives again became the loyal opposition.

Parnell was a fine horseman, a fair shot and a good-enough cricketer to captain the Wicklow Eleven. He was educated at Magdalene College, Cambridge, but came down without a degree. Tall, taciturn, magnificent of beard and presence, he rarely spoke in the House. But when he did, he could attain a bleak and biting eloquence.

Parnell's lineage was not very different from that of many other members of the Protestant gentry. The family came over from England during the Restoration of Charles II, short years after the Cromwellian conquest. An ancestor, Thomas Parnell, was a poet and friend of Dean Swift. A great uncle, Sir Henry Parnell, held British office under Melbourne and became the first Baron Congleton. His mother was the daughter of an American Naval officer, Commodore Charles Stewart, who once commanded *Old Ironsides*. Delia Stewart Parnell inherited her father's fierce hatred of the English and passed it along to her son intact.

While in school in England Charles Parnell showed that his mother's inheritance had not been wasted. "These English," he said to his brother, "despise us because we are Irish, but we must stand up to them. That's the way to treat an Englishman—stand up to him."

Parnell was an amateur metallurgist, a mathematician—and a man of deep superstition. He had a mortal fear of the number 13, and believed that the month of October was his most dangerous month. He hated the color green and was convinced that much of Ireland's woe could be attributed to the fact that it was the national color.

Spurned in his youth by a Miss Woods, he remained a bachelor for most of his meteor-like career. In the words of

22

Michael Davitt, leader of the Land League and for a time his close colleague, Parnell's "mind was barren of all faith except a boundless faith in himself."

This driving faith almost made his dream for Ireland come true. It appeared to be only a matter of time and tactics for Home Rule to be achieved at last. Even the unalterable hostility of the House of Lords would somehow be circumvented by the magic of Parnell!

But it was not to be. Parnell's dream, like Gatsby's, was already conditioned by the past. As early as 1881 he had started an affair with Kitty O'Shea, the wife of one of his henchmen. Lulled by a retainer's fee and hopes of political advancement, Captain O'Shea seemed complaisant enough. For a time he and Parnell shared Kitty's favors, but this seems not to have suited the fire-and-ice leader at all. There was a famous scene in which Parnell, silent as ever, simply entered the O'Shea bedroom, threw Kitty over his shoulder and carried her off.

When Kitty bore Parnell's daughters (1883 and 1884) O'Shea still remained quiescent. Suddenly, in 1889 he filed suit for divorce, naming Charles Stewart Parnell as co-respondent. An uncontested divorce was granted on November 17, 1890.

At first the factions which formed Parnell's block in Parliament rallied behind him, and he received a resounding vote of confidence. Then the British, tired of his sway, moved smoothly to bring about his fall.

Gladstone, in a celebrated letter to a colleague, made it known that he could no longer support the cause of Irish Home Rule with the tarnished Parnell as its spokesman. "Poor fellow, poor fellow!" Gladstone exclaimed, shedding a crocodile tear or two. His letter noted "the splendid services rendered by Mr. Parnell to his country" even as he drove home the knife.

High Churchmen, both in Ireland and England, discovered rather late in the day how shocked they were over affair and divorce. Parnell's following was riven. By splitting into factions, his fellow Home Rulers were in fact throwing him—as he clearly saw and said—"to English wolves now howling for my destruction."

With the scandal breaking over him, he refused to bow his head one inch. His fall was like the Archangel Lucifer's, long days falling.

In July, 1891, Parnell married his Kitty. All that summer he fought, by public meeting and bitter by-election, to clear his name and regain his mastery. But the strain was too great. On October 6, in the month he feared most, he died of exhaustion and general debility. He was only forty-five.

He was buried in Glasnevin Cemetery among Ireland's great, with thousands of hushed mourners. Kitty placed a withered rose in his coffin, the rose which she had given him on first meeting and he had cherished across all those stormy years.

Parnell's great contribution to Ireland's cause was the splicing of the twin strands of Land Reform and Home Rule. All the disparate leagues and associations and clubs—including the American-based Fenians—closed ranks behind him. To his eternal credit, he abhorred the use of violence for his ends. But he did create the techniques of passive resistance and ostracism which—first tested on a luckless land agent called Captain Boycott—gave the word *boycott* to the language. Even though he failed in his quest for Home Rule, he was able to force Parliament to pass a great deal of land reform legislation that vastly improved the lot of small landowner and tenant. In Shane Leslie's phrase, "he did more for the Irish peasant than the Russian Revolution did for the Russian serf."

Parnell was away from Avondale so much that he even moved his stables to England. To his fellow members of the Ascendancy his absences and his actions were viewed with mixed feelings.

He was in the paradoxical tradition of Henry Grattan

and Wolfe Tone, Lord Edward Fitzgerald and Robert Emmet —Protestants all who espoused the cause of Catholic Ireland. Like Mr. Charles Barton, he had served his term as High Sheriff of Wicklow. Much as they feared what Parnell was trying to bring about, a few of his fellow squires still drank his whiskey when he did come home. No man could be all bad, they argued, who rode a horse and shot and played cricket the way Charles Parnell did. Besides, all the Parnells back to old Lord Congleton (who took his own life) and beyond were a touch on the eccentric side. . . .

The Bartons took the firmer line. Back in the 1870's there had been home-and-home cricket matches on the pleasant lawns of Avondale and Glan, with Charles Barton and Charles Stewart Parnell the respective captains. After Parnell took over the leadership of the Home Rule party, he was banished by the Unionist Bartons, and all communication between the two houses ceased.

Erskine Childers was eight years old when Parnell first came to power, nineteen when he fell. From the great career, and talk about it that swirled around him, Childers learned subliminal lessons that would surface years later.

At the time of Parnell's final ordeal, Childers was an undergraduate at Cambridge. He actually defended the leader's right to a certain amount of private immorality. This was during a meeting of an undergraduate Debating Society as the next chapter tells.

Later, in his vast and scholarly work on *The Framewor of Home Rule* (1911), Childers gives an account of the Parn lite triumphs and trials, and shows his awareness of wh Parnell sought to achieve.

Growing up, Childers was drawn to Parnell for seve reasons. They shared a basic trait, for self-reliance was the root of each's character. Of all those Emersonian dicta t Childers read and re-read the one that he hewed to most fa fully was *trust thyself: every heart vibrates to that iron strii*

25

Parnell too had a quote-of-quotes that was his lodestar. It was Polonius' admonition to the young Laertes: *This above all: to thine own self be true.* No man ever lived more completely to its command.

There was branch as well as root to their similarities. Neither Parnell nor Childers cared very much what any man thought as long as he felt himself to be acting truly by his own instinct and rules. Both were solitary men, although Childers had a gift for the friendship of the few that was lacking in the older, icier man.

Each had one love that became his life and more.

4.   A Sunlit Time

Erskine Childers went up to Cambridge in the fall of 1890. His College was Trinity—most magnificent of all the colleges along the Cam, with its Tudor Great Court and its elegant Wren Library. He read the Law, and for the first time his gifts for concentration and hard study were taxed to the full.

Among Childers' friends in Trinity was the handsome and popular Eddie Marsh. Marsh had a high reedy voice and a puckish sense of humor. He never married but was the Establishment's favorite best man, usher and god-father. Later in life he became a patron of the arts, a writer of graceful prose and the perennial private secretary of Winston Churchill. For personal services to the Crown he was created a Knight Commander of the Victorian Order.

In his book of reminiscences, modestly called *A Number of People,* Sir Edward recaptures the flavor and mood of Cambridge in the sunlit, late-Victorian time of the 1890's. "Till the war came to confound all epochs," Marsh writes, "my life divided itself in retrospect into three parts: Before Cambridge; Cambridge; Since."

Despite such precedence, it was in retrospect a surprisingly eventless time. As Marsh describes it, people bulked larger than happenings:

"What strikes me most when I look back on the life

27

which I and my companions led at Cambridge is an extraordinary innocence and simplicity . . . . We were all tingling with intellectual curiosity, arguing on every subject in the firm belief that we should thus arrive at Truth. . .keen politicians, nearly all Liberals, aware of the 'storms that raged outside our happy ground' but not much irked by them; great readers in general literature, both English and foreign; respectfully and rather externally interested in the other arts, especially music, but hardly at all in any form of sport."

In addition to Childers, there were, in the small, mostly ex-Etonian world that Marsh gathered around himself, such promising men as Bertrand Russell, who was reading Mathematics, Robert Trevelyan, son of Sir George the historian, and great nephew of Lord Macaulay, Oswald Sickert, budding poet and brother of artist Walter Sickert, and George Warrington Steevens, soon to win fame as a correspondent in the Boer War. Maurice Baring, novelist and man-of-letters in the making, came up from Eton in 1893.

Two Classics scholars whom Childers and Marsh admired played a large part in setting the intellectual tone of Cambridge in those days before the University's excellence turned to the scientific. Both R.D. Archer-Hind and A.W. Verrall were brilliant on the lecture platform, and Marsh has given us vivid glimpses of them both in action:

Here is Archer-Hind, the great Grecian scholar and eccentric "padding up and down the lecture room with his little red Socratic pug nose in the air pouring out on the wood-wind of his beautiful voice translations of Plato in an English as exquisite as the Greek."

And here is Verrall during his lecture on the Choephori of Aeschylus: "His commentary was a series of surprises which burst on us like bombshells, and with his mastery of the arts of preparation he worked us up into excruciating suspense for the next."

Like Haileybury, the Light Blue University was a proving

ground for service to Queen and Empire. But the scope was broader now. Debating and learned societies flourished, and they were ideal places to whet one's skills of voice and pen.

One of the most celebrated of the debating societies was the Magpie and Stump in Trinity which Childers joined shortly after entering the College. Its President, presiding from a chair placed on a table, wore a dinner jacket and a large red tie. Facing him in a glass case were two stuffed magpies on a stump. All speeches and motions were directed to His Majesty the Bird; anyone who addressed or referred to his Consort was ruled out of order by the President.

The minutes of the previous meeting were usually the subject of fierce debate, and often a motion would be made to reject them *in toto*. Any member who did not speak for at least two minutes a term was fined a half-crown. When an Australian with an almost impenetrable accent attempted to make a motion, it was moved "that all participants be required to speak in the English language."

Some debates were serious, some funny and some just plain silly. Serious, funny or silly, they all served the same purpose: to give the members an opportunity to develop forensic skills, especially the humor, patience and simulated anger so useful in debate. Among the more lighthearted topics debated in Childers' day was the proposition that "The Early Worm Catches Cold," which was affirmed by 14 *ayes* and 4 *noes*. "Things Have Come to a Pretty Pass" was another subject of lively discussion. "Penny Plain Is Better than Tuppence Colored" was a hardy perennial for the ritualized deliberations of the Magpie and Stump.

The Society suited Childers very well indeed. He was elected Treasurer in December, 1891, and President the following June. Later, he chose to campaign for reelection to the top office by plastering the town with posters favoring his candidacy, and by making long mock-serious speeches in public places. His main purpose was to attract attention to the Magpie and Stump, whose membership was falling off.

According to Basil Williams, later one of his closest friends, Childers stirred up a "glorious row", but most undergraduates simply thought it a hilarious rag. Although Childers was not reelected, the campaign succeeded in publicizing the Society, and so in gaining new members.

Childers was never in danger of having to pay the half-crown fine. He seems to have had views on everything, and to have been particularly articulate on the more serious motions.

On May 8, 1891 (the 529th Meeting of the Society), the motion was "that in the opinion of This House private immorality should not necessarily exclude a man from taking a prominent part in public affairs." It was obvious that the horrendous fall of Charles Stewart Parnell was very much on the minds of the debaters. For this debate took place just two months before Parnell married Kitty O'Shea, at the time when he was fighting for his political survival.

The Victorian undergraduates rejected the motion by a vote of 11–10. Chivalrous by nature, and sympathetic to his Wicklow neighbor's plight, Childers spoke against the majority vote for a terse three minutes.

A meeting in February, 1893—the 569th—debated the proposition that "This House Approves the New Home Rule Bill." Childers spoke a full 30 minutes in opposition. The thrust of his argument was that an independent Ireland so near to the main British isle would not be compatible with "our own safety." He was still speaking as a proper young Anglo-Irish Unionist, more concerned for the defense of Britain than the dream of Irish freedom. This argument of the unique geographical position of Ireland in relation to the larger isle was one he would ingeniously turn completely inside out when he came to champion Ireland's cause.

So the Ascendancy mold into which Childers had been born was still unbroken. A tendency to play the pedant was beginning to show, and it might be noted that his long-windedness caused one rival debater to refer to "the intolerable gas" of Mr. Childers.

These Cambridge years were full and happy ones. with prowls across the Cambridge fens and sailing on the Norfolk Broads on the occasional weekend. And often there was Glan between terms for long, sustaining summer days.

Vacation reading parties were another variation on Cambridge life. In order to do some concentrated study, more than the absorbing social life of Cambridge in term-time allowed, small groups would meet in some remote place, usually in the company of a professor or tutor. Bertrand Russell, Eddie Marsh and Erskine Childers shared one such vacation in Wales. For recreation, Childers, the outdoorsman and, again, something of the pedant, taught his companions the fine points of angling for trout. From their mountain hideaway Marsh wrote laconically that "Childers has turned us all into fishermen."

On graduation Erskine Childers achieved First Class honors in the Law. Then he took the examination for the British Civil Service and passed third highest. This considerable exploit allowed him to pick his first post himself.

In character, with his developing love of procedure and debate, he chose that of Committee Clerk in the House of Commons.

After many years of separate ways, Childers and Edward Marsh were to meet again in a London Conference room. The time was November of 1921. British and Irish delegations had assembled to hammer out a Treaty which would end the bitter fighting of the first phase of the "Trouble." Childers was Secretary to the Irish delegation, Marsh in his familiar role of *alter ego* to Churchill. This is the way Marsh recalled the meeting: "I had a painful moment when I first saw Erskine Childers sitting at the council table. We had been great friends at Trinity and later, and I knew him as one of the sweetest natures in the world: but now, when our eyes met, in his there was no recognition."

31

Erskine Childers in the British Army, 1900—*photo courtesy of Radio Times, London*

5.   Late Afternoon of Empire

To all outward appearances, everything was in its proper place. *Pax Brittanica* still seemed at high noon. The Queen Empress sat sedately on her throne as her Jubilee drew near. The prosperity created so long ago by the Industrial Revolution was firmly maintained and advanced by the triumphs of technology. The Fleet ruled the seas unchallenged.

Yet by the year 1895, when Erskine Childers took up his Parliamentary duties, there were some long shadows across the Empire. Increasing economic and political isolation from the Continent was one symptom of new stress. Those frequent changes of Government, caused in large degree by the divisive strain of the Home Rule question, was another symptom. The splendid little wars, as remote and as bracing as the winds that whistled down the Khyber Pass, seemed to be coming closer to home. Even Mr. Kipling's tone was getting a little shrill.

Irish freedom was dead for a generation. In February of 1893—and his own indomitable 83rd year—Mr. Gladstone had actually introduced a modified Home Rule bill which passed the Commons by a pasted-together majority of 40. Shane Leslie in his memoirs calls it "a muffled salute to the dead Parnell," which indeed it was.

Sensing disharmony, rallying to its own entrenched interests, the House of Lords killed it. Peers from the deep country, some even from asylums and mental homes, were rounded up to assure the outcome.

Later, a General Election confirmed the Lords' judgment. So, in 1895, the Marquess of Salisbury became Prime Minister for the fourth time. Sophisticated and cynical, as jingoistic as his political mentor Disraeli, Lord Salisbury had no great taste for the ways of democracy. His bent was foreign policy and his touch accommodating. He worked hard to close the gap with the Continental powers. In so doing he was away a good deal.

Inevitably, the managing of Empire was left to his formidable Colonial Secretary, Joseph Chamberlain. Once a popular Mayor of Birmingham, first a Radical then a Liberal, Chamberlain had broken with Gladstone over Home Rule. Once headed to the right, he never looked back, and was rapidly becoming the greatest imperialist of them all.

From 1895 to 1906, eleven still-formative years in the life of Erskine Childers, the Salisbury-Chamberlain brand of Conservatism was continuously in power. As a Civil Servant, Childers could show no Party inclination of his own. But he watched, and learned, and sharpened his Parliamentary skills.

The Committee system of the House of Commons was designed to assure an equable distribution of the work load of lawmaking. Under one "Committee of the whole house" there functioned six Grand Committees to examine and report on legislation. Clerks like Childers formed the permanent staff of these Committees. The drafting and re-drafting of clauses and amendments and enabling acts was their daily fare. The Parliamentary skills which they sought to perfect were clarity and precision of language, and the necessary art of compromise.

Childers took up bachelor quarters in Chelsea. More permanently, he and his three sisters—Dulcie, Constance and Sybil—settled into a flat in Carlisle Mansions, then as now a stronghold of good solid Victorian comfort.

Sailing remained Childers' favorite pastime. One of the first things he did after reporting to his new duties was to buy

34

a shallow-draft, gaff-rigged sloop called *Vixen*. Strongly-built, with double-diagonal teak planking and a big center-board, she was 30 feet overall and had a nine-foot beam. Although heavy and slow to windward, and with cramped living quarters below, she was well-suited to her skipper's favorite cruising country, the shoal waters and sandy estuaries of the northern European coastline.

When Parliament was not sitting he would go off for long, leisurely cruises. Sometimes his brother Henry crewed for him, or his new friend and fellow Committee Clerk, Basil Williams, but often enough he went alone.

We have a glimpse of him near the start of one of his solitary voyages at a harbor down the Thames a way. He ties up and asks the Dockmaster what the weather is like along the Belgian Coast. Soon he is off again downriver, after reefing his main against a freshening gale.

Out the Thames estuary, then up-Channel into the North Sea—often lumpy and never really safe—such was the usual preliminary course. Once across, Childers was in his element, prowling among the Frisian islands and exploring the myriad creeks and inlets at the mouth of the Maas and the Scheldt, the Ems, the Jade and the Elbe. When time permitted—and often in those unhurried days it did—he would go on through the Kiel Canal to the Baltic coasts of Denmark and Germany.

Some years later Childers would draw on his incomparable knowledge of these waters when he came to write *The Riddle of the Sands*, and gain his lasting fame.

His North Sea lore was also the main reason that the Royal Navy sought his services so eagerly at the outbreak of World War I.

Childers and Basil Williams became boon companions. They shared a taste for literature, and their Committee assignments brought them a good deal together. In the affectionate memoir of Childers which he wrote and printed privately after his friend's death, Williams gives us an interesting glimpse of the new boy in the House.

"I first knew Erskine Childers in 1895, when he joined

35

the staff of clerks in the House of Commons, of which I had already been a member for a year or two. In those days he seemed a particularly quiet, almost retiring colleague who did the work allotted to him efficiently and without fuss, but for the rest made no great mark and in his leisure moments had a peculiar power of abstracting himself from all extraneous interests and of being absolutely absorbed in his own thoughts or in some mysterious writings . . . ."

Born in 1867 into an old Somerset family, Williams was three years older than Childers. He went to Marlborough and New College, Oxford, where he took a First in the Classics. After World War I Williams held Chairs of History at McGill and at Edinburgh.

The more Basil Williams observed his quiet new friend, the more intrigued he became. From other sources Williams learned the story of Childers' campaign for the Presidency of the Magpie and Stump with its "mock hustings and having the College walls plastered with posters". Williams took a closer look. Childers' long voyages in a "little cockle of a boat" and boyhood as an orphan on a great Wicklow estate were discovered in due course, and lent new dimension and new mystery.

In the Williams memoir there is a glimpse of another facet of Childers which added to Williams' interest. For Childers, like many another mild man ashore, was something of a tyrant aboard ship:

"A week-end expedition on his new and larger yacht, *Sunbeam* of fifteen tons, is also very vivid. We cruised about in Southampton Water and to the Isle of Wight. Here Childers was in his element. Aboard *Sunbeam* there were no fits of brown study, no undue modesty in the skipper. He was undoubted despot there and we landlubbers had to do what we were told and to look sharp about it without any back-talk, whether it were hauling at a rope, or taking a hand at the helm, or doing

36

something mysterious with a marling spike and the lee-scuppers. . . .Of course he was entirely responsible for the navigation—though his powers were not put to any very severe test on this occasion; but one saw enough to feel one would be perfectly ready to trust oneself to him in any gale or sudden squall off the most treacherous coast."

This particular outing aboard *Sunbeam* came in the early 1900's, but the description belongs here. For it enhances our understanding of Childers' character. Childers aboard *Vixen* was already the complete and confident sailing man, with a touch of the martinet in his make-up.

Childers never did quite realize that ambition which he had confessed in his letters to Dulcie about disappearing for a year or two. But one autumn in the late 1890's he did ship out of Liverpool aboard an old tramp steamer West Indies-bound.

Later Childers described some of his shipmates to Williams in a way that foreshadowed his own fictional skills: the third officer was "an old, dour silent, grizzled man of 62, looking like some gnarled tree trunk on a blasted heath. He never speaks or unbends except to the cabin-kittens when he thinks he is unobserved; and then he expands in an elephantine tenderness. A strange silent riddle of a man." The captain was more human, "a wiry little Welshman, flaming red. . .he had a little brig of his own once and sailed her up and down the world with every sort of adventure." He was a man who would talk "of his early days of distant voyages in sailing ships in wondrous lands, with strange adventures among strange men." Here, obviously, was a man after Childers' own adventurous heart.

Once arrived in the Caribbean, Childers chartered a boat with an all-black crew and actually did, Ulysses-like, "wander from island unto island." The entire crew was so seasick that he had to do everything himself, including the delicate matter of piloting his craft in unfamiliar waters, past many a jagged coral reef.

Through his continuing friendship with Eddie Marsh, who was cramming for the Civil Service exams, and his own fondness for reading and the theater, Childers was able to share in the intellectual ferment of the mid-1890's. Marsh had not yet taken up quarters in the Raymond Buildings, where his famous "attic" would become a meeting place for the world of art and letters. But, with his gifts of ready charm and wit, he was already making many friends among the new talent, and sharing them with his Cambridge comrades.

One such friend was George Bernard Shaw, whom suddenly everyone was talking about. Shaw's play *Mrs. Warren's Profession*, with its theme of the economics of prostitution, had been turned down by the official censor. But his next and more agreable play, *Arms and the Man* (1894) had a splendid run and *The Devil's Disciple*, three years later, enhanced his reputation.

Oscar Wilde, too, was at the top of his sparkling form. Both *The Importance of Being Earnest* and *Lady Windermere's Fan* appeared in 1895, when people were still talking about his bold and mocking novel *The Portrait of Dorian Gray*.

Many of the old standards and virtues were under assault. Ibsen's plays, with their harsh and heightened realism, were probing into dark corners of the human condition. The brilliant and disturbing drawings of the young Aubrey Beardsley were running regularly in the *Yellow Book*, and it was clear that a growing public preferred their delicate perversity to the narratives-on-canvas of Sir Laurents Alma-Tadema, Sir Edward Burne-Jones and Sir John Millais.

As the Jubilee year of 1897 neared Rudyard Kipling caught the mood and faint malaise of England better than anyone else. Drawing on what John Bowle calls his "queer chameleon genius", he reflected in his *Recessional* "the push and the pride and, occasionally, the misgivings of Empire":

If, drunk with sight of power, we loose
Wild tongues that have not Thee in awe,
Such boastings as the Gentiles use,
Or lesser breeds without the Law—
Lord God of Hosts, be with us yet,
Lest we forget—lest we forget!

Although never quite clear exactly what kind of a warning note these beautiful sonorities were sounding, their tone reminded his vast and delighted audience that, whether the Empire disintegrated from some form of false pride or managed to hold on a little longer, the whole operation was at a level not far below the Lord's.

The hollow sound at the bottom of the well of Victorian plenty was getting louder. Troubles with those "lesser breeds" were beginning to have a particularly metallic ring, the focus now being on the South African scene.

When in 1899 tensions with the stubborn Boer led to the outbreak of war, it was believed at first that the regular Army could handle the situation. But by late December the campaign was in deep trouble, and volunteers were badly needed. Erskine Childers and Basil Williams were among the first to answer the call to the colors.

The seeds of South African discord were planted years before. As far back as 1815, when the Cape settlement became a British colony, the Boers—who had pioneered there—began to chafe. The Boers (Boer is Afrikaans for *farmer*) were a hardy and ingrown race, mostly of Dutch extraction but with some German and French antecedents as well. Unlike the British, their ties with their homelands had gradually weakened. They had become Boers or Afrikaners first, with their own tribal laws and a fierce love of freedom. Although they shared with the British a recognition that it was their divine duty to subdue and exploit the native Kaffirs, they wished to be beholden to no one.

So, in 1837 began the Great Trek of the Boers across the

Orange river and up into the high veldt. Boer Republics soon mushroomed, the two most permanent being the Transvaal and the Orange Free State. Although still nominally under British suzerainty, the Boers were for all day-to-day purposes free to breathe the high, clear air of freedom there.

The trouble was that British adventurers and other settlers could not keep away from those wide uplands. The Boers called these intruders *uitlanders* or outsiders, and resented them greatly. By the 1880's the uitlanders were beginning to outnumber the Boers. Discovery of gold in the Transvaal (1884) simply accelerated the process of infiltration.

Apart from their own attractions, the two Boer republics lay directly athwart a great two-part British dream—of Imperial lands reaching all the way to the Zambesi, and of Cape-to-Cairo rail and telegraph communications. Two remarkable men, Cecil Rhodes and Sir Alfred Milner, were the principal dreamers. By 1890, Rhodes was Prime Minister of the Cape Colony—and the possessor of one of the world's vast fortunes, based originally on the Kimberly diamond mines. Milner, who came out to South Africa as High Commissioner in 1897, was a financial wizard with ice-cold administrative skills and the firm conviction that Britons were born only to be rulers.

Under great pressure from his people, Oom Paul Kruger, Boer leader and tribal patriarch, laid down certain laws which made citizenry a long process for the uitlanders. When they did achieve it, theirs was a second-class citizenry with no vote and heavy taxes.

On New Year's Day, 1896, something happened which made a bad situation infinitely worse. Dr. Leander Starr Jameson, one of Cecil Rhodes' more irresponsible colleagues, led 500 armed horsemen into the Transvaal to rally dissident uitlanders in Johannesburg and to bring Kruger to heel. One of Oom Paul's commando units—born horsemen and dead shots like all the Boers—rounded the raiders up with ease and they were left to cool their heels in Boer prisons. "Old

Jameson has upset my applecart," said Rhodes, with perfect truth.

The ill-starred Jameson Raid is a watershed date in late Victorian history. There ensued, in John Buchan's words, "an apparent loosening of civilization's cement, which is a reverence for law and order and a general goodwill. A more violent, a less equable temper was growing in the world . . . . Politics became more feverish and party feeling more extreme . . . . Britain's possessions acquired at random were suddenly seen as the material for a world-wide polity which offered illimitable opportunities to her youth . . . . Her poets sang of it with an Elizabethan passion. No statesman omitted it from his perorations, and Mr. Chamberlain was recognized as its 'business manager'."

There seems to have been very little doubt that the jingoistic Joseph Chamberlain knew in advance about Dr. Jameson's plans, and in a larger sense about Cecil Rhodes'. The question whether he had actually connived at the Jameson Raid was raised in the House of Commons. Since a nice point of Victorian honor seemed to be involved, a Select Committee was appointed to look into the whole affair. It so happened that Basil Williams was designated Committee Clerk. In due course, the Committee came up with their answers: condemnation of the actions of Rhodes and Jameson, full vindication of the elegant Chamberlain and his Colonial Office so far as any suspicion of complicity was concerned.

Basil Williams' work as clerk for this particular Select Committee marked the beginning of his lifelong interest in South African problems. Later he would write a full-dress biography of Cecil Rhodes.

By 1899, Britain was spoiling for a fight. Even though the Boers very tolerantly resisted the understandable impulse to hang Dr. Jameson and his top lieutenants, the situation rapidly worsened. Oddly enough, the British civilians in South Africa were much more warlike than the military, for the

41

latter knew first-hand in what short supply everything was, from cavalry swords to modern rifles to remounts.

Journeying to England, Sir Alfred Milner was able to persuade his master, Joseph Chamberlain, that the cause was a good one and time was ripe. Impossible ultimatums were exchanged. The British demands, sent unaccountably by mail packet, stipulated home rule for the new settlers in the Rand (where the gold was) and the disarming of all Boers in the Transvaal. The latter demand, as they well knew, was totally unacceptable.

Encouraged by the rattling of friendly sabres in Germany, Kruger too was peremptory beyond any hope of peaceful solution. He demanded that the British withdraw their troops from territories adjacent to his republic and turn back reinforcements already on the high seas. He threatened war if they did not do so.

Time and the Boer ultimatum ran out on October 11, 1899.

In short order the confident British won two small victories—Talana and Elandslaagte. Their brutal use of the lance in the latter made mortal the Boers' hatred of the invader.

In those early days of the war each side had about 20,000 men in the field. But the Boer rifles were better—Mausers that could kill a man at 2200 yards—and they used them better. They had 1200 trained artillerymen, well-equipped with guns from Le Creusot and Krupp. Also in the Boers' favor were their interior lines of communication, and the burning faith that their cause was just.

So the tide swung quickly over to the defenders. Drawing on every able-bodied boy and man, from 15 to 60, the Boers were soon able to field some 40,000, and for a time this was enough. Even when General Sir Redvers Buller, VC, arrived with 40,000 reinforcements, the Boers went right on winning.

Beefy and rock-solid, Buller looked like the ideal man for the job. But behind the calm exterior, and under the

42

proven courage, lay a self-doubt and stupidity that made him one of the most inept military leaders in British history. Oddly enough, through many disasters he kept the loyalty of his men. As one of his officers said, "such a man could do anything with soldiers, if he could but invent anything to do." All Sir Redvers could think of was frontal attack in close order, and his men went down in windrows.

The war hit the aging Queen Victoria hard. Instinctively, she knew that her ministers and generals were taking the campaign too lightly. Then came December 1899 and the terrible awakening. Within one "Black Week", England learned of three shattering defeats: Stormberg, Magersfontein and Colenso.

News of Colenso reached the half-blind Queen in despatch form early one morning, before her daily dose of belladonna. Squinting, she misread the news, and rejoiced at breakfast over victory at last. Then the daily papers came and with them the truth: another bitter loss, the worst defeat of the three. She was silent for a moment. Then she said quietly, "Now perhaps they will take my advice and send out Lord Roberts and Lord Kitchener as I urged them to do from the first."

This time the ministers took heed. Britain's two most celebrated soldiers were ordered to take over the South African campaign, with General Kitchener to act as Chief of Staff to the small, much-loved Field Marshal.

The ministers also called for volunteers. Shocked out of long complacency, deeply involved emotionally, Englishmen responded by the thousands.

Basil Williams was already a member of the Honourable Artillery Company, most ancient and prestigious of all the British volunteer units. As one immediate result of the Black Week disasters, the Company was called to active duty in its entirety. On vacation in Ireland, Erskine Childers, who had no military affiliation, sent his friend a frantic cable that he

43

was returning to England immediately and wished to be enrolled in the ranks of the HAC.

Although the HAC battery that was being activated was already almost fully manned, Childers talked his way not only into the unit but into Basil Williams' section.

So, very rapidly indeed, Childers and Williams together made what Childers called the transition "from the ease and freedom of civilian life to the rigors and serfdom of a soldier's."

Orders for South Africa came after a few perfunctory weeks' training. On a wild February night of swirling snow, the mounted artillerymen of the HAC rode out of their London barracks. They "filed silently out into the slushy streets from under the dim lamps of the barracks gateway." With the flakes thickening, they pulled down their broad-brimmed slouch hats as they rode, and huddled gratefully into their Army cloaks.

Thirteen miles down the Thames, "in the first ghastly dawn", the troop reached the Albert Docks and clattered along the sheds which bordered the berth where their transport, the SS *Montfort* lay.

6.   Not So Splendid, Not So Little. . .

Erskine Childers at first glance did not seem a very promising soldier. He wore glasses, which was most unusual for an enlisted man in those days, and he had that sciatic leg. But he turned to with a will, for his was the wish to excel in whatever he did. His Boer War diary (called *In the Ranks of the C.I.V.* when it was published in book form) and his letters to his sisters show—despite their characteristic modesty and understatement—how well he succeeded.

The horse-carrying transport *Montfort* took three weeks to slog her way to Capetown. Childers' duties as stableman kept him almost constantly with his charges—feeding and watering them, leading them round the horse-deck for exercise, shoving them back into their stalls . . . .

The first few days out, the North Atlantic was in boisterous mood, and most of the soldiers were sick. Childers, the sailing man, had a great advantage, as this entry in the diary records:

"Our sergeant, usually an awesome personage to me, helpless as a babe, and white as a corpse, standing rigid. The lieutenant feebly told me to report when all horses were watered and feeds made up. It was a long job, and at the end I found him leaning limply against a stall. 'Horses all watered, and feeds ready, sir.' He turned on me a glazed eye, which saw nothing; then a

45

glimmer of recollection flickered, and the lips framed the word 'feed,' no doubt through habit; but to pronounce that word at all under the circumstances was an effort of heroism for which I respected him."

Anchored for a few hours off Las Palmas in the Grand Canary, *Montfort* had her first news of the war. Ladysmith—invested since October—was still heavily besieged by the Boer, but General Buller's relieving force was at last nearing the beleagured city.

Soon they were headed south again. The diary notes the transition:

"Then came the tropics and the heat, and the steamy doldrums, when the stable-deck was an 'Inferno,' and exercising the horses like a tread-mill in a Turkish bath, and stall-cleaning an unspeakable business. Yet the hard work kept us in fit condition, and gave zest to the intervals of rest."

To keep cool Basil Williams and Childers slung their hammocks on deck. They started a ship's newspaper, making four copies in manuscript, as there was no printing press on board. One or two entries reflect their high spirits. Here is Childers' recipe for "something of a dubious, hashy nature" which was the main breakfast staple:

"Catch some of yesterday's Irish stew, thoroughly disinfect, and dye to a warm khaki colour. Smoke slowly for six hours, and serve to taste."

Here is Basil Williams' "prophetic" description of their arrival in Capetown, done in the style of the Baroness Ouida:

"It was sunset in Table Bay—Phoebus' last lingering rays were empurpling the beetling crags of Table Mountain's snowy peak—the great ship *Montfort*, big with the hopes of an Empire, was gliding majestically to her moorings. Countless craft, manned by lissome blacks or tawny Hottentots, instantly shot forth from the crowded quays, and surged in picturesque disorder round the great hull . . . ."

46

The first real view of the splendid Table Mountain, with "a table cloth of white clouds spread on it", came on February 26. They lay off Capetown all day on the 27th. Unlike Williams' fervent and fanciful description, the actual landing on a great deserted key was something of a letdown, without even a crane to help them.

While *Montfort* was still lying in the roadstead, the news was flashed to her that the Boer General Cronjé had capitulated at Paardeberg, and that 4,000 prisoners had been taken along with him. And the questions that soldiers always ask themselves on their way to combat began to form: *Are we still needed? Will we get there before it's all over?*

Ladysmith was actually relieved on February 28, after a siege that lasted 118 days. In character, the plodding Sir Redvers Buller allowed the numerically-inferior Boers to slip away.

After Lord Roberts' stunning victory at Paardeberg and their own failure to take Ladysmith, the Boer high command realized that their forces could no longer stand up to the British armies in set battles. So they instituted Phase II of the contest, a guerrilla warfare of swift attacks on convoys and small outposts—the kind of hit-and-run tactics that suited the Boers best. Despite the enormous numbers now arrayed against them, and the beginnings of a scorched-earth policy laid down by the vigorous Lord Roberts, Paul Kruger the patriarch politician, along with the military leaders like Louis Botha and Christian de Wet, re-affirmed their determination to fight to the last man. In Kenneth Griffith's phrase the Boers "lived off their burning land and fought at the gallop."

All that spring of 1901 the HAC Battery trained—and chafed. Inching northward they finally reached Bloemfontein, capital of the Orange Free State, which had fallen to Lord Roberts' hard-marching offensive in mid-March.

Enteric fever was rife there, and morale sank lower. Still, as one of the troopers picked by lot to witness the Annexation Proclamation, Childers remembers a thrilling moment. Colonel Pretyman, the Governor of the newly-acquired

47

Orange Free State, read out the Annexation Proclamation, renaming it the Orange River Colony. How properly-English Childers' sentiments still were is shown by his account:

"I couldn't hear a word except 'colony' at the end, at which everyone cheered. Then the flag was unrolled, and hung dead for a minute, till a breeze came and blew out 'that haughty scroll of gold', the Royal Standard. Bands struck up 'God Save the Queen', a battery on a hill above the town thundered out a royal salute, everybody cheered, and I was standing on British soil."

Alternating between driver and stableman, Childers chafed along with all the rest. The job of driver was more interesting, as it took considerable skill to wheel the gun into position, get the ammunition wagons to the rear (in the combat drill) and then run ammunition to the simulated firing line as required.

A message to members of the Battery from Lord Roberts himself helped: *they were not to be disappointed at not yet having gone to the front. . .there was plenty more work to be done.* The dapper little Field Marshal, "Bobs" to the British public and his adoring troops, knew the mind and heart of the man in the ranks very well indeed.

Pushing on in triumph toward Pretoria, capital of the Transvaal, Roberts was by-passing many thousands of unconquered Boers who in particular harassed his right rear. Commanding their will-o-the-wisp forays was Christian de Wet, the finest guerrilla fighter that the war produced.

On June 22 news came to Roberts' Headquarters that de Wet had cut the vital rail line to Pretoria and that his forces were swarming in the vicinity of the town of Lindley, where Lieutenant General Arthur Paget commanded. A convoy was ordered to help relieve and re-supply the town. Among the forces escorting the convoy was the full HAC Battery of four 12½ pounders (Vickers Maxim quick-firing) along with 3200 rounds of its still-unused ammunition.

Childers describes the slow-moving convoy and its long

halt at midday "in deference to the habits of the trek-ox whose pensive progress over level ground, sullen obstinacy at critical spruits (half-dry river beds) and acute sensitiveness to the hours of his meals make up one of the many difficult problems of warfare in a country such as this."

June 26th—the day after Childers' 29th birthday—was the unforgettable day for the Battery. The convoy and its escort came to a crest which ended in an abrupt, typically flat-topped kopje commanding the road, and the kopje was bristling with Boer riflemen. The Lancers were ordered to work their way round to the rear of the hill, while the HAC Battery was to engage it frontally. A staff officer galloped up with the orders.

"Walk—March!, Trot!" rang out, and "down we went into the most villainous gully, splashed through a stream, galloped up a steep and crumbling bank, formed line on the level and trotted methodically into action."

Under fairly intense rifle fire the guns were unlimbered, the wagons withdrawn and the range of the hostile kopje quickly found. Childers was preoccupied at first with a pack-saddle on his off-horse that was slipping. "Then I noticed the whine of bullets and dust spots knocked up and felt the same sort of feeling that one has while waiting to start a race, only with an added chill and thrill."

"Our shrapnel are bursting beautifully over the Boer lines," he notes while waiting to run more ammunition to the guns.

In the course of the next hour, the four HAC guns fired 225 rounds. They were the first shots fired overseas by the HAC in the three-and-a-half centuries of its previously-domestic existence. One gunner and one driver were wounded in the action, and four horses hit.

And so at last Erskine Childers learned the glorious uncertainties of combat.

Childers with an "Honourable Artillery Company" gun, 1900 —
photo courtesy of Radio Times, London

7.   A Swirling Summer, a Fragmented Fall

The next day saw more action. Seven miles on, behind another of those ugly little spruits, the Boer was waiting for the slow-moving convoy. A ridge with undulations sloped down to the stream bed. Beyond were kopjes, and from the summit of one of them a Creusot gun commanded the spruit.

The left section of the HAC Battery, under Captain Budworth, and with Erskine Childers serving as a driver for one of the two guns, was in the post of danger, protecting the rear of the convoy. Now, for the first time, the Battery experienced, "in its list of new emotions," that of shell-fire from a big enemy gun. Mostly bursting on impact, the shells did little damage. "We are already getting used to them," Childers noted in his diary, "but the first that fell made us very silent, and me, at any rate, very uncomfortable."

To add to the confusion, the Boer set fire to the veldt and, "with a favoring wind the flames, licked their way to our very guns and horses." The enemy, however, failed to press home the attack, and in good time the convoy lumbered into Lindley.

Childers' reaction to these first days of combat is properly understated and soldierly. "Of course we are all delighted that the days of waiting are over, and that we have had fighting and been of use."

His admiration for Captain Budworth, later a general

and already a first-class soldier, was almost schoolboyish. Some years later, writing to Basil Williams, he reconjured how he felt:

> "I cannot get over a feeling of shyness for Budworth. As a man in the ranks I had a profound reverence for him, and it is almost unpleasant to realize that he is a mortal man and a fellow-sinner. I like him very much."

All that summer the Battery played its useful part—protecting convoys, helping to relieve outlying garrison towns, trying to intercept the ubiquitous yet quicksilver de Wet. In a letter to one of his sisters Childers analysed his feelings about the enemy, after the novelty had worn off:

> "The most curious part of it all is that one has no feeling of enmity for anyone when fighting. It is all blissfully impersonal, like a game. I never can connect shells and bullets with a malicious sender, nor do I bear any grudge against the people I am trying to kill . . . ."

As early as March, 1901, before he had actually tasted the joys of combat, Childers was already developing this sporting feeling of his for the foe. De Wet had been accused of brutality to prisoners. In a letter to *The Times,* Childers wrote that the Boer general was "not only a gallant soldier but a humane and honorable gentleman . . . . We gain nothing and only lose in self-respect by slandering him." Endorsing the letter, *The Times* called Childers "a fair type of the best kind of English fighting man."

As summer turned to fall and it became clear to everyone except perhaps de Wet that the Boers were on the run at last, Childers makes another revealing entry in his diary:

> "As for de Wet, the plucky Boer who is fighting us down here. . .now that his cause is hopeless, we have sworn to get him to London and give him a dinner and a testimonial for giving us a chance to fight."

52

Basil Williams and Childers took more and more to sleeping in the open. Rather than cramming themselves into a bell tent with eleven other enlisted men, they would, in Williams' words, "doss out together under one of the guns."

"There," the Williams Memoir goes on, "when we were tired of playing picquet with a precious but greasy pack of cards, we would talk of all things under the sun until we rolled over to sleep."

According to Williams, their "basically hidebound Tory philosophy" began to change. Out of their running dialogue and the easy democracy of life in the ranks more liberal ideas were emerging. It would be tempting to project this trend to include sympathy for a small nation like the Boer republics in their struggle to be free. There is in fact no hint of such sympathy, either in Williams' memoir or in Childers' wartime diary.

Nor is there any awareness of the fact that several Irish and American-Irish Brigades fought on the side of the Boers. One of the latter performed well in the siege of Ladysmith and evacuated a big Krupp gun when the Boers raised the siege. Major John Macbride was the second-in-command of the Irish-American Brigade. He was the fiery little Irishman who later married Maud Gonne and was shot for his part in the 1916 Easter Rebellion . . . .

The Childers' diaries do contain several cheerful references to the Munster Fusiliers, one of the traditional regiments serving with the British. Here is a typical entry, showing that Childers' somewhat patronizing Ascendancy views had not yet changed much:

"Had a jolly talk with some Paddies of the Munster Fusiliers about Ireland etc. They were miserable, 'fed up' but merry; that strange combination one sees so much of out here. They talked about the revels they would have when they got home, the beef, bacon, stout, but chiefly stout . . . ."

In a more generalized way, Shane Leslie's autobiography contains a comment which sheds an amusing light on Irish attitudes toward their service under the British:

"Irish regiments won glory in the darkest days of the Boer War. The Boers were also a small nation and Irish soldiers on departure gave three cheers for Kruger to ease their conscience. After spells of heroic fighting, they celebrated their return by giving three more cheers for the vanquished on Dublin quay, like a team after a football match. English critics, who cannot appreciate this duplicity of soul, need never try to understand the Irish."

What the Childers' diaries do have is some excellent combat reporting. They perfectly reflect that narrow world of blinkered reality and rumor in which each small section of an army invariably functions. "I am getting used to the blank ignorance in which we live," he notes on July 5. Because—at least in theory—they had to plan ahead, the soldiers assigned to the cook-shop were the source of many of the rumors. Officers' servants were also the origin of many. "Both are always false," Childers remarks briskly, "but there is a slightly more respectable mendacity about the latter than the former."

This account of a typical action gives that whole swirling summer in microcosm:

"We and the Munsters and some Yeomanry were marching down a valley, whose flanks were supposed to have been scouted, the infantry in columns of companies, that is, in close formation, and all in apparent security. Suddenly a storm of rifle-fire broke out from a ridge on our right front and showed us we were ambushed. The Munsters were nearest to the ridge, about 600 yards, I should say. We were a bit further off. I heard a sort of hoarse murmur go up from the close mass of infantry, and saw it boil, so to speak, and spread out. Our section checked for a moment, in a sort of bewilderment (my waggon was close behind our gun at the time), but the next, and almost without orders, guns were unlimbered and whisked round, a waggon unhooked, teams trotting away, and shrapnel bursting over the top of the ridge in quick succession. All this time the air was full of a sound like the moaning of wind from the bullets flying across the valley, but strange to say, not a man of us was hit. Some of them were explosive bullets. The whole thing was soon over. Our guns peppered their quickest, and it was a treat to see the shrapnel bursting clean and true along the ridge. The infantry extended and lay down; some Yeomanry made a flank move, and that episode was over."

In Pretoria on August 15, the HAC Battery had the honor of being reviewed by Lord Roberts. Standing on the steps of his headquarters with a large staff, the Field Marshal looked "very small, fit and alert;" the Childers diary then enthusiastically quotes the soldiers' ditty about their leader:

" 'E's little but 'e's wise,
    'E's a terror for 'is size!''

"We are not interested in the possibilities of defeat," Queen Victoria had said at a dark hour early in the war. "They do not exist." The Queen died in January of 1901, knowing that her prediction was true.

Yet there was a lot still to be done. The reliefs of Ladysmith, of Kimberly and of Mafeking were well past now, each in turn blown-up by the press into major triumphs. The overreaction of the British people to the lifting of the sieges, especially Mafeking, left them momentarily drained of further emotion. Their attention wandered to the Boxer Rebellion and to the Gold Coast, where there was trouble again with the Ashanti.

Phase three of the war began in September, 1901. Paul Kruger, sick and old now, crossed the border into Portuguese territory, never to return. He left the conduct of the war to his generals and to Marthinus Steyn, the once-mild Orange Free State leader, now one of the bitterest of the bitter-enders.

The generals re-formed their ranks again, turning their best men and horses into commando units of 300, with commandants appointed by Louis Botha himself rather than by election. Each 100-man increment was led by a field cornet, and every ten by a corporal—a far cry from the old "every man his own officer" of the early days of the war.

From the gray-green plains of the high veldt, where the eye travels immense distances, to the mountain rim that runs from Drakensberg to the Rhodesian scarp, where it breaks down in wild kloofs—or gorges—to the bushveldt, the Boers fought on. (The streams, starting as strings of pools on the high veldt, become torrents as they drop down, and end as sleepy tropical rivers in the lowlands.)

It was tough country to fight over, and the Boer was still a tough foe to fight.

By November, it had become Kitchener's war, with Lord Roberts homeward bound for honors richly earned, and Sir Redvers Buller relieved at last. On Roberts' way home, he stopped at Colenso to see the grave of his only son, lost as part of Buller's vast folly there.

In October came the British "Khaki Election," so-called because the waging of the war was the only issue. In the voting Lord Salisbury and Joe Chamberlain earned overwhelming support, and Kitchener had his blank check to finish it all off.

Kitchener's war was more merciless than Lord Roberts'. Block-houses and barbed wire stretched across the land now, and massive drives by mounted soldiers swept many Boers— women and children mostly—into concentration camps, where they died in droves.

Still the end did not come until May 31, 1902. When the Peace was finally signed at Vereeniging, more than 20,000 Boers were still in the saddle. Many smashed their rifle stocks on the rocks rather than pile them in surrender.

Exactly 59 years later, on May 31, 1961, the Republic of South Africa came into being. With its creation, the dream of freedom for which the Boers had fought and died was realized at last.

The HAC Battery, along with many of the other volunteer units, was ordered home in late September of 1901. General Paget spoke warmly to the men of the Battery before they entrained for Capetown: "I am sorry to lose you and I shall miss you very much." He cited three actions where the guns were particularly well served under heavy fire. "I hope you will sometimes think of me as I certainly shall of you. . . Goodbye."

Running under the modest surface of his diaries is the fact that Erskine Childers had, during the months of combat, turned into a fine soldier. Basil Williams' affectionate testimonial confirms this.

". . .though so very different in many ways from most of his comrades, though liable, even on active service, to fall into his fits of brown study, these periods of abstraction never came upon him when there were any soldierly duties to perform, and he earned the liking and respect of officers and men not only for his thoroughness and unassuming courage as an artillery driver, but still more for his unselfishness in all the little difficulties of campaigning life, his modesty and the transparent fineness of his character."

The Battery sailed on October 7 on the transport *Aurania*, horses and all. Continuing what would be a lifelong fascination with South Africa, Basil Williams remained behind to look around a bit on his own. Childers, very much in character, stayed with the horses and the arduous routine until the end of a voyage every bit as uncomfortable as the trip out ten months before.

London gave her homecoming citizen-soldiers a thundering welcome and the Freedom of the City. There was also a

57

service of Thanksgiving, and Childers remembers the "sudden dim hush in the great cathedral."

Describing the Guildhall and the Mayor's welcome there, the final entry in Childers' diary well embodies his feeling about the whole enormous South African experience:

"I expect the feelings of all of us were much the same; some honest pride in having helped to earn such a welcome; a sort of stunned bewilderment at its touching and passionate intensity; a deep wave of affection for our countrymen; and a thought in the background all the time of a dusty khaki figure still plodding the distant veldt—our friend and comrade, Atkins, who had done more and bloodier work than we, and who is not at the end of it yet."

8. The Book That Became a Legend

While Erskine Childers was still campaigning in South Africa, his adoring sisters were circulating passages from his diary to family friends. Several of these reached Reginald Smith, senior editor of the London publishing house of Smith, Elder and Company.

When *Aurania* docked in Southampton, the enterprising Mr. Smith was waiting for Childers on the pier. Right then and there he extracted a promise from the homecoming soldier to pull the diaries together into book form.

In the Ranks of the C.I.V. came out late that fall of 1901. Its title may seem somewhat confusing: the "City Imperial Volunteers" referred to in it was simply the overall name for all the London civilian detachments serving in South Africa. Dedicated not surprisingly to "My Friend and Comrade Gunner Basil Williams," the book found swift favor with a ready-made audience of English readers still half-enamored of the war that continued to be fought so heartily. By Christmas it was in its third printing.

In a letter to his sister Constance, Childers wrote a description of one of his new admirers that shows how characteristically he reacted to the fame now coming his way. At the time, Childers was staying in Scotland with Reginald Smith for a shooting party. One day his host took him to see "a dear old chap, yellow as a guinea from India and a keen sportsman. We got onto books and rather to my annoyance Reginald said, 'I wonder if you have read Mr. Childers' book?' . . . . Suddenly he leapt to his feet and shouted, 'What, are you the man who wrote this?', bounded across the room, burrowed in a heap of untidy literature, plucked out a thumb-worn copy of *In the Ranks*, chucked it down and wrung my hand with embarrassing vigour. The poor old chap got quite pathetic. 'I've often felt such a jiggins,' he said, 'sitting at my club having a good dinner, when you others were roughing it out there.' Wasn't it nice? It touched me awfully. I felt I was the fraud, because I enjoyed the outing and dislike clubs!"

With its quick strokes of local color, cheerful gentleman-ranker humor and fine action sequences, *In the Ranks* continued to find favor with British readers until the jingoistic Boer War fever began to recede.

Although Childers dutifully resumed his work as a Committee Clerk to the Commons, what he wanted to do most, after his dusty year of soldiering on the veldt, was to sail again. So, in 1902, he bought *Sunbeam*, bigger and heavier than *Vixen* (15 tons, 40-feet overall) but still well-suited to the North Sea waters that were his favorite cruising grounds.

During that same year he wrote *The Riddle of the Sands*, filling it with his fresh delight in the beauty and mystery of the Frisian Islands and the great tidal estuaries behind them.

The year 1903 was a banner year for Childers. Not only did it see publication of *The Riddle*, destined to become a classic of seafaring adventure, it was also of course the time of his visit to Boston with the HAC and the providential meeting with Molly Osgood that changed his life.

The Riddle of the Sands was published by Smith, Elder in May. To understand its lasting appeal, a summary of the plot is essential, even at some diminution of suspense for the new reader.

The narrator, Carruthers, is a rather light-hearted young Foreign Office employee. When we first meet him he is passing a boring September of a not-specified year, condemned by his duties to stay at his desk and live in a half-deserted club. Meanwhile, all his friends are on country house parties or pursuing other cheerful long-vacation pleasures.

Toward the end of his time of enforced incarceration, a letter from an acquaintance named Davies comes, urging Carruthers to join him in some late-season duck shooting in the Baltic. Carruthers, who is by his own admission rather a smart young man-about-town, remembers Davies as an energetic if somewhat dull fellow undergraduate at Oxford. Later, as Carruthers went his upward way in London society, he had deliberately allowed an incipient friendship to lapse.

What irritates Carruthers about the letter is the assumption that he *will* accept—and bring a whole shopping list of items like foul-weather gear, a pound of Raven Mixture smoking-tobacco, and a prismatic compass along with him.

Out of boredom with his half-empty club, and a slight feeling of guilt about Davies, Carruthers does accept, in what he terms "an act of obscure penance." Davies' telegram in answer to his acceptance instructs his guest to bring a Number Three Rippingill Stove, an order which Carruthers considers "a perplexing and ominous direction." Nevertheless, he obeys. Before leaving London, he also buys the Raven Mixture "with that peculiar sense of injury which the prospect of smuggling in another's behalf always entails."

Heavily laden, Carruthers arrives at Flensburg, which sits pleasantly on its Baltic fjord. He finds Davies even seedier than he had remembered. Dressed in an old Norfolk jacket and wearing a tweed cap and muddy brown boots, "he clashed on my notions of a yachtsman—no cool white ducks or neat blue serge; and where was that snowy-crowned yachting cap, that precious charm that so easily converts a landsman into a dashing mariner?"

Davies greets him in an awkward, rather off-hand way.
" 'I say, you've brought a good deal of stuff.'
'You gave me a good many commissions.'
'Oh, I didn't mean those things,' he said absently."

The question of who is to carry Carruther's gear to the dinghy next comes up.

" 'Aren't your men here?' I asked faintly.

'Men?' He looked confused. 'Oh, perhaps I ought to have told you, I never have any paid hands; it's quite a small boat you know.' "

So begins Carruther's apprenticeship aboard *Dulcibella*, twin of Childers' real-life *Vixen* even to her 30-foot overall length, her nine-foot beam and her two skins of diagonal teak. There are mysteries about Davies that trouble Carruthers, landsman that he is. One is Davies' diffidence about discussing the early phase of his holiday, when *Dulcibella* was working her way through the East Frisian Islands. Frank and hearty in all else, the skipper slides away from any details of his Frisian passage.

Then Carruthers notes that a leaf from the ship's log has been torn out. The discovery is another little pebble of discontent and worry flipped into the clear pool of their pleasant days at sea.

And there is another odd clue. Although there are plenty of duck about, Davies keeps complaining that the Baltic is too tame and mild a place for good shooting and urges a return to the wilderness and worsening weather of the Frisians.

A casual contact with the master of a coastal sailing barge adds to Carruthers' puzzlement. Davies greets Schiffer Bartels of the galliot *Johannes* with nervous indifference when the latter comes aboard. Yet the newcomer seems very fond of him, "smiling affectionately out of a round grizzled beard."

Bartels, it seems, had helped Davies out of a bit of a mess in the North Sea. At one point he tells Carruthers that his friend is "as brave as a lion and as quick as a cat." At another, Bartels speaks cryptically about *Dulcibella*: " 'She is strong and good, your little ship, and—heaven!—she had need be so.' "

After Bartels has gone, the truth comes tumbling out. It seems that, during his time in the Frisians, Davies had fallen in with a German yachtsman called Dollmann and his pretty daughter. In the course of this new friendship, Herr Dollmann, an icy Junker, proposed that they sail to Hamburg and the Baltic together, with Dollmann's smart 60-ton *Medusa* showing the way. The idea struck Davies, already quite taken with Fraulein Dollmann's charms, as an excellent one.

They started out in worsening weather. As the winds reached gale force and the seas grew short and steep, they hove to within hailing distance. Dollmann proposed a short-cut through the sands and Davies yelled back his agreement.

At the exact critical moment when Davies needed guidance most, Dollmann vanished, relying on his own speed to windward and local knowledge to get through. Deserted now, with his charts of no use in the shifting sands, Davies' cause seemed hopeless. By sheer luck the flooding tide carried him into a narrow safe channel. Finally, he went aground, with a mile of sand acting as a breakwater against the young gale. It was at this point that Bartels turned up, also living out the storm in a branch of the same channel. With his help, Davies broke out his big anchor, secured to fifty fathom of warping hawser. With the anchor firmly embedded in the sand, and the powerful winch supplying the strain, *Dulcibella* then clawed herself off the sandspit in the classic kedging operation.

For weeks thereafter Davies lived with the knowledge that the German had wished and planned his death. Brooding, rehearsing every detail of his relationship with Dollmann and the fair daughter, Davies had finally come to a startling conclusion: Dollmann, the elegant German aristo-crat, was actually an Englishman on the run—a spy perhaps, certainly a man up to the devil's own work in those remote islands.

The evidence as he presents it to Carruthers is tantaliz-ing. Just as Dollmann was pulling away at the height of the storm, he had shouted his plan in English, *a language he had previously said he knew nothing of*:

63

" 'Short-cut through the sands. Follow me!' "

The lapse into English was simply to make sure that the victim understood. Since the words were the last that Davies would hear on earth, the slip did not much matter in any case.

Davies also bases his identification of Dollmann on plain, stubborn Anglo-Saxon instinct (an instinct that also tells him that Clara Dollmann is a perfect English rose, and that she is totally unaware of her father's perfidy).

So now Carruthers knows why he has been summoned, and why they must go back to solve the riddle locked somewhere in the shifting sands and treacherous channels of those remote islands.

Carruthers' sense of adventure responds to the challenge, even though he knows that his fluency in German was the main reason why Davies recruited him in the first place. His sense of humor helps, as he realizes that he has in effect been "kidnapped as neatly as ever a peaceful clerk was kidnapped by a lawless press-gang, and, in the end, finding as the arch-conspirator a guileless and warm-hearted friend, who called me clever, lodged me in a cell, and blandly invited me to talk German to the purpose, as he was aiming at a little secret service on the high seas."

Threading their course west again, there is plenty of time to talk of hopes and aspirations as well as plans. We are reminded of Childers and Basil Williams when they "dossed out" in South Africa under the southern stars and discussed everything under the sun. Davies confesses that, early in his uneven career, he had failed his entrance tests for the Royal Navy. He believes deeply that a Naval Reserve should be created in advance of any actual emergency by a maritime power like Britain, and he dreams of putting his small-boat knowledge to his country's service in such a unit. He looks on the upcoming Frisian adventure as an unexpected and fulfilling chance to serve at last.

The skipper grows quite eloquent about the Germans, and their right for equal sea-space:

64

" 'I don't blame them,' said Davies, who, for all his patriotism, had not a particle of racial spleen in his composition. 'I don't blame them: their Rhine ceases to be German just when it begins to be most valuable. The mouth is Dutch, and would give them magnificent ports just opposite British shores. *We* can't talk about conquest and grabbing. We've collared a fine share of the world, and they've every right to be jealous. Let them hate us, and say so; it'll teach us to buck up, and that's what really matters.' "

As they negotiate the Kiel Canal by night—lit up like a great London street—Davies bursts out in admiration of this symbol of new forces astir: " 'Isn't it splendid? He's a fine fellow, that Emperor.' "

Arrived back in the Frisians again, they pick up Dollmann's trail and also that of an amiable German naval officer called von Brüning, commander of a "low gray rat of a vessel," the torpedo gunboat *Blitz*. Von Brüning is obviously working in close conspiracy with the master of *Medusa*.

To overhear more about what this pair is up to, Davies and Carruthers row their dinghy by night and fog across sixteen miles of tide-swept sands. By this beautifully-described exploit they achieve total surprise, and fit another piece into the jigsaw puzzle which they are assembling.

Dollmann and Von Brüning, it seems, are posing as officials of a salvage company doing some desultory dredging for sunken gold. A meeting of the company, the British adventurers finally learn, is simply their cover for the real purpose of their late-season activity: *the rehearsal by single tug and lighter for a full-dress amphibious invasion of England.*

Here is how Carruthers describes the moment of truth— a moment which comes while he is hiding in a dinghy aboard the German tug herself:

"Yes, I understood at last. I was assisting at an experimental rehearsal of a great scene, to be enacted, perhaps, in the near future—a scene when multitudes of

65

seagoing lighters, carrying full loads of soldiers, not half-loads of coal, should issue simultaneously, in seven ordered fleets, from seven shallow outlets, and, under escort of the Imperial Navy, traverse the North Sea and throw themselves bodily upon English shores."

Even in his hazardous listening post, Carruthers can marvel at the boldness of the idea:

". . .to draw on the resources of an obscure strip of coast, to improve and exploit a quantity of insignificant streams and tidal outlets, and thence, screened by the islands, to dispatch an armada of light-draught barges, capable of flinging themselves on a correspondingly obscure and therefore unexpected portion of the enemy's coast; that was a conception so daring, aye, and so quixotic in some of its aspects, that even now I was half incredulous."

The importance of the trial operation is underlined by the presence aboard the tug of a superior whose identity is mysterious. He is the man "for whose behoof this secret expedition has been planned" and who has insisted on being present in person. In the moment of sudden action aboard the tug, Carruthers cannons into him and verifies an old conjecture: "It was one who in Germany had a better right to insist than anyone else." By such beautiful and Childers-like understatement, the author tells us that it is none other than Kaiser Wilhelm himself.

Silly playboy no longer, in fact rather amazingly adept for an erstwhile landlubber, Carruthers wrecks the rehearsal and makes his getaway. Soon he and Davies, with Dollmann and daughter aboard, head for England on the sturdy *Dulcibella*.

Like all good storytellers, Childers-Carruthers knows well when to get off-stage:

"From that point our personal history is no concern to the outside world, and here, therefore, I bring this narrative to an end."

66

By Christmas of 1903, *The Riddle of the Sands* was well into its third printing. Two impressions were run off in 1904, one each in 1907, 1908, 1910 and 1913. A new, inexpensive edition appeared in 1914 as the approach of World War II gave the novel an added immediacy.

The fact that it was quickly banned in Imperial Germany contributed to the public's curiosity. Nor does there seem to be any question but that the novel had a direct impact on British naval thinking. The development of a naval base in the Firth of Forth—much nearer the German coast than the great Fleet anchorage at Scapa Flow—was certainly hastened by the warning that *The Riddle* contained.

Another fillip to sales was the arrest and imprisonment by the Germans of two British naval officers who went to the Frisian Islands to check on the real-life possibilities of Childers' fictional invasion. . . .

By 1938, the book had gone through 17 British editions. With the outbreak of World War II, and Britain again in hazard from the sea, there was fresh interest in the novel. It was in fact coming to be regarded as a sort of harbinger of wars.

The first U.S. edition came out in 1915 without any marked impact. But the American publishers, Dodd Mead, reissued it in 1940—largely because of the enthusiasm of Christopher Morley, who praised it in the pages of the *Saturday Review of Literature*. In the preface to this edition Raymond Bond explains why it is more than a fine adventure story:

> "Substitute for the Imperial Navy the great German air fleets of today, and extend the possible ports of invasion from the Frisian Islands, where the *Dulcibella's* crew went 'duck shooting,' to the French channel harbors and beyond, and Erskine Childers' novel takes on a fantastic timeliness."

Since World War II there has been a proliferation of editions on both sides of the Atlantic. The Mariner's Library Series in London issued *The Riddle* in shipshape form in 1955, and has reprinted it twice since. J.M. Dent in London, jointly with E.P. Dutton in New York, added it to their series of Illustrated Classics, with deft pen-and-ink drawings by Charles Mozley that spring spontaneously from the text. The Barre Press coffee-table edition (1972) has moody illustrations deriving in part from J.M.W. Turner, and an affectionate introduction by Brigadier E.F. Parker.

It is estimated by one old publishing hand that Childers' only novel, in all editions so far, including a Penguin paperback, is approaching the two-million mark.

From first publication, the novel received an excellent press. *The New York Times'* review on May 9, 1915 is a fair sample: "Apart from the political significance of the book, *The Riddle of the Sands* is fiction of a high quality . . . . its style and its permeating atmosphere of the sea suggest Conrad."

Some years later John Buchan, whose *The 39 Steps* has often been compared to the Childers novel, called *The Riddle of the Sands* "the best story of adventure published in the last quarter of a century." His tribute, which ran in the Christmas issue of *John O'London's Weekly* in 1926, is an excellent summary of the novel's virtues:

"It is a tale of the puzzling out of a mystery which only gradually reveals itself, and not till the very end reaches its true magnificence; but its excitement begins on the first page, and there is a steady crescendo of interest . . . ."

Buchan in conclusion makes the same comparison to Conrad which the *New York Times* reviewer did: ". . .the atmosphere of grey Northern skies and miles of yeasty water and wet sands is as masterfully reproduced as in any story of Conrad's."

Reviewing the "sumptuous" Barre Press edition as

recently as 1972, the *Washington Post* stressed the appeal of *The Riddle* to the sailing community:

> "Not surprisingly *The Riddle's* most loyal readers have always been amateur yachtsmen, and it is easy to see why. It is not just the evocative descriptions of seascapes and sailing episodes, but also the classic sketches of real 'boat people' who are obviously drawn from Childers' own experiences at sea. Davies, the rumpled and pipe-smoking small-boat enthusiast, is a durable portrait of the besotted mariner, victim of a bad attack of sea fever. . . .
>
> "It must be this human quality which has made *The Riddle* such an international favorite with yachting readers."

Word-of-mouth among mariners has in fact been one of the great preservatives as applied to *The Riddle*. There exists —today more than ever—a cult of admiring readers, which includes both shallow-draft boatmen and deepwater sailors. They are not unlike the Baker Street Irregulars.

Another reason that the novel has lived so long is that a good deal of the mystery that has grown up around Childers himself has rubbed off on it as well. There is something legendary, something fabulous, about both creator and creation. The fact that most of the legends concerning Childers are fairly wide of the mark—such as the belief that he was a British spy during all his roving career—is irrelevant. A novel by a man who was on the run for the good part of his last years tends to have more appeal than a book by a musty scholar or commuting bank clerk!

As a longtime admirer of *The Riddle of the Sands* this biographer can only add a few points to the exemplary praise of John Buchan and others. One is that the book seems forever young in spirit. It has the exuberance of youth, the innocence that precedes first-love, and that sense of adventure that knows that the race is to the bold. ("Fortune loves rough wooing," Carruthers reminds himself in his precarious hiding place aboard the German tug.)

Another point is that the story affords considerable insight into the author's character, as fiction so often does. Carruthers, as he learns his new craft of apprentice seaman, becomes more and more like Childers. Davies starts out bearing a marked resemblance to the author. The patriotism of his that wishes to serve is very much the author's. When Davies falls in love with Clara Dollmann, he dims out a bit. For love, to the still-uninitiated Childers, was a kind of aberration or weakness which rendered the victim something less than his own man.

So, in much the same way that Dick Diver in *Tender Is the Night* starts out as Fitzgerald's friend Gerald Murphy, and ends up as Scott Fitzgerald himself, Carruthers begins as a London dandy and then takes on the virtues of courage and competence that Childers admires (and himself possessed in large degree).

It is the world's loss that Erskine Childers never wrote another work of fiction. Lord Vansittart, in his erratically-brilliant autobiography, *The Mist Procession,* makes a flippant comment on this matter, as part of a paragraph concerning the senseless loss of life in the Irish Troubles: "Erskine Childers also got himself shot—a pity, for he had written a good book, *The Riddle of the Sands.*"

The celebrated diplomat begs the question. During the remaining nineteen years of Erskine Childers' life there were harsher claims on his talents than the penning of novels of suspense however fabulous.

9.   Solstice

The ten years (1904–1914) following Erskine Childers' marriage to Molly Osgood were a happy and creative time. Their idyllic quality is captured in a letter which Childers wrote, early in his marriage, to one of his sisters whose wedding was imminent: "This will be our last word probably before you marry. Well, it is a very loving and very hopeful word. . . .I pray that you may be as happy as Molly and I— I can't say more for that is the most wonderful happiness I know."

Their first child, Erskine Hamilton, who became President of Ireland in 1973, was born in December, 1905. Robert Alden arrived five years later. Molly had one miscarriage in between, also a son.

The Childers settled in a Chelsea flat where many came because of the author's growing fame, and came again because of the hospitality and charm of both Erskine and Molly. A glimpse in the Basil Williams memoir shows that Childers, in the midst of considerable activity, continued to slip away into his own world from time to time:

"He and his wife entertained their always growing circle of friends with a simple and generous hospitality in that quaint room. . .which served as dining and drawing room, as study where Childers did his work, and at times also as nursery for the two boys. . . .Here sometimes when only intimates were there, one would talk to his wife and perhaps the children, while he would go on writing, seemingly oblivious to all the talk around him."

Like half the London world of letters and politics, the Childers dined often with the irrepressible Eddie Marsh, ensconced now in his famous top-story flat in the Raymond Building. Other good friends were Sir Frederick and Lady Pollock. Sir Frederick, the third Baronet, came of a celebrated family of lawyers and jurists, and was himself a world authority on Torts and on the Law of Partnership. A Trinity Cambridge man like Childers, though his senior by 25 years, Pollock had been, from 1883 to 1903, Corpus Professor of Jurisprudence at Oxford. He had also written books on Spinoza and on the Monroe Doctrine, a novel in epistolary form called *The Etchingham Letters* and a retelling in light to not-very-light verse of famous English law cases.

Sir Frederick's most popular book, *Introduction to the History of the Science of Politics,* published in 1890, was among Erskine Childers' favorite books.

Humorous without malice, somewhat brusque on first meeting, and with several layers of shyness, Pollock was basically the most vigorous and direct of men. A humanist above all else, he was in many ways Childers' ideal. Certainly, they resembled each other greatly.

In Pollock's celebrated correspondence with Justice Oliver Wendell Holmes, which lasted from 1874 to 1932, there is a cheerful entry (July 6, 1906) which gives a glimpse of the young Childers:

> Tomorrow [writes Pollock] I am going to see two charming Americans . . . Mrs. Erskine Childers of your state, with whom I am reading Dante's *Purgatory* in such times as we can steal, and Elizabeth Robins of Kentucky: Mrs. Erskine Childers' is a modern marriage by capture—her husband went to Boston with the Hon. Artillery Company and brought her home. They are devoted to sailing a small boat (she can steer a course)

Mollie Childers —from a family portrait

and their baby rising some six months is known as the Admiral."

By the summer of 1905, Erskine and Molly were cruising far afield in *Asgard*, the sturdy 49-foot gaff-rigged ketch that Dr. Osgood had given them as a wedding present. *Asgard* was designed by Colin Archer, a famous Norwegian marine architect of Scottish descent. She was built in Norway and bore a marked resemblance to Nansen's *Fram* of Arctic fame, also Archer-designed. (*Asgard*, in Norse mythology, is the citadel of the gods, which contains Valhalla. It is also the Norwegian equivalent of Osgood.)

Despite her lameness, Molly Childers was a passionate sailor and a more than competent one. In one cruise the Childers covered 2,500 miles, ranging as far north and east as Finland. At times they had a green crew of friends aboard, at others one paid hand.

"I count Molly as a trained seaman always or the thing would have been impossible," Childers wrote Basil Williams with pride. "She can navigate, keep watch and steer."

On his return from South Africa, Childers resumed his duties as Parliamentary Clerk, a position he held until 1910. He finally resigned after fifteen years to devote his time to his writing, his Liberal politics and the cause of Home Rule.

Although he never again turned his hand to fiction, he produced five more books during the years leading up to World War I. The first of these was a brief, formal history called *The H.A.C. in South Africa*. It came out in 1903 under the joint by-line of Basil Williams and Childers. Actually Childers did most of the writing, for Williams went back to South Africa (as he would again and again) leaving the projected book unfinished. Brisk and stylish, with a good deal of the charm of *In the Ranks of the C.I.V.*, it enhanced Childers' professional standing as a military historian and critic.

Then, for several years after his marriage, Childers

worked on Volume V of the *Times' History of the War in South Africa* under the general editorship of L.A.S. Emery. In it he covered the period of guerrilla warfare, some of which he had himself seen first-hand. Over and above the vivid accounts of the forays of de Wet and Smuts and the other Boer leaders, there is down-to-earth criticism of British errors that makes the book one of the most valuable of the series of six.

Childers' study of the Boer War was directly responsible for his two next publications, *War and the Arme Blanche* (1910) and *German Influence on British Cavalry* (1911)—both extremely critical of traditional British army training.

In military jargon, the *arme blanche* is the cavalry saber, used along with the lance in the kind of frontal charge which the Boer magazine-rifle and marksmanship relegated to the Stone Age. Childers advocated training the cavalry as mounted infantrymen, expert in the use of the rifle rather than cold steel. His views were endorsed by none other than Field-Marshal Earl Roberts in a lively introduction. Commenting on the Childers argument that the rifle is the horseman's best weapon and that the saber always fails, either in tactical offense or reconnaissance, Lord Roberts has this to say:

"With every word of this I agree, and it must be remembered that my judgment is based upon personal and first-hand knowledge. Why did our Cavalry fail? Because they did not know, because they had never been required to know, how to use the principal and most useful weapon with which they were armed."

By now the onetime gunner and the Field Marshal are blood brothers, each doing the Empire credit in his own way. A quote from the final chapter shows with what resonance Childers still thinks of himself as patriotic Englishman:

"I have written strongly, because I feel strongly on a point about which every Englishman, soldier or civilian, has a right to feel strongly. We have wasted too much

75

energy, brains and splendid human material on the perverse pursuit of a phantom ideal . . . ." [The cold-steel cavalry charge.]

  German Influence on British Cavalry is a sequel to *War and the Arme Blanche,* with many more arguments in favor of more modern weapons and training.

Together, at a time when the main thrust of his thought and involvement was already turning to Ireland and Home Rule, the two studies gained for Childers a somewhat overblown reputation as military thinker—and by extension as guerrilla fighter and saboteur—which would later on come back to plague him.

During these halcyon years, the Childers made many new friends. One was Robert Woodhead, not long down from Oxford, and a favorite cruising companion. He was fated to be killed early in World War I. Another was Alfred Ollivant, who learned the art of sailing from the Childers and later would write a tender tribute to Erskine. But of all the friends old and new, the favorite next to Basil Williams himself was Gordon Shephard, a young professional soldier who shared the Childers' love of adventurous cruising. Shephard went on to become one of the first fliers in the British Army, earning the Distinguished Service Order and the Military Cross for his valor. At the age of thirty-two he became the youngest brigadier in the Flying Corps. He was killed in an aircraft crash in 1918 while on a routine patrol.

After his death Shane Leslie edited the *Memoirs of Gordon Shephard* with running commentary. Here is Leslie's first mention of the Childers in relation to Shephard:

"In the following summer (1909) he made the acquaintance of Mr. and Mrs. Erskine Childers, an acquaintance which ripened into deep friendship and under their roof in Chelsea he could almost be said to have found a second home."

Then Leslie quotes Shephard's own brief entry about the

meeting itself (August 13, 1909) which took place just before Shephard was off on a North Sea cruise:

"I dined yesterday with a great yachtsman, a Clerk in the House of Lords but nevertheless a good Radical. He strongly recommended me to go to the Texel and work south to Flushing or only to the Hook and then back. His name is Childers . . . ."

Either "House of Lords" was a mistake, or Childers was on loan at the time. In any event it is obvious that Childers and Shephard hit it off from first meeting, with their exchange of views on good cruising country.

Shephard soon became a younger brother in all but fact to Childers. With the growing fame of *The Riddle of the Sands* the supposition arose that he was the actual model for Davies or Carruthers. Since the book was written in 1902–03, when Shephard was still a schoolboy at Eton, this was just another of those Childers legends with little grounding in reality.

When Shephard was not cruising with the Childers, he often borrowed *Asgard* from them. In an entry for October, 1913 he calls *Asgard* a "fine sea-boat; and besides being weatherly, she rides the seas with a very easy motion, a quality which many sea-boats, especially yachts, do not possess."

Late in that summer of 1913, the Childers and Gordon Shephard vacationed in the northern Baltic. "You cannot imagine the pleasure of cruising far north in midsummer," Childers wrote to Basil Williams, ". . .the shore from Petersburg by Finland and Aland to Sweden is all fringed by tiny islands and rocks and shoals, but there are passages between them marked by buoys and lights and, if you like and have a fair wind, you can sail in there, like threading a needle or sewing a very intricate hem." Despite a great deal of deep-water sailing, Childers remained a small-boatman at heart.

In October of 1913 Shephard put *Asgard*, weatherly craft that she was, to a stern test. The Childers had left her in Christiania, and there Shephard and a crew of three took over for a spectacular voyage. First they went up the Norwegian

coast all the way to Bergen, then across the North Sea to the Hebrides and so down the Scottish and Irish coasts to Holyhead in Wales. For this exploit, in the worst of off-season weather, Shephard received for a second time, the Challenge Cup of the Royal Cruising Club.

After Brigadier Shephard's death, the *Yachting Monthly* paid tribute to his boldness: "We know that he found himself considerably endangered on more than one occasion, and his feats of seamanship were accomplished by sheer daring."

Erskine Childers took exception to this. His letter to the *Monthly* tells us a good deal about Childers as well as Shephard:

"I would like to say that he was not one who courted risk, but who, desiring to extend the limited field of small yacht cruises and having decided to undertake some distant voyage, would carry through what he had undertaken. In his flying work the same quality was displayed. If a necessary undertaking presented difficulties, those difficulties were not allowed to stand in his way. Once having made up his mind to do a thing, he did it. Those who watched him at work would tell you of his singular wit and skill in minimising danger and his delight in exercising these powers. But to imply that he sought risk for risk's sake and out of a dare-devil spirit is to ignore his purpose and fine intelligence, and the fact that in all he did every detail was planned out beforehand and difficulties were weighed and allowed for. He was of the type of Frobisher who, desiring to extend his knowledge, accomplished great things in spite of many dangers."

It is small wonder that Shephard and Childers became brothers, for their cool way of looking on danger's bright face was exactly the same.

10.   The Framework of Home Rule

Charles Stewart Parnell once stated the heart of the matter in ringing words: "No man has the right to fix a boundary to the march of a nation, no man has a right to say, 'thus far shalt thou go, and no farther. . . .' "

Nevertheless, with Parnell's fall and death, the cause of Ireland, with its twin strands of Land Reform and Home Rule, came unspliced. The former strand remained strong and pliant; the strand of Home Rule seemed for a time to fray and unravel.

We have seen how Parnell's bold tactics did succeed in ramming through some long-overdue agrarian legislation. By the Land Act of 1881 and the Land Purchase Act of 1885, the "Three F's"—Fair Rent, Free Sale and Fixity of Tenure—were inscribed in the rule book at last.

During the long years of Conservative rule (1895–1905) there was full recognition that continuing improvement in the lot of the Irish small landowner was necessary. It was a substitute—and a sop—for the Home Rule for which the natives were considered so unready.

A forward step was the Wyndham Land Purchase Act of 1903, which went a long way to correct the Ascendancy's assumed right to the best soil and the best pasture land. The Act made it possible for tenants to buy their holdings from their landlords on the installment plan, with the Government putting up the necessary capital.

Such practical innovations as the Irish Cooperative movement also helped the peasant farmer. First in Parliament and then as President of the movement itself, Sir Horace Plunkett provided the motivating force. George Russell, "AE" the poet in his more mystical moments, was an articulate and active lieutenant.

It is interesting to note that by 1921, when Ireland was in flaring revolt against her English masters, the Land Reform problem was actually quite near its final solution, with two-thirds of all arable acres in the hands of the native Irish by voluntary transaction.

Home Rule had a stormier passage. Lacking the iron discipline imposed by Parnell in the years up to 1891, the Irish delegation in Parliament splintered into factions. John Redmond was the acknowledged inheritor of the Parnellite tradition, but he never did quite mould his countrymen into the same kind of weapon. A Wicklow landowner with the face of a weary hawk, he was a man most accomplished in Parliamentary procedure. By 1900 Redmond had established his leadership of all the national elements in the Irish representation. There was only one trouble: when, in the rapidly-evolving years from 1911–1914, the chance came and came again, he was a little too pro-English, a little too tame, a little too gentlemanly . . . .

In Ireland itself the cause of freedom seemed, in the 1890's and early 1900's, to be in limbo. "Ireland sat crouched by her dying fire," is the way historian Redmond Fitzgerald puts it. Fitzgerald also calls it a "time of fungus growth." In actual fact, there was considerable growth of several varieties that would burst into flower some years later.

One form was a renewed interest in the preservation and extension of the native language. In 1893 Dr. Douglas Hyde and six compatriots founded the Gaelic League with this object in mind. Padraic Pearse, the poet and leader of the 1916 Rising, was one of the first to see clearly what lay behind the act: "If there is one thing that has become plainer than another it is that when the seven met in O'Connell Street to found the Gaelic League they were commencing ... not a revolt but a revolution."

Many other tributary streams were beginning to flow —streams that, in confluence, would form the broad river of the Irish Renaissance. The Irish Literary Theatre gave its first performance in 1899. William Butler Yeats, Lady Gregory and Edward Martyn were the guiding spirits behind the project, the first play in the all-Irish repertory being Yeats' *The Countess Cathleen*. By 1904, with George Moore and "AE" actively contributing their talent now, as well as exciting newcomers like J.M. Synge and Padraic Colum, the great Abbey Theatre itself was born.

Another contributing freshet was the Sinn Fein movement, founded by Arthur Griffith in the early 1900's. A newspaperman with a gift of trenchant phrase, Griffith did not believe that the English Parliament was the place where Irish freedom would be achieved. By contrast to the long-established Irish Republican Brotherhood, with their secret meetings and caches of arms, Griffith was an advocate of passive resistance, self-reliance and economic independence. But Griffith's basic message was the same. Its sturdy essence lies in the Gaelic phrase *Sinn Fein* itself, which translates into "We ourselves."

The rise of Labour under the leadership of James Larkin and James Connolly was another manifestation, for they sought to organize all Irish workmen under the banner of the Transport Workers Union. The kind of social reform which they began could not but contain national aspirations.

A revival of Irish art and crafts had the same motivating force: a pride in the national inheritance. So did a proliferation of literary societies and sporting clubs. Behind the pride, in the shadows still but growing year by year, was the feeling that Parliamentary action just might not be quick enough or drastic enough to obtain the longed-for freedom.

Erskine Childers became a champion of Home Rule not

by emotion but by a gradual intellectual process. He is supposed to have been strongly stirred to pity and to action by a trip he made to the west of Ireland in 1908, when he saw first-hand the hard lot of the peasants in the sparse and rock-strewn counties of Galway and Mayo. But his letter to Basil Williams that autumn tends to belie this. He wrote of a "very quiet and happy holiday in Ireland, including a jolly motor trip with my cousin Robert Barton through a good deal of central and western Ireland mainly to inspect cooperative societies. . .in which Sir H. Plunkett and a good many other well-known people look for the economic salvation of Ireland."

We are reminded of the "plucky Boers" whose hard lot seemed hardly to affect Childers at all. Surely a "jolly motor trip" is not one in which the motorist is deeply troubled by the poverty he sees around him!

What actually converted Childers was his own growing liberalism, the beginnings of which were those long talks with Basil Williams under the South African stars.

In succeeding years, he came to believe in the rights of small nations to govern themselves. Then, out of his deep study of Irish history and his observation of such contemporary phenomena as Sir Horace's well-organized co-operatives and the whole explosion of national pride, he made up his mind that Ireland was not only deserving but ready:

"I have come back finally and immutably a convert to Home Rule, as is my cousin, though we both grew up steeped in the most irreconcilable sort of Unionism."

In his decision he was fully supported by Molly. She threw herself, her fervor and her charm, into the cause which would put them both on a collision course with their whole Ascendancy way of life.

In 1910 something happened which thrust Home Rule to stage-center again, after so many years in the wings. Four years before, the Liberal Party had been swept back into

82

power in the most startling landslide the country had ever seen. The Liberal majority was so great that the party had no need of Redmond's support. But now, in the General Election of January 1910, the Liberals were returned to power with no clear majority or mandate. Only with Irish National and British Labour support could they even remain in office. So, H.H. Asquith, the Prime Minister, reached a working agreement with John Redmond. Its essence was that Redmond and his followers would vote with the Liberal Party *provided* a Home Rule bill was re-introduced and every effort made to give it a fair wind.

As it turned out, Mr. Asquith, whose temperament was as benign as a bishop's and whose methods were bland and dexterous, and Redmond, the tame hawk who loved the ritual of Parliamentary give-and-take, would work almost too well in the loose harness of their verbal understanding.

Asquith's Liberal party itself was, by George Dangerfield's brisk definition, a mixture of "Whig aristocrats, industrialists, dissenters, reformers, trade unionists, quacks, and Mr. Lloyd George." The doctrine of *laissez-faire* was its anchor, and compromise its most valued tactic.

Spurred on by the awareness that Home Rule was once again a live issue, Erskine Childers now applied himself to writing what would turn out to be his most important work of non-fiction. He called it *The Framework of Home Rule.* It is part history and economics, part eloquent argument in favor of Dominion status for Ireland. Freed from his daily chores as a Parliamentary clerk, he drafted a good deal of it at Glan, which had been such a stronghold of Unionism in his youth. "What a place to work in!" Childers wrote to Williams, rejoicing in his freedom: "We have invented a new game, squach rackets against the coach-house door, and an hour of that gives one exercise enough for the whole day."

The rest of the time, Childers put his good brain and great capacity for concentration on the problem in hand.

In the historical section he makes it clear that, from the

83

12th century on, Ireland was treated by England as a colony. Earlier she had styled herself a kingdom (sometimes with many kingly chieftains), and she had indeed been in many ways a nation. But Strongbow's invasion changed all that.

The Dublin area known as the Pale became the seat of central authority. From behind its ring of fortresses the British sought to control the native majority, which outnumbered them many times. To do so they worked sedulously for centuries to perpetuate the myth that the Irish were literally "beyond the Pale"—ignorant, depraved, perverse and quite incapable of governing themselves.

The Act of Union (1800), the direct result of the abortive rebellion of '98, abolished the Irish Parliament in Dublin. Ever since, Childers reminds us, the British had justified the Act by this same "systematic defamation of Irish character."

Childers goes on to make the excellent point that this antipathy on the part of the British was a political not a social one. Nothing could change the geographic fact that, at their nearest, the larger island and the smaller were (and are) separated by a mere 60 miles of open water. Any military strength that Ireland developed, any alliance she contracted with a foreign power, was inevitably a threat to England's security.

The argument that Ireland's proximity made her situation special, even "abnormal," crops up again and again, just as it had when Childers was telling his fellow debaters in the Magpie and Stump that England could never take the risk of giving Ireland her freedom. It was far easier, Childers now reminds us, for Britain to give a good measure of independence to outlying parts of the Empire like Canada and South Africa.

Childers does allow that there were some hazards involved. But here is the ingenious way that he turns the premise of his undergraduate days around:

"As for the risk to Great Britain, I have only this last word to say: Let her people, not for the first time,

84

show that they can rise superior to the philosophy, as fallacious in effect as it is base and cowardly in purpose, which sets the safety of a great nation above the happiness and prosperity of a small one."

This is the thrust of his argument. Writing as the Englishman he still was, caring deeply still about the country of his birth, he is asking England to live up to her own finest instincts. *Have trust in Ireland,* he says, *realize that what is best for Ireland will be best for the Empire, recognize at last that she is a nation not an appendage* . . . .

Sharp counterpoint is his filial but critical recognition that England's understanding of Ireland is nil:

"So long as one whole island democracy claims to determine the destinies of another island democracy, of whose special needs and circumstances it is admittedly ignorant, so long will both islands suffer."

Childers' argument that Ireland was indeed a democracy economically and politically ready to take its place as a Dominion is formidable and learned. The weakest part of the book is his failure to identify the dangers implicit in the problems of the Protestant North. In 1911, to him as to many, it was still a cloud no bigger than a man's hand.

He does recognize the fact that Ulster, with its shipbuilding and linen industries as well as its predominant Protestantism, had always been closely linked to England. He is also well aware that certain Conservative elements in England, back to Lord Randolph Churchill in the 1880's, encouraged a split between North and South should Home Rule ever come. "Ulster will fight," Lord Randolph said in this regard, "and Ulster will be right."

By 1911, the Conservatives were discovering all over again that opposing Home Rule and encouraging the separateness of Ulster were good bludgeons with which to belabor the hated Liberal majority.

Sanguine and idealistic, Childers, in the *Framework* expresses confidence that all Irishmen of good will, Catholic and Protestant alike, would pitch in and work together for the national good, once a reasonable measure of political freedom was achieved. "No Home Rulers after Home Rule," was his hope. He hits hard at the weary shibboleth of its enemies that "Home Rule Means Rome Rule," citing the tolerance with which Protestants were treated in the Catholic South.

Childers also reminds us that the Protestant counties in the North were not really so unlike the rest of Ireland. Many of the settlers who came over from Scotland and England at the time of the Ulster Plantation and the Cromwellian Settlement had, in three centuries, become quite Irish. It was England that for her own purposes cultivated the myth of the dour and different Ulsterman, just as she perpetuated the legend of the feckless if more cheerful native to the south.

Enlarging, he also reminds us that a good number of the Protestant Members of the Parliament from the northern constituencies were Home Rulers, not Unionists, and that this was true of many Protestant landlords, tenants, capitalists and laborers as well. In a terse phrase he says that the Irish Unionist Party in the Commons was "absolutely unrepresentative of the practical, virile genius of Ulster industry."

Childers, the trained Parliamentarian, holds out some hope for a middle way: "Compromise enters more or less into the settlement of all burning political issues. That is inevitable under the Party system; but of all questions under the sun, Home Rule questions are the least susceptible of compromise so engendered."

Being the most generous-spirited of men, Childers admits that good progress had been made in the matter of agrarian reforms. But to him, this in no way diminishes the Irish need for Home Rule, for the birthright of a nation was the basic involvement. *If Ireland did not crave her freedom with all her heart and soul she was not worthy of achieving it.*

The Framework of Home Rule was published in 1911. It was a year when that once-small cloud of opposition in the

North and in England was spreading and becoming septic. In a letter to one of his sisters Childers showed his awareness that the cause he had espoused was unpopular with many of his English contemporaries: "The book is just out and I hope will get to you soon. I feel it is a terribly forlorn hope, like the *Arme Blanche* books! An unpopular cause—I seem to be thoroughly identified now with such: but one must follow one's bent and speak one's thoughts regardless."

In the next year, something happened which made Home Rule seemingly inevitable, and filled the whole sky with mingled hope and foreboding.

Asgard

11.   The Mottled Sky

The happening which for a time improved the prospects of Home Rule—and then turned the years from 1911 to 1914 into a turmoil—was Mr. Asquith's Bill stripping the House of Lords of its control by veto.

As early as 1909 the Liberals had been determined to create a situation by which the Lords were seen to be blocking the will of the people. The Budget for that year appeared to be the perfect means to do so. The man whose duty it was to present the Budget was the Chancellor of the Exchequer—David Lloyd George. Under his magnetism and his eloquence, the small, buoyant Welshman had an unerring sense of timing, and of his own high destiny.

In the 1909 Budget, he undertook to raise 16 million pounds of new income by taxation. One-third of the money was for eight new dreadnoughts, to allay the public's fears of Germany's growing seapower. The other two-thirds was for Old Age Pensions, embodied in an Act that was close to the core of the Liberal mystique.

Misjudging the mood of the people, the House of Lord's rejected Lloyd George's Budget by a vote of 550 to 75. Now Mr. Asquith had his desired pretext. Although a second inconclusive General Election in December of 1910 did nothing to change his tenuous majority, he moved smoothly to shear the Lords of their power.

The Prime Minister's reform Bill, known simply as the Parliament Bill, finally cleared the House of Commons in May of 1911 (long after the controversial Budget which had triggered the greater issue had slipped through with little change). In the Bill was the fateful provision that any measure the Commons passed three times in succession would automatically become law *despite the continuing veto of the Upper House.*

On July 24, in a scene of indescribable din, Mr. Asquith tried to announce to the Commons his intent to send his reform Bill to the Lords. If it failed to pass, his plan was to advise the new King, George V, to "exercise his Prerogative to secure the passing unto Law of the Bill." The Old Conservatives shouted him down with cries of "Traitor! Traitor!" Sometimes he got a word or two in edgewise, then the roar would roll over him again. After 45 minutes he sat down with great dignity, his mouth a hard line in his slightly-flushed face. It was the first time in Parliamentary history that a Prime Minister had been denied the courtesy of a hearing.

Published the next day, the statement of intent made Mr. Asquith's plan unmistakably clear. The "King's Prerogative" would be to create 500 new Liberal peers on Mr. Asquith's advice, and so assure the passage of the Bill. The King was willing to accept the Prime Minister's advice and act on it.

To show what was in store, Mr. Asquith drew up a not-too-private list of nominees. Some of the rumored names were profoundly shocking to the diehards among the blue-bloods. There were writers like James M. Barrie, Thomas Hardy and even Anthony Hope Hawkins of *The Prisoner of Zenda* fame. . . several lawyers, including Erskine Childers' mentor Sir Frederick Pollock. . . upstarts like Sir Abe Bailey, the South African millionaire. . . even a "grocer" in the person of Sir Thomas Lipton.

July and August of 1911 were the hottest months anyone remembered. On the surface, the mood of London was festive enough, for it was Coronation Summer, with many balls and fetes. But underneath there was nervous unrest. The Agadir incident in July added a frisson of real terror. For, by steaming into Moroccan waters, the German gunboat *Panther* stretched the delicate membrane of peace among the great powers to the limit. Her ostensible mission was to support German economic interests; but it was in fact defiance of the French and British, and seen for some anxious weeks as such. . . .

August 10 was the day when the Lords, turning out in unprecedented numbers, met to decide their own fate. The temperature was exactly 100 degrees, with no breeze stirring.

Was the Prime Minister bluffing? Did the King really mean to go along? Would the Lords vote down a reform which the people so clearly supported?

Right down to the last ditch, the diehards or "Ditchers" in the Lords fought to put together a majority to kill the Bill. It was known that many of the peers were undecided up to the day of the voting. The Ditchers sequestered the particularly-prized hat of one of the Dukes whom they considered safe but nervous. The Duke bolted without voting—and without his hat.

When it was all over the vote was 131 to 114 (with many abstentions) in favor of the Parliament Bill. The more enlightened peers, who saw that the House of Lords was doomed either way, supported it as the lesser evil. The diehards snarled that the vote was produced by a coalition of "Rats and Bishops."

Now it seemed that no one could stop Home Rule for Ireland. Now Mr. Asquith would keep his word. In their easy double harness he and John Redmond would jog across the finish line.

They reckoned without Sir Edward Carson. They reckoned without Andrew Bonar Law, the new leader of His Majesty's not-so-loyal Opposition, and Field Marshal Earl Roberts of Kandahar, and F.E. Smith (later the first Earl of

Birkenhead). They reckoned without an Ulster Member of Parliament called Captain James Craig, and Mr. Rudyard Kipling, and General Sir Henry Wilson of the War Office.

Such were some of the rather odd bedfellows that history drew together in the fall of 1911 to make sure that Home Rule did not come into being without a mighty struggle—and to make sure that, if it *did* pass, Ulster would flare into open rebellion.

Sir Edward Carson was in his late fifties. He was a big pale man with dark eyes and a jaw like one of the rocky promontories along the Antrim coast. Member of Parliament for Dublin University, he espoused Ulster's cause with the ardor of a fanatic. The wish of the Protestant North to stay within the British Empire seemed to him neither treason nor rebellion. Yet his actions, in a less curdled time, might well have been considered close to both. He made speeches "instinct with passion." He caused his vast Ulster audiences to swear great oaths never under any circumstances to submit to Home Rule and Catholic domination.

He organized Volunteer forces all over the Northern Counties. By the fall of 1913 there were over 100,000 of them—drilling and cheering him to the echo at mass rallies.

Sir Edward had many English as well as Irish allies in his burning cause. It was a paradoxical fact that there were times when the Home Rule issue seemed to have very little to do with Ireland and a very great deal to do with turning the Liberals out of office.

Mr. Bonar Law, a Scotch-Canadian with a sad, rumpled face, supported every Carsonite move, both in the Commons and out.

The aging Lord Roberts offered his military expertise and vast prestige to the Volunteers. Then, realizing that the offer was a little out of line for a Field-Marshal still on the active list, he recommended a model Lieutenant-General, Sir George Richardson, "a retired Indian officer active and in good health," in his stead. The offer was enthusiastically accepted.

F.E. Smith, *arriviste* whose ambition knew no limits and the boldest Parliamentarian of his day, saw in the Ulster situation just the kind of murky waters he liked to fish in. He went so far as to serve as aide-de-camp, or galloper, to General Richardson at one of those big military reviews. Inevitably he became known as "Galloper" Smith, and the nickname stuck all the way to his Earldom and his days as Lord Chancellor of England.

Captain Craig and six friends drew up a document along the lines of an ancient Scots Covenant solemnly pledging its signers to "use all means which may be found necessary to defeat the present conspiracy," and, should a Home Rule Parliament come into being in Ireland, "to refuse to recognize its authority." All told, 471,444 men and women of the Northern Counties signed the great Covenant.

As for Rudyard Kipling, his antennae were as sensitive as ever to the public mood. He became more Orange than many of the native Orangemen (Orangemen being simply another way of saying Ulster Protestant, deriving from William of Orange and his famous victory of the Boyne).

On April 8, 1912, Kipling's inflammatory poem *What Answer from the North?* ran on the front page of the London *Morning Post*. These were the blaring lines:

> "One Law, one Land, one Throne.
> If England drives us forth,
> We shall not fall alone."

Sir Henry Wilson, a resourceful Ulsterman in charge of Military Operations at the War Office (and later a Field-Marshal) was much closer to the Opposition than to the Liberals in power. He was in fact in almost open conspiracy with Sir Edward and Bonar Law to make sure that the Army would be slow to act in any real showdown over Ulster.

What were Mr. Asquith's and John Redmond's reactions to all this eloquence and swashbuckling?

93

After his show of vigor in pushing through his Bill of Parliamentary reform, the Prime Minister withdrew into an Olympian calm. Not for nothing was his family motto *Wait and See*, for now he obeyed its injunction to the letter. In Harold Nicolson's phrase, he was a man who "believed in the strict avoidance of evitable pain; he allowed sleeping scorpions to lie."

Mr. Asquith did manage to put through a perfunctory Bill forbidding the import of arms to any part of Ireland. He continued to carry out his Prime Ministerial duties punctiliously and with style. But he seemed to be moving in a dream world.

John Redmond watched him, and worried, and hoped against hope that developments in his beloved Commons would prove to be real and solid and not just part of the dream. . . .

During March and April of 1914 two events shook his hopes, and even dented Mr. Asquith's apathy.

In March, some British troops stationed at the Curragh of Kildare in Southern Ireland were ordered to four key points in Ulster as a precautionary measure. Fifty seven officers of Unionist persuasion, including Brigadier Hubert Gough, commanding the Third Cavalry Brigade, indicated that they would turn in their papers rather than entrain for the north and for possible conflict with like-thinking Protestants.

Such was the famous Curragh Mutiny, for mutiny it was. After much coming and going between Dublin, the Curragh and London, the orders were watered down, and finally allowed to lapse. The mutineers remained on duty, their actions somehow condoned. To give some illusion of action, Mr. Asquith himself manfully took over the portfolio of Secretary of State for War.

With deep apprehension John Redmond watched the widening gap between Constitutional authority and reality.

In April, an Orange gun-runner called Major Crawford delivered 20,000 rifles and three million rounds of ammunition to three ports in the Belfast area. The bulk was off-loaded at Larne from the *S.S. Fanny*, a converted collier. Volunteers cordoned off the town and locked the police in their barracks. Outnumbered and embarrassed, the Belfast Government simply looked the other way.

All spring, the idea of Ulster as a separate entity gained ground. The concept of Ireland as a "seamless garment," with one coastline, one Parliament, one culture and language—the concept so dear to the southern Nationalists—was unravelling.

Sir Edward Carson's theme was now "Peace but Preparation," indicating some room for negotiation. Mr. Asquith yielded at last to the brutal facts implied in "Preparation." John Redmond buckled in his turn.

By July, it was not a question of whether *Ulster* would be excluded from Home Rule but *where* the borders would be drawn, especially through and along the County of Tyrone—a veritable checkerboard of Protestant and Catholic communities.

How bitterly the South felt about this decline in its aspirations is shown by the striking and prophetic editorial in Arthur Griffith's newspaper *Sinn Fein* which ran on July 11, 1914:

"We would give much to see a national legislature, no matter how limited its scope, reestablished in this country for, poor though the thing might be, it would give us again a national center. But this 'Home Rule' no longer proposes to set up such a legislature—instead it proposes to cut Ireland in two and to stereotype the vanishing differences between Southern and Northern, Catholic and Protestant. We tell those who would accept such a measure and think it gain that they will bring not peace to Ireland but a poisoned sword."

For several years Southern Ireland had been in a state of ferment. The main surface manifestation was the Dublin strikes in 1913. Organized by Larkin and Connolly, they were suppressed with great brutality by the British.

To William Butler Yeats, writing in September 1913, it seemed a gray time, petty and mean, a time when the fires of nationalism were banked not burning:

> "Was it for this the wild geese spread
> The gray wing upon every tide;
> For this all that blood was shed,
> For this Edward Fitzgerald died,
> And Robert Emmet and Wolfe Tone,
> All that delirium of the brave?
> Romantic Ireland's dead and gone,
> It's with O'Leary in the grave."

(John O'Leary (1830–1907) was an early Fenian leader.)

Beautiful as the lines are, Yeats could not have misread the mood of his country more completely. For the calm was only a surface calm. *Surely Romantic Ireland was dying + Practi-*

In that same year of 1913 a militant new movement *fighting r* called the Irish Volunteers came into being. It was an off- *living as* shoot of the secret Irish Republican Brotherhood and sought to convert the pioneer work of the Gaelic League and the other societies of the Irish Revival into more direct action. To the hotheaded Volunteers, Home Rule and its slow maturation in Parliament was simply too drawn-out and unpromising a process.

Padraic Pearse, the young poet-revolutionist, saw this more clearly than many: "Ireland unarmed will attain just as much freedom as it is convenient for England to give her. Ireland armed will attain ultimately just as much freedom as she wants."

Many good liberals and Home Rulers on both sides of the Irish Sea realized that the creation of the southern Volunteers was necessary to counterbalance the forces in the North. They saw it simply as a measure of self-protection at a time when the situation was going from bad to worse.

One group took direct action. Alice Stopford Green, the

96

spirited widow of British historian John Richard Green (author of *A Short History of the English People*) was a prime mover. Eoin MacNeill, founder of the Volunteer Movement in the south and professor at University College Dublin was in the group, and so was The O'Rahilly, chief of an age-old Irish clan. Darrell Figgis was a key member, a romantic Irishman with a chestnut beard. There was also the tall, also bearded and even more romantic Sir Roger Casement, an Ulsterman who had been knighted for his work in the British Consular Service.

MacNeill, Figgis and Casement met at Mrs. Green's London flat in early May. Its windows gave out on the Thames. It was a gray day and the tide was out. In his *Recollections of the Irish War*, Darrell Figgis recaptures the scene: "Beside the distant quayside some coal-barges lay tilted on the sleek mud of the river-bottom, with their sides washed by the silver waters that raced seaward."

The *Recollections* are full of such detail. Without ever playing down his own considerable role, Figgis makes others come vividly alive: "Looking outward before the window-curtains stood Roger Casement, a figure of perplexity, and the apparent dejection which he always wore so proudly, as though he had assumed the sorrows of the world. His face was in profile to me, his handsome head and noble outline cut out against the gray day."

Back and forth they argued how best to help the Irish cause.

"Let's buy the rifles," Figgis suddenly said with great urgency, "and so at least get into the problem."

"That's talking," said Sir Roger, his face alight with battle. In actual fact, Figgis recalls, it marked the end of talking and the beginning of action.

Since the group's limited funds would all be needed to buy the guns themselves, a boat was needed at no additional cost, and a man who could sail the boat.

Shortly after the meeting at Mrs. Green's, Casement

wrote Figgis that he had found exactly the right man—an Englishman with impeccable Liberal credentials, a famous yachtsman who owned his own yacht, and a man devoted to the cause. His name was Erskine Childers.

"I went at once to see Mr. Childers at his flat in Chelsea," Figgis remembers. "He told me that Casement had spoken to him fully concerning the project, and that he was willing to help in every way possible, recognizing the risks that were involved, and the necessity for absolute secrecy."

Such were the origins of Childers' most adventurous cruise, and the only one that belongs to history.

Mollie and Erskine Childers on board *Asgard*, 1910

The Running of the Guns (1)

There was as yet no whiff of treason. Erskine Childers volunteered because he had misgivings about the prospects of Home Rule, and felt strongly that some measure of prepared-ness was needed in the South to balance the massive arming and drilling in the North. He also happened to be quite avail-able.

His political life was at a standstill. He had done all he could, as both consultant and writer, to assure the success of the Home Rule Bill. Its first passage through the Commons in January of 1913 had been duly celebrated by a dinner graced by the Olympian presence of Mr. Asquith. During the toasts, Childers' role was signalled out for high praise.

Starting in 1912, Childers had made a try for a seat in Parliament. Selected by the Liberals to stand for Devonport, he proved a conscientious but not very effective candidate. The Liberal tradition of free beer for all at the hustings, with much contingent noise and merriment, was particularly irksome to his own reticent temperament.

When, in the late summer of 1913, the local Committee Chairman complained to him about some aspects of his candidacy, he resigned with few regrets.

Alfred Ollivant, the English writer who learned to sail aboard *Sunbeam* and *Asgard*, has described the essence of Childers in a way that makes it easy to understand another reason why the arms-running appealed to him: "He was by temperament one of that great company of gentlemen-adventurers which our country has given perhaps in fuller measure than any other to the roll of history."

Darrell Figgis had some reservations about Childers at that first meeting. He seemed a little too much the proper Englishman. But then Figgis remembered that his help was only needed at sea "where his services for Great Britain had been such that he would hardly be suspected of trafficking with those who wished to run guns to her peril."

In other words Erskine Childers' cover was perfect. So Figgis took him on faith. They quickly agreed on a plan of operations, with as few members of the group as possible actually involved in the details. Over and above his concern for total secrecy, Childers had only one request: that Molly be part of the plot, starting as "communications center."

Alice Stopford Green would act as Treasurer, collecting and distributing all the funds.

Darrell Figgis would buy the guns in Belgium or Germany and get them to a North Sea port.

Erskine Childers and his ketch *Asgard* would pick up and deliver them to Ireland by sea.

Childers actually accompanied Figgis on his shopping trip to the Continent. After a failure at Liège, they found two brothers called Michael and Moritz Magnus in Hamburg who happened to have 1,500 serviceable second-hand Mauser rifles available, and 49,000 rounds of ammunition. After all the publicity over Larne, the Magnus brothers were wary of sales to English-speaking strangers. On a sudden inspiration Figgis told them that he and Childers were Mexicans, and so well outside any British embargo. Since the Magnus brothers were anxious to be convinced, they allowed themselves to be, and warmed immediately to the work in hand. Much to Childers' amazement the deal was consummated, with Figgis staying on in Hamburg to settle final details.

By June 21 Childers was in Wales, where *Asgard* had

100

been left after her fall cruise the year before. He had already written the boatyard at Criccieth that she was to be put in commission as quickly as possible. Arriving there, he wrote to Molly that he found "the condition of the yacht rather dispiriting—very behind-hand and everything done rather slackly . . . . All the gear in different places so that I could not properly check it." The compass was missing, and the sails were not ready.

Childers, at his crispest, gave the boatyard crew their priorities and deadline. Then he hurried on to Dublin to work out plans for the actual landing of the guns in Ireland.

Since The O'Rahilly was under close surveillance and Eoin MacNeill too prominent a figure, the choice for an Irish contact settled on Bulmer Hobson, a young Volunteer with time and energy to burn. Meeting in secret, he and Childers decided on the tidy little harbor of Howth, just north of Dublin for *Asgard's* landfall. Their bold plan was to unload the contraband in broad daylight there, and so avoid the dangers and confusions of a night operation.

The rendezvous with Figgis would take place off the Ruytigen Lightship at the mouth of the Scheldt. Figgis would have the arms aboard a tug. The time for the transfer was set at high noon, on either Saturday, July 11, or Sunday, July 12.

There was too much contraband for *Asgard* to carry by herself so a second yacht, *Kelpie*, was called into service. She was owned and skippered by hot-tempered Conor O Brien, architect by profession and sailing man by inclination.

Asgard, out of Wales, and *Kelpie*, out of Foynes, would meet at Cowes, near Southampton, on July 7 to agree on final details and to exchange last messages with Figgis, firming up the all-important rendezvous.

(On the world scene the skies seemed clearer than they had in months. There was one small dark cloud causing some diplomatic disturbances: on June 28, at a place called Sarajevo, the Archduke Franz Ferdinand and his wife had been assassinated. But everyone hoped that this event could be kept in a Balkan context.)

By late June *Asgard* was at Conway, moored below the great Welsh castle and in reasonable shape for the expedition. Childers arranged for his crew to assemble there on July 1.

In addition to Molly, there was the invaluable Gordon Shephard, a pilot now with two years in the Royal Flying Corps behind him, and with sailing skills to match Childers' own. A less-familiar crew member was the Hon. Mary Spring-Rice, 34-year-old daughter of Lord Monteagle of Mount Brandon in County Limerick. (Lord Monteagle, an Anglo-Irish peer and a dedicated Home Ruler, was an uncle of Sir Cecil Spring-Rice, then British Ambassador in Washington—another bit of excellent cover for this not-so-innocent voyage.)

It was Mary Spring-Rice who first inspired Sir Roger Casement with the whole idea of running arms from the Continent, and who actually recommended Erskine Childers to him. Her only sailing experience had been playing around in small boats in the Shannon estuary below Foynes, where the Monteagle lands were located. But her proficiency in the galley, and her intrepid spirit, were to prove great assets. As Gordon Shephard wrote to his mother part way through the cruise, "Miss Spring-Rice is a wonder. She has never been far to sea before, yet she was hardly ill at all and looks and is most useful."

Such was *Asgard's* afterguard. Two paid hands completed the crew, both Donegal fisherman. Their names were Patrick McGinley and Charles Duggan. Once at sea Childers explained the secret mission to them. Their exuberant response at the chance to strike a blow for Ireland was a boost to everyone's morale.

The first few days underway had a dampening effect on both body and spirit. As *Asgard* worked her way down the Welsh coast she ran into head winds, steep seas and pouring rain. Despite ample foul-weather gear, everyone was soaked to the skin. Even Erskine was seasick. He also managed to run a marlin-spike through one of his fingers, and the cut turned

102

nasty. Until it mended, Molly had to do more than her normal trick at the wheel.

Then McGinley was bashed over the eye by a swinging block-and-tackle, so badly that he took to his bunk. Mary Spring-Rice—by necessity learning fast—had to stand his watches for him.

In her log for July 6, Mary noted that the capable Gordon Shephard was also the heaviest sleeper on board: "All efforts to rouse Mr. Gordon proved in vain until a tin of golden syrup was got out . . . ."

That was the day they left the seemingly-endless Welsh coast at last and stood out across the mouth of the Bristol Channel for Cornwall. Now for the first time they felt the full drive of the long Atlantic rollers. The wind remained a maddening south sou' west, so that *Asgard* had to buck head winds all the way. By now Childers had to face the fact that they would be late for the meeting with OBrien at Cowes, and hard put to reach the Belgian coast in time.

On July 7, the sun shone at last, and the white cliffs of Cornwall were a dazzling white below the purple line of the headlands. They passed St. Ives, looking attractive in the sunlight, and the crew longed to put in, to stretch and dry out. But Erskine Childers, in his element as leader responsible, ruled that they must push on.

That afternoon *Asgard* rounded Land's End at last, with the wind still southerly and a heavy sea running. Later, in the misty twilight, there was a bad moment. The deep fog-bell on the buoy just to seaward of the Runnelstone Rocks suddenly sounded alarmingly close. Gordon Shephard instantly put *Asgard* about. Then Molly, who had the sharpest eyes on board, spotted the Runnelstone Buoy safely to port and Shephard resumed course with a sigh of relief.

Their first real break was a fair up-Channel wind just after rounding the Lizard. With topsail and spinnaker set, *Asgard* ran joyfully before it. Dead on course now for the

Solent, she managed to clock a splendid 8 knots.

Late on the night of July 8—two days behind schedule—they raised Cowes. Mary Spring-Rice's entry in her log described the actual arrival at the famous yachting center: "We got in at 1 a.m. It was quite beautiful passing through the searchlights with the water all gleaming and rippling under a sort of unearthly glow. While the men stowed the sails, I went down hastily to make hot drinks, and so to bed at 2 a.m."

Conor OBrien was predictably furious. In a letter from Cowes to Alice Stopford Green, Molly Childers noted his behavior when he boarded *Asgard* the next morning. He "swore dreadfully at Mary (his cousin)—in a rage at our keeping him waiting—absolutely brutal. Cheered up later and worked hard helping us." Battered *Asgard* needed all the help she could get, with much gear lost overboard and several ripped sails.

(The swashbuckling, short-fused Conor OBrien was a most capable seaman. Shortly after taking part in the arms-running, he joined the Royal Navy Volunteer Reserve and served from 1914–1918. In the early 1920's he sailed his celebrated yacht *Saoirse* around the world. Although nearly 60 when World War II broke out, he skippered badly-needed small vessels from America to England. Next to sailing, his favorite past-time was barefoot mountain climbing.)

Molly Childers' self-appointed task was to keep Mrs. Green informed of the progress of the expedition. Her warmth and charm come through in a characteristic excerpt from the Cowes letter: "Do you remember I said the first bird that followed us was you yourself? A great white gull was with us on the wing for a long time one day and I knew it was you. Oh, if only you could have come!"

Two huge meals ashore at the Royal Marine Hotel, two good nights' sleep in harbor, and the taking on board of plenty of fresh fruit and vegetables, did a great deal to revive the spirits of the crew. The high moment for Mary Spring-

Rice was at lunch when she downed an enormous iced lemon squash that she had been dreaming about for three days.

The rendezvous off the Scheldt was confirmed by an exchange of telegrams with Darrell Figgis in Hamburg. Obviously it had to be the later day: Sunday, July 12.

Waiting for Erskine Childers at Cowes was a letter from Figgis mailed in Hamburg just two days before. He reported that all details were seemingly going well. He also managed to convey, in slightly cryptic style, the identity of the tug that would deliver the arms: "By the way, what do you think of *Gladiator* for the name of that boat? It sounds good, don't you think? It struck me at once when I saw it on a tug on the river here."

To reach *Gladiator* at the appointed time, the two yachts still had to cover 150 miles. *Kelpie* caught the morning tide up the Solent on July 10.

Owing to delays while the sailmaker finished his repairs, the slower, beamier *Asgard* did not leave Cowes until slack water in mid-afternoon of the same day.

Now all depended on wind and weather, for neither *Asgard* nor *Kelpie* had any power but sail.

Darrell Figgis, meanwhile, was finding final arrangements in Hamburg not quite as smooth-running as he had anticipated. The German police were on his trail, the Mexican cover was wearing thin, and worst of all the Magnus brothers were now warned that all out-going shipments had to be inspected by a Customs Officer.

The resourceful Figgis, a man not easily discouraged, managed to find a loophole: regulations did permit a pilot to act as Customs Officer. He and the Magnus brothers engaged one who, they hoped, had "suitable qualities."

Without much time to spare, *Gladiator* was loaded with the guns, which were wrapped in straw and tied in canvas, twenty to the package. The ammunition boxes did not arrive until three hours before casting-off time, which was eight o'clock on the evening of Friday, July 10.

At last the pilot showed up. "On him," Figgis recalls, "and on the handling of him, depended everything. I do not believe I have ever scanned any man's face so anxiously, yet so guardedly, for signs either of beneficence or of corruptibility. Either would have been equally suitable. But he was a grave and stern man, with a face like a mask, out of the mouth of which dropped a very big pipe."

They talked in English as the pilot spoke no "Mexican." It developed that the cigar which Figgis offered him found favor, and a full box quickly changed hands. With enormous dignity the pilot also accepted three large English banknotes, over and above the regular fee.

Figgis' description of the crucial moment shows his own gift for very un-Irish understatement:

"We took a few further turns on the deck before he went down to examine the cargo. I walked the deck awaiting his return in an anxiety I could scarcely contain. I found it even difficult to breathe, and only by steady pacing could I control myself, for it would never do to let my anxiety reveal itself. Then I heard him coming up the ladder from the hold. He walked past me, and only as he passed me did he turn for one quick moment and look at me. The light of understanding was in his eye.

"He went up on the bridge and spoke to the skipper. The skipper called to the crew, the hawsers were cast off, and the tug began to make a way down the river. All was well. They had chosen a good pilot, who was also a Customs Officer."

The night of July 10 brought head winds that continued all the next day. By 8 p.m. of July 11, *Asgard* was still trying to fetch Beachy Head, half way between Cowes and Dover. "A depressing day, full of doubts and anxieties," Mary Spring-Rice recorded.

Sunday, July 12, the day of days, dawned to reveal a calm

106

sea, with a favoring but very light breeze. To avoid the powerful mid-Channel tide, Childers stayed close inshore. Raising Folkestone, they ghosted along within a pebble's throw of the beach which was "full of the 'smart set' parading their best clothes in the brilliant sunshine."

To starboard lay four or five British warships, bells ringing peacefully for Sunday service.

With the Ruytigen Lightship still a good 45 miles away, the unspoken worry now was how long past noon *Gladiator* would be willing to wait.

Molly Childers, Gordon Shephard and Pat McGinley busied themselves making cabin and saloon ready for the rifles. First they sawed up the two bunks in the saloon. Then there ensued a lively argument whether the big table there would have to go as well.

Suddenly a joyful shout came from Duggan, who had the wheel.

"There's a west wind!"

It was the needed lift. Mainsail and mizzen were freed, spinnaker and topsail quickly broken out, and *Asgard* surged. The tide had turned now and was sweeping her north— helping, of course, but leaving the delicate question of just how much they were being set.

Then came another stroke of good fortune. They heard the fog-signal on the eastern end of the Goodwin Sands booming away, and then spotted the buoy itself to port, exactly where it should have been. So Erskine Childers knew that he was compensating correctly, and still on course.

By 2:30 in the afternoon the weather was thickening alarmingly, with a dense sea-mist choking off the sun. Childers posted all hands on deck as lookouts. Even Gordon Shephard, drowsy from an arduous night watch, had to give up his cherished afternoon nap to man a sector.

Precisely at 7 p.m. Childers' dead reckoning told him that they were in the vicinity of the Ruytigen Lightship. By now they were an anxious five hours past rendezvous time, and the visibility had shut down to less than a cable's length.

The lookouts strained to spot the dark hull of the Lightship. . .or its ancillary buoy. . .or *Kelpie*. . .or *Gladiator*. . . or indeed *anything* that would fix their position and end their vigil.

But all they saw were the long North Sea swells that came rolling out of the brown-gold mist, swept past without tumbling, and vanished again.

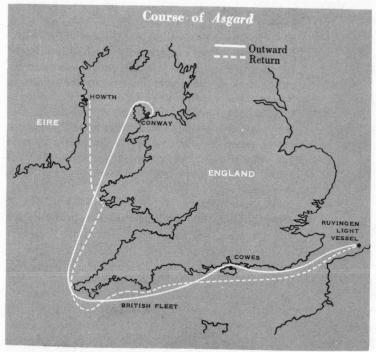

The course of *Asgard*, July 1914

13.

The Running of the Guns (2)

Molly Childers' sharp eyes were the first to see them: the buoy and then the dark-hulled Lightship. But of *Kelpie* and *Gladiator* there was still no sign. They cruised about in the gathering dark, thinking that Conor O Brien of the short fuse had blown it again, and had left the scene in disgust. In order not to arouse curiosity, they gave the Lightship a wide berth.

Molly spotted a sail through a rift in the fog, but it turned out to be a fishing smack. Fog and dark and low spirits closed down . . . .

Then came the indelible moment. A delighted cry from Molly triggered it: "Conor and the tug! Do you see! A steamer and a yacht mixed up—lying close to one another—now the tug is coming towards us."

Gladiator was bearing down on *Asgard,* black and larger than they had expected. From her deck Darrell Figgis called his news.

"Conor's loaded and off now, with 600 rifles and 20,000 rounds."

There was a pause as the news sank in.

"He's left you 900 and 29,000 rounds," Figgis shouted again.

This was more than they had bargained for. It meant breaking out the canvas bales on deck, throwing away the straw and stowing the heavily-greased rifles one-by-one.

For six hours they worked, with the German crew of the

109

tug passing down bale after bale from her high deck, alternating with the heavy ammunition boxes.

First the saloon was filled, level with the top of the table, which proved a useful stabilizing influence. Then cabin and passage. And still the guns kept coming, until even the area at the foot of the companionway had its quota.

Molly's description for Mrs. Green caught the excitement well:

"Darkness, lamps, strange faces, the swell of the sea making the boat lurch, guns, straw everywhere. . .no room to stand left save on guns, guns everywhere . . . . It was all like a mad dream, with a glow of joy and the feeling of accomplishing something great at the back of it to keep the brain steady and the heart unperturbed."

Childers' one burning wish was to take everything they could, even if it meant reducing their freeboard and their margin of safety in heavy weather. Finally "the last box was heaved on deck and the last rifle shoved down the companion." Several tell-tale boxes of ammunition had to be left on deck while room was found below to stow them in fo'castle and sail lockers.

By now it was two in the morning, with a faint glimmer of false dawn beginning to show. No one had noticed that tug and ketch, locked in their mutual absorption, were drifting down on the Lightship. *Asgard* quickly cast off and both craft, picking up steerageway in the strong tide, were carried past the moored vessel.

During the loading operation, mattresses and clothing had been stowed aft of the mizzen. Now, while *Gladiator* was taking *Asgard* in tow for a quick getaway, the crew spread the mattresses over the stacked guns as best they could. Those not still needed on deck, including Molly and Mary, fell on them, and were soon deep in exhausted sleep.

With little or no wind now, so that the sea turned glassy, tug and tethered ketch averaged ten knots during the next four crucial hours. Off Dover, where the Germans had agreed

110

to put Darrell Figgis ashore, *Gladiator* cast them off. The big tug soon disappeared in the early-morning mist.

The last thing they saw was Figgis waving a long good-bye from the tug's fantail, almost as if he were blessing them for the anxious days ahead.

There was plenty of time. The agreed date for the unloading of the guns at Howth was Sunday, July 26. That meant that they had 13 days to cover about the same distance that they had already accomplished in nine.

So the narrative is of small hardships endured and hazards experienced rather than of a race against time and wind and tide.

There was no room below to store the final three boxes of ammunition. With bitter regret, Childers ordered them thrown overboard—4,000 rounds, leaving 25,000 for delivery. *Asgard* rode more easily now, and Molly and Mary at least were glad to have the extra space.

The afternoon of Monday, the 13th of July brought a scare. Off Folkestone again, *Asgard* passed a group of gray British warships in line ahead. One started firing and they thought guiltily they were being ordered to stop. As no further action ensued, they kept on, realizing at last that it was only target practice. . . .

To Gordon Shephard, the cabin was now too stuffy to sleep in, and he moved his mattress to the passage. "It is almost a gymnastic feat to get by without walking on him," Mary Spring-Rice noted. "How Molly manages to get about with her leg is a constant wonder to me."

Molly more than managed. She was seized with a kind of exaltation, as another of her reports to Mrs. Green made clear: "We sleep, crawl over, sit on, eat on guns . . . . They catch us in our knees; odd bolts and butts and barrels transfix us from time to time but we are all so happy and triumphant, so proud of ourselves that we swear we are comfortable . . . . It is all glorious fun and, joy of joys, Mary and I are up to it. . . ."

111

Keeping the guns and ammunition dry was a continuing task, especially on wild wet days, of which there were many. At one point Gordon Shephard spilt some coffee and Molly cried in terror, "Gordon, you're ruining the guns with that coffee!" But carbolated vaseline in quantity was on hand to repair the inroads of tea, fruit juice and seawater as well as coffee. Two waterproof sheets were found, and also proved a great help.

Food became a critical matter with water growing scarce, and the taste of oil and grease ever present. To add to their woes, some eggs which had been soaked by seawater turned "a bit musty for boiling." Mary worked wonders. Pat McGinley showed signs of becoming a first-class ship's cook, and one night the versatile Gordon Shephard produced a much-praised "Sweet omelette," of buttered eggs, cooked in his favorite golden syrup.

Off the Devonshire coast (July 16) they found themselves in the midst of a fleet of picturesque Brixham Trawlers with red-brown sails. On Gordon Shephard's inspiration, they hailed one and, for two shillings, bought a fine mess of pollock, bream and mackerel. After endless rations of tinned meat and greasy potatoes, everyone looked forward to fresh fish for dinner. But while Mary was cooking, a mean swell came up, and most of the fried pollock spilled between the guns.

That same night brought new anxiety. *Asgard* was off Devonport, making good time on a broad reach. Suddenly, units of the British Grand Fleet seemed to be on all sides, cutting across their course at standard speed. Dreadnoughts of the *Iron Duke* class. . . other battleships hardly less formidable. . . battle cruisers. . . loomed to port and starboard, their towering superstructures faintly aglow. Destroyers in good numbers went tearing about, chattering to each other by searchlights after the manner of their kind.

Or were some of them trying to signal Asgard?

One destroyer in particular came very close, bearing

112

down from dead astern. Sent aft by Childers, Mary held the stern light high to make sure the tiny ketch was seen at all. At the last minute the four-stacker—still blinking some admonitory warning—changed course and like a greyhound went tearing off on a fresh scent.

On and on the great warships came, like citadels of the sea. To add to the sense of awe and mystery, searchlights on the far northeast horizon were turning cartwheels across the night sky.

It was well past midnight when the last capital ship disappeared to the northeast, with two destroyers barking at her heels.

Later, they learned that the Fleet units were on maneuvers out of Spithead. It was all part of that full-dress Review which would become an enduring symbol of the last peaceful days before Armageddon.

Normally small craft like *Asgard* would have been left to fend for themselves during a Fleet exercise. But with King George V aboard one of the dreadnoughts, especial care was taken to avoid the ramming or sinking of any of his loyal subjects.

They rounded Land's End on the grey, misty night of July 17th. Two days later, well ahead of schedule, *Asgard* dropped her hook at Milford Haven, bowered in green Welsh hills. There Gordon Shephard had to catch a night train for London, as his leave was up. Mary Spring-Rice and her "Mr. Gordon" spent the day ashore. After a big hotel breakfast and a shopping expedition for the needed provisions, Shephard, in character, had an enormous sleep while Mary "wrote letters, read the magazines and day-dreamed," just possibly of Mr. Gordon.

By late afternoon the glass was falling. Gordon Shephard rowed Mary back to *Asgard* for a last farewell and then he was gone in a sudden downpour, promising to meet them at Howth in a week's time for the final act of the drama.

Asgard reached the Welsh port of Holyhead, some 40 miles due east of Dublin across the Irish Sea, on Thursday, July 23. They were glad to be in safe harbor, for the weather was worsening and the wind, howling in the rigging, boded no good for the final run.

The next morning turned out slightly better than they had feared, and they were making good time in cloudy, squally weather when Erskine Childers spotted a tear in the mainsail. This meant back to harbor, and some heavy work by Molly and Mary with the sail-needle.

Three hours behind, with the wind dropping now, they left Holyhead again. For a long time that afternoon a great gull kept them company, floating gravely along just above the mizzen. Molly was sure it was Mrs. Green again, "coming to wish us well." The less-fanciful Erskine identified the bird as the gull that had polished off the remains of the breakfast bacon and was now undoubtedly hovering in hopes of more leftovers.

Toward dinner-time a nor'easter began to build up and by midnight *Asgard* was fighting a full gale. The crests were steep hills for climbing now, and the troughs were valleys into which they plunged with the sinking sensation that each drop might be the last.

Not wishing to be caught below, Mary Spring-Rice spent half the night crouched in the cockpit or the hatchway. Finally she joined Molly in the cabin, but could not sleep.

With no Gordon Shephard now as trusted deputy, Childers stayed on deck the entire night. At the height of the storm, he had to go up the mainmast to lash down a broken tackle. While there is no full description of this episode in Mary Spring-Rice's log, an account by Alfred Ollivant of a similar exploit brings Erskine Childers under stress into full focus:

"Childers, already gray, lame, and the eldest of us by some years, went aloft to do it. A little figure in a fisherman's jersey, with hunched shoulders and straining arms, the wind tearing through his thick hair, his

114

face desperately set, he tugged, heaved, fought with hands and feet and teeth, to master the baffling elements and achieve his end. That is how I saw him then: that is how I shall always see him now—a tussling wisp of humanity high overhead, and swirling with the slow swirl of the mast against a tumult of tempestuous sky."

Next morning it was still blowing a diminished gale but the worry of not making Howth on time was gone now. Thanks to his skillful navigation, Childers had brought *Asgard* to a point ten miles southeast of the Howth promontory, which was exactly where they wished to be.

The natural thing to do after weathering such a storm would have been to head for Kingstown Harbor on Dublin Bay to dry out and repair the damage. By breaking out their prestigious Royal Cruising Club pennant, they might well have avoided search parties and awkward questions. But it was too great a chance to take. Childers elected to cruise upcoast for the rest of the day, and to anchor off the wild and beautiful island of Lambay for the night.

Despite exhaustion and battering from the storm, spirits were high. Childers and his four crew members had been at sea for 23 days, with less than five nights in harbor—something of a record for a yacht of *Asgard*'s size. They had weathered what they later learned was the worst storm in the Irish Sea since 1882. And they had brought the guns.

In celebration, Mary Spring-Rice made a special effort over the stew. In a careless moment, she managed to add a few drops of paraffin, but Erskine Childers was so hungry he did not even notice.

The vital day—Sunday, July 26—dawned gloriously clear, but the Irish Sea was still a green delirium. According to the plan worked out so long before, Darrell Figgis was to meet them in a small boat on the seaward side of Lambay if all was well. The time of the rendezvous had been fixed for ten in the morning. Then Figgis was to escort them into Howth

Harbor, where Bulmer Hobson's Irish Volunteers in good numbers would unload the precious cargo.

Ten o'clock came and went. Childers sent lookouts forward, and posted Mary Spring-Rice with a pair of binoculars to see if there was any evidence of welcome or warning from Lambay itself.

10:30. . .10:45. . .and still no sign of any craft, large or small. And all Mary saw were birds by the thousands on the grass-grown cliffs—great black-backed gulls bickering and wheeling at the summit, comical puffins in their nests along the cliffside, kittiwakes and fulmars diving and gliding near sea level . . . .

Since Howth Harbor drains to mud when the tide is out, *Asgard* had to go in on the flood tide, unload the guns and make her getaway before the ebb. If no craft or message materialized in time to do so, the agreed plan was for *Asgard* to sail to Shannon in the west.

With the tide flooding fast now, and time running out, Childers had his lonely moment of decision. His was the bold solution made in awareness of how tired his crew was, and how long the slog to Shannon would be:

"We'll go in anyway!"

All action now, Erskine ordered jib, main and jigger trimmed, for *Asgard* would be close-hauled almost all the way. At the same time he pointed her bow toward the lighthouse on the Howth Harbor breakwater.

Not without misgivings, Darrell Figgis reached Howth Harbor at 9:30 a.m. Matters had not gone exactly as planned. The men with the motor boat had endured a rough passage from Bray early that morning and refused to put to sea again.

There were already glimpses of *Asgard* from time to time as she cruised about waiting for welcome in some form.

One piece of luck did favor the basic plan. The British gunboat HMS *Porpoise* had left Dublin Bay on a false scent. Both Figgis and Hobson had planted rumors of a gun-running in Wexford, and *Porpoise* obligingly headed south in the

116

small hours. (Figgis' contribution was a "clumsily-coded tele-gram" to a political leader in Wexford mentioning a rendez-vous. Hobson dropped word of an arms landing well south of Dublin to a member of the Volunteer Committee called John Gore, "an ancient solicitor . . .not noted for his reticence," and soon many a client learned in strict confidence of the phantom plan.

So Dublin Bay was clear of patrol craft. As an added pre-caution, Hobson detailed 20 volunteers to infiltrate Howth Harbor with orders to look as much like tourists as possible. They were to help the yacht make her landing, and also to cope with any police interference that might arise before the main body arrived.

At 10:30 Gordon Shephard, true to his promise, reached the little harbor. He immediately spotted *Asgard* "a long way off behind Lambay Island." Finding Figgis crouching on the pier, he learned that the motor boat had never even left port. Trying to persuade Figgis to help him find any craft at all—sail or power—with which to reach *Asgard* proved unavailing.

Then *Asgard* appeared off the southern tip of Lambay, and both Figgis and Shephard breathed more easily. Shephard scouted the eastern pier, "arranged where the yacht should lie and told off men to catch the wraps." It was fortunate that he was there, as none of the advance party even knew that wraps were the lines one heaved ashore to make fast.

From the western breakwater, Coast Guardsmen were studying the approach of *Asgard* with the greatest interest. Finally they were able to make out a woman in a red jersey at the wheel, and this seemed to allay their suspicions that something serious was afoot.

The woman was Molly Childers, and the red jersey was the agreed signal that all was well on board.

Exactly at 12:45 *Asgard* entered harbor, dropping her sails as she did so.

But where were the Volunteers?

117

The plan called for them to be there at 12:45. If Erskine Childers could make it through so many seafaring hazards, it seemed odd that the land-based group could not do so.

(The Volunteers had already staged three Sunday outings to divert suspicion. The earlier outings were made to seem more like picnics than military maneuvers, and police interest had shown a gratifying falling-off.)

As *Asgard* rounded the small lighthouse on the break-water, her crew saw a small group of men at the pier-head just across the narrow harbor entrance. They spotted Gordon Shephard and Darrell Figgis among them.

From *Asgard's* deck Charles Duggan threw a light line to the pier, with a heavier one attached. He was a shade late, and the ketch, still with some way on, overshot.

Guided by Gordon Shephard, the men on the pier grabbed the light line and then the heavy, and were able to haul *Asgard* alongside at last.

Where were Bulmer Hobson's men?

Just as *Asgard* was being made secure, those on board heard the tramp of many feet in cadence. Four abreast, at the double, the Volunteers over eight hundred strong came swinging down the pier.

Some wore uniforms of sorts; most were in civilian clothes. Some wore bowlers, some straw hats, and some had bandoliers slung across their shoulders. A few of the officers carried revolvers, and a hundred of the men had been issued long batons with leather handles in case of trouble with the police.

(The secret of the guns had been well guarded, so that only three or four of the Volunteers Committee knew what was in store. To the rest, the 7–8 mile march from Dublin followed by the run on the double down the long pier was simply another test of stamina.)

Arthur Griffith was there, less passive in his resistance now. Eoin MacNeill was there too, and Padraic Colum, and a tall, intense man called Eamon de Valera. The O'Rahilly, also in the ranks, was just as ignorant of what-next as the many who had not shared the early planning.

It was The O'Rahilly who later found words to express the feelings of the eight hundred: "When the White Yacht, harbinger of Liberty, suddenly appeared out of nowhere, and, on the stroke of the appointed hour, landed her precious freight at Howth, history was in the making."

Gordon Shephard jumped aboard *Asgard*. Joining Molly Childers and Mary Spring-Rice at the mizzen, he watched what happened.

Under Erskine Childers' direction, the guns were already being handed up the hatch. Seeing the first rifles, realizing at last what their mission was about, the nearest Volunteers let out a yell of triumph.

"There was some scrimmaging at the start," Gordon Shephard wrote his father shortly afterwards. What actually took place was that some Volunteers broke ranks in their excitement and their wish to get their hands on the guns.

With his usual calm, Childers held back the flow of rifles until the officers restored order. They lined up their men in two columns all the way to the end of the pier.

Then each man in turn received his gun without confusion.

Meanwhile a Coast Guard cutter had snaked her way through the harbor shipping and was crossing the open water on *Asgard's* starboard side. A cry went up when she was spotted. Rifles and revolvers were quickly trained on the approaching craft. Taking the hint, the Coast Guardsmen contented themselves by firing rockets to summon the Royal Navy patrol craft which by then was many sea miles away.

The unloading took less than an hour. By Hobson's forethought there were taxicabs on hand to take the extra guns and the heavy ammunition boxes, and these too were quickly loaded. Just before the order to march was given, the troop raised three cheers for *Asgard* and her crew.

When the long column reached shore—rifles jauntily

119

shouldered—the Volunteers in turn were greeted by cheer on thunderous cheer from townspeople and holiday makers attracted by the scene.

The day was turning sour, with rain squalls now and a half-gale blowing. It was high time for *Asgard* to be off for her Welsh sanctuary. In a last ritual, Gordon Shephard helped Childers set the storm trysail.

Mary Spring-Rice and Shephard were to lunch with friends in Howth, and then go their separate ways. They stepped onto the pier, and Shephard helped Childers cast off. Soon *Asgard* was standing out to sea.

The pier was almost empty now. From its vantage point, Gordon and Mary watched the little ketch until she disappeared at last in the mist and rain.

14. The Spilling of the Waters

Shortly after they reached England Erskine and Molly Childers heard good news about Conor O Brien's share of the arms. At a rendezvous off Wales, the rifles and ammunition had been trans-shipped from *Kelpie* to Sir Thomas Myles' *Chotah*. Sir Thomas, a distinguished Dublin surgeon and a former President of the Royal College of Surgeons, was felt to have a lower profile than the colorful O Brien, and his yacht was a more familiar sight in the Irish Sea and Dublin Bay. The arms were safely landed at Kilcoole in Wicklow on August 1.

The Childers also learned for the first time of the tragic sequel to their own exploit.

All had gone well with the Volunteers on their march back to Dublin until they reached Clontarf, on the outskirts of the city. There they found their way blocked by a Battalion of the King's Own Scottish Borderers, and by police in good numbers as well. A police official told them they would have to surrender their arms, and a scuffle ensued in which a few of the guns were seized. There followed a long dialog, with both Hobson and Figgis taking vociferous part.

While the discussion was going on, the Volunteers and their guns simply melted away by two's and three's across the nearby gardens, parks and fields. All but nineteen of the rifles found their way to safe hiding places.

Frustrated and empty-handed the Battalion withdrew

toward Dublin. A crowd that grew and grew jeered at them as they marched. In the narrow confines of Bachelor's Walk the British rear-guard took a stand. Suddenly, with no orders from their officers, the soldiers began firing indiscriminately into the crowd. Two men and one woman were killed and 38 wounded.

Now the world knew that there was one law for the North of Ireland and another for the South. In the North, Sir Edward Carson's men paraded openly by the thousands, with machine guns and bayonets as well as rifles. Although they were in full defiance of the law, neither the British Army nor the Ulster police lifted a finger against them.

In the South, the landing of a few hundred guns, in good part to support the Government policy of Home Rule, had to be paid for in human lives.

By what Dangerfield calls "this little spatter of blood and bullets," Catholic Ireland learned that it was still a conquered nation under military occupation. "It matters very little," the indignant historian goes on, "whether 3,000 civilians were slaughtered, or 300, or 30, or three: there are stains in Bachelor's Walk which nothing will ever quite wash away."

Remember Bachelor's Walk! became an Irish Republican battle cry. And revolution was more than whisper now.

During those same last days of July of 1914, the skies of Europe were growing black with foreboding.

Now, as the storm broke, the floodwaters of fear, of hatred and misunderstanding and ambition began to surge over the spillway.

— *On Tuesday, July 28, Austria declared war on Serbia.*
— *On July 31, Germany and Russia mobilized, and within 24 hours a state of war existed between them.*
— *On August 3, Germany declared war on France. The next day German troops crossed the Belgian frontier.*
— *By the night of August 4, Great Britain, guarantor of the sanctity of Belgian territory, was in the war.*

The age-old saying had always been, "England's difficulty is Ireland's opportunity." But now John Redmond, who aspired to be the leader of all the forces driving for Irish freedom, showed his true colors. Like so many others, he yielded to the centripetal pull of one of the great moments of history.

The scene was a packed House of Commons on the afternoon of August 3. Sir Edward Grey, the Foreign Minister, had just told the Members how totally committed England was to her pledge to Belgium. Closing ranks, Mr. Bonar Law had said a few supportive words for the Loyal Opposition.

Before a hushed House, John Redmond rose to make his great and self-ruinous offer:

"There are in Ireland two large bodies of Volunteers. One of them sprang into existence in the South. I say to the Government that they may tomorrow withdraw every one of their troops from Ireland. I say that the coasts of Ireland will be defended from foreign invasion by her sons, and for this purpose armed Nationalist Catholics in the South will be only too glad to join arms with the armed Protestant Ulstermen in the North. . . We offer to the Government of the day that they may take their troops away, and that, if it is allowed us, in comradeship with our brethren in the North, we will ourselves defend the coasts of our country."

The applause, scattered and partisan at first, swelled to a great roar as it spread to the Opposition benches. Slumping a little as he took his seat, John Redmond listened to the accolade with no sign of emotion.

"How do you think they'll take it?" he asked a colleague, knowing in his heart that he was no longer even the shadow of Parnell's ghost.

"They" was the South of Ireland, his full constituency as leader of the Home Rule party.

Most of the Anglo-Irish and many of the Irish rallied to England in face of the greater danger of the Hun. But the fiercer Republicans, in sufficient numbers to keep the fires of

123

liberty burning and to destroy John Redmond's faltering and token leadership, went secretly to work.

Ireland's opportunity had come again and at last.

A Short seaplane, 240 h.p. Sunbeam engine, circa 1914

"Roundels Is Us"

From the flat East Anglian countryside around Felix-stowe, the North Sea looked as moody and lumpy as ever. And its steep, shallow seas and sluicing tides were much as he re-membered them. The rules of the game were what had changed. Now there was no more late-season duck shooting in the Frisians, no more searching for safe anchorages in delightful little coves and sandy estuaries. For, north by east of Felixstowe, and less than 200 miles away, enemy battle-ships by the dozen and cruisers by the score lay on constant alert behind those barrier islands he knew so well. Shoals of U-Boats were patrolling the entrances to the Elbe and the Weser, the Ems, and the Jade. Hovering overhead, when the weather was fine, were airships or small zeppelins, with the blunt, explicit Iron Cross painted on their canvas sides. . . .

Wearing the dark blue uniform of a lieutenant in the Volunteer Reserve, Erskine Childers reported to the Naval Air Station at Felixstowe on August 18, 1914. Less than a month had passed since his exploit of running contraband arms through the Grand Fleet in all its panoply and power.

Childers' response to the same Fleet's urgent request for his special skills was neither contradictory nor out of charac-ter. It was just one more example of that Parnell-like trust-in-self, that Emersonian vibration to the iron string of self-reli-ance.

To some, including his more extreme colleagues in the search for Irish freedom, it looked odd and over-zealous. To a man like Childers, how it looked was a matter of total indifference. His passionate concern was still freedom for Ireland. But now the rights of another small nation had been violated, and England—his England still—had promised to protect those rights. The Hun represented clear and present danger. There had to be an England, and an Empire, for it was within their vast scope that Ireland would obtain her Dominion status.

Such was the rationale of many a Home Ruler. Add, in Childers' case, the call of adventure, the wish once again to see "the shrapnel bursting beautifully over the enemy lines," and his volunteering becomes logical, even inevitable.

At 44, he was lean and weather-worn and as fit as many a much younger man. His skin, stained by sun and bitten by salt seas, was stretched taut over the high cheekbones. The eye, clear but remote, added to that look of the ascetic and the dreamer which would increasingly be his.

Yet there was little time for dreaming. By a minor miracle of Admiralty staff work, he had been assigned as observer on one of the seaplanes carried by HMS *Engadine,* working out of Felixstowe.

The seaplanes, built by the Short brothers, were useful workhorses of the Harwich Striking Force of cruisers and destroyers based at Harwichport just across the harbor from Felixstowe. Limited of range (some 250 miles) and of ceiling (9,000 feet), capable of speeds of just over 90 miles an hour when the wind was right, the Short seaplane, like its sister planes the Schneider Cup, the Fairey and the Sopwith Baby, was a brand new instrument of warfare. The Short was a biplane on twin pontoons or floats. In the early models the pilot sat in the after cockpit. Operating from the forward one, the observer—as Childers quickly learned—performed multiple duties which included almost everything but the actual flying of the plane. Among them were navigation (his skill of skills), photography of enemy ships and installations, radio communications, and the firing of the Lewis light machine gun through the biplane's many wire struts. Another responsibility was the accurate release of the five 20-pound bombs housed suspended from a little trolley under the fuselage for use against "targets of opportunity."

Engadine and her near-twins *Riviera* and *Empress* were converted Channel steamers, quite fast and with a low freeboard suitable for launching planes. They were seaplane carriers in the sense that they could each house three planes with folded wings in the metal deck hangers installed behind their stacks by the Royal Navy. But they had no flight decks for the actual launching.

One of the survivors of those pioneer days, William Guy Carr, describes in suitably jaunty style the way the planes became airborne:

"When they wanted to launch a birdie, they stopped the ship, hooked the birdie onto a fall dangling from the end of a derrick and then by the Grace of the Lord and a lot of good management, they hoisted the birdie off the deck, swung it overboard and lowered it into the water. Meanwhile, the pilot [and observer] prayed there were no enemy submarines in the vicinity who could be so unladylike as to take a pot shot. . . . Try to picture the fun they had hoisting out seaplanes on derricks when the sea was anything but smooth as a mill-pond."

At the end of the mission, the pilot landed his seaplane as near as possible to the mother ship, and the plane was winched back on board.

Naval aviation was still an inexact science a little more than four years old. In March of 1910 a Frenchman, Henri Fabre, after a surface run of a thousand feet on a French lake, made the first take-off from water. Then he flew over the lake for a third of a mile at an average height of six feet.

There were other firsts.

In May, 1912 the battleship HMS *Hibernia* launched a

127

Short seaplane from a makeshift platform constructed over her forecastle. The plane circled the Fleet, drawn up at Weymouth, and landed safely in the drink.

On July 28, 1914, a Folder seaplane, also of Short design, lumbered into the air with a torpedo slung between her pontoons, and proceeded to make the first successful torpedo drop.

Each training exercise and sortie, that summer of 1914, brought new knowledge. Proficient and eager for action, Childers learned as he flew, and of necessity learned fast.

In those early days, the British planes both land and sea were known simply by the serial number assigned to them when construction was completed. Childers for example flew in Short 136. But too many Allied planes were being shot down by their own trigger-happy AA batteries and their own fellow fliers. So bull's eyes, "roundels" as they were called, were painted on the fuselage and wings of British, French and Russian planes—and later on Italian and U.S. ones. When the circle with its sharply-colored concentric bands was seen, the cry would go up, "roundels is us". And the gunners would hold their fire.

The phrase caught on. "Roundels is us" went into the language of the day, carrying its message of momentary safety, and also, less directly, a cheerful promise of ultimate victory.

Lieutenant Childers was lucky in the men he served under. Commodore Reginald Tyrwhitt led the Harwich Force. He was a seaman through and through. Tall and powerfully-built, clear-headed and solid as a rock, he was direct of action and of speech. His command consisted of two flotillas of twenty destroyers each, and some half dozen light cruisers, some ancient, some new—as well as those three hybrid seaplane carriers. He was known as Com. (T), T being for Torpedo boats, the old-fashioned name for destroyers.

Closely associated with Tyrwhitt was another Commodore, (Com. (S) for submarines), also working out of Harwich-

128

port. Com. (S) was the redoubtable Roger Keyes, later of Dardanelles and Zeebrugge fame. Keyes, whose sharp features and pointed ears gave him the look of an intrepid faun, was the bolder man, with a taste for glory and a commendable wish to grapple with the enemy. HMS *Lurcher,* a fast destroyer, was his flagship; his command consisted of a score or more of rather elementary submarines.

In their own good time and England's, both Commodores would become Admirals of the Fleet. Together, week in and week out during those first anxious years, they saw more action than any other units of the Royal Navy.

Simply stated, their mission was to support the Doctrine of Distant Blockade. This was the overall strategy by which Admiral John Jellicoe's battleships at Scapa Flow in the Orkneys sought to contain and to destroy the *Hochseeflotte.* (Thanks in some degree to the warning of *The Riddle of the Sands,* the fast battle cruisers under Vice Admiral David Beatty were in late 1914 moved south to Rosyth on the Firth of Forth to be nearer the foe, but they also figured in this strategy.)

The Doctrine called for the sealing-off of the North Sea area by the Channel Fleet in the south and by units of the Grand Fleet in the north (both Jellicoe and Beatty). "Occasional driving or sweeping movements carried out by the Grand Fleet traversing in superior force" was one of the agreed tactics. Supplementing these majestic sweeps was the hard, unending grind of observing and patrolling Germany's 150 miles of North Sea coastline to make sure that the enemy did not sally out unseen. This assignment was given to Tyrwhitt and Keyes. They were also instructed to harass the foe. They were in effect to act as bait to lure his capital ships from their snug sanctuaries without themselves being destroyed in the process.

It was Keyes who gave his and Tyrwhitt's beautifully coordinated philosophy a name. He called it "creating the right atmosphere." By this he meant conditioning the enemy to a defeatist and defensive posture of never quite knowing when or where he was going to be hit and hit hard.

Ten August days after Childers reported in, Com. (T) and Com. (S) had a close call. Their ships and submarines were patrolling aggressively in the Heligoland Bight, on a tip that German units were also out in force. Beatty's battle cruisers had been alerted too, but this the Harwich Force did not know. At precisely the crucial moment in a morning of confused fighting, Beatty came crashing through the mist with three of his magnificent ships, and went straight into flaming action. German losses: three cruisers and a destroyer sunk, three more cruisers badly damaged. Only one British ship was seriously hurt, and there were less than a hundred casualties.

By dash and good luck the British had gone a long way to creating the "right atmosphere."

Later, as historian, Winston Churchill makes one of those large statements of which he was so fond: "Henceforth, the weight of British naval prestige lay heavy across all German sea enterprise. . . . Except for furtive movements by individual submarines and mine-layers not a dog stirred from August to November."

At the time of the Battle of Heligoland Bight, Mr. Churchill was First Lord of the Admiralty. Characteristically, he pressed for further action. Along with Tyrwhitt and Keyes he was anxious to launch a new type of foray in which the three seaplane tenders and their gadfly planes would serve as the live bait.

One might well ask why the Royal Navy, after a successful first experiment, did not put flight decks on more capital ships, and so create a force of genuine seaplane carriers. The answer is that naval aviation was still so new that the Sea Lords were unwilling to commit even one battleship or cruiser—badly needed for more conventional duties—to such hazardous and untested activity.

Another question is why Erskine Childers, a military thinker and strategist of some reputation, a middle-aged man whose spy novel was in part responsible for moving the battle cruisers to Rosyth, was willing to undergo the relative obscurity and modest rank of an observer. The arduous duties would seem at first glance to be something for a much younger man to perform. The answer is that he was very good at what he was doing and even as far back as the Boer War, a low-ranking job of danger and hardship appealed to something in his nature.

Absorbed as he was in the problems of day-to-day training, Childers still kept a weather eye on Irish developments. In September the Home Rule Bill passed the Commons for the third time, and so became law. When they delayed the passage for the last time the previous May, the Lords had excluded Ulster from it. Now, overriding them, the Commons included Ulster, so that the long-awaited law embraced all Ireland.

But a Contemporaneous Act was also passed providing that the Home Rule Law would not actually come into effect until after the War was over.

Many reluctant Republicans came to believe at last the refrain that firebrands like Padraic Pearse had been telling them for years:

"Ireland unarmed will obtain just as much freedom as it is convenient for England to give her. Ireland armed will attain ultimately just as much freedom as she wants."

The usefulness of the Gaelic League grew less, as the secret societies stepped up their drilling and made their plans for insurrection. The Volunteers had some guns now—the Howth rifles, and more coming in from America and elsewhere. Pearse, relinquishing his secretaryship of the League for sterner matters afoot, knew where it would all end and found the words to say so:

"I set my course ᚐᚱ ᚐᚅ ᚱᚑᚋ᚜ seo Roman
To the road before me, mio ᚷᚐᚔᚖᚆ ᚛ᚑ ᚈᚔᚏᚆᚐᚄ .
To the work I see, ᚐᚏ ᚐᚅ ᚗᚅᚔᚑᚋᚆ ᚛ᚑ ᚲᚔᚅ
To the death that I shall get." ᚔᚄᚐᚋᚐᚅ bᚐᚄ ᚛ᚑ ᚷᚂᚔᚅ .

131

On the afternoon of November 23, conditions were ideal for a reconnaissance raid by seaplane carriers with escorting cruisers and destroyers. The task force put to sea at 1700, and Childers and his fellow pilots and observers rejoiced at the prospect of action at last. But an intercepted German wireless message reported German armored cruisers in great numbers scouting off Heligoland—in exactly the area where the planes were to be launched. Reluctantly, the Admiralty ordered Tyrwhitt to abandon the operation.

In mid-December the Germans gave sharp evidence that the lesson of the "right atmosphere" had not been fully absorbed. Admiral Hipper and a powerful task force headed by four battle-cruisers bombarded Scarborough and Whitby in Yorkshire. In rapidly-worsening weather Hipper managed to elude all British attempts at interception and regained the Jade unscathed.

On December 24, a German land-based plane, flying at great height, bombed the outskirts of Dover—the first time that bombs were ever dropped from the air on British soil.

Although the German armies had been stalled at last in France, and the Western Front was stabilizing, a sense of uncertainty if not alarm began to spread through England. So far as the Royal Navy was concerned, people began to ask exactly who was teaching what to whom.

16.   Cuxhaven Revisited

Everyone was hoping for a nice quiet Christmas in port. But there were warnings that this was not to be. During the night of December 23, Commodore Keyes, flying his broad pennant from HMS *Lurcher,* had slipped out of harbor. On the morning of the 24th it was clear that ten of his submarines were also missing from their berths.

Normally, if no operation was imminent, pilots and observers bunked ashore at Felixstowe. Flight Commander Cecil Kilner, the pilot of Short 136, and Erskine Childers, its observer—along with the crews of the other two planes housed by *Engadine*—had on the 23rd been ordered to sleep aboard. . . .

There had been snow flurries during the night, but the day before Christmas dawned clear and very cold, with a glassy sea. Some of the stewards and messmen were already ashore buying Yuletide turkeys and geese when Commodore Tyrwhitt's flagship *Arethusa* broke out the unequivocal signal: "Raise steam with the utmost dispatch."

By 1130 the carriers *Engadine, Empress* and *Riviera. . . Arethusa* and two other cruisers, *Undaunted* and *Aurora. . .* along with eight destroyers. . . had all cleared harbor under sealed orders.

They had gotten underway so fast that many of the stewards and messmen were left ashore. From the stone quay the stragglers waved the geese and turkeys they had bought as the task force moved smoothly seaward.

Plan X, which the sealed orders contained, had been drawn up by the Admiralty on December 2, and initialled by Mr. Churchill. Opened at last, the plan turned out to be simplicity itself:

The task force was to rendezvous sixteen miles north-north-east of Heligoland an hour before light. The ten submarines were to station themselves between Commodore Tyrwhitt's ships and the German coast.

Concerning the seaplanes' role, the plan was so direct it sounded easy: "The seaplanes will proceed to drop their bombs on the Cuxhaven airship shed, noting what men-of-war are lying in the Elbe and its mouth en route there. On their return they should note what men-of-war are at Wilhelmshaven and in the Jade River."

Then there came a forthright warning to which no one could take exception: "Except when attacking the air sheds, the seaplanes should endeavor to keep out of gunfire."

After leaving the Jade, the little squadron was to fly along the coasts or islands to Nordeney Gat "to meet the flotilla which will be steaming south in line abreast."

Should the enemy attack, it was the destroyers' and submarines' task to rescue the pilots and sink the planes. To lighten the planes for easier take-off, each was to carry three 20-pound bombs, not five.

In the Official History after the raid was over, the underlying purpose was given: "As before, it was hoped that the enterprise might provoke a fleet action, and the whole Grand Fleet was concentrated in the middle of the North Sea."

To Commodore Keyes, reading the instructions, it seemed the Fleet, maneuvering some two hundred miles away, would hardly be in a position to lend support with any immediacy. He realized with pride that his submarines would have to carry a heavy responsibility. In a message to his command he expressed confidence that their skippers would "drive

134

home their attacks, proceed to the assistance of seaplanes, or carry out any other service that might arise."

Studying his own orders, Childers felt a mixture of elation and nostalgia: *because of his special knowledge of the terrain, Kilner and he would lead the little squadron into action.*

So the stage was set.

In good time the Task Force reached the launching area. The twenty minute drill, rehearsed so often, went without a hitch: the swinging open of the heavy hangar doors, the "running up" of the seaplane engines, the actual hoisting out of the planes.

With the first streaks of dawn Kilner and Childers took off. Six of the other eight planes followed. Two suffered engine failure and had to be hoisted in again.

The presence of the flotilla had not gone undetected. Cruising north of Heligoland, U-Boat 6 spotted the expedition just as the planes were being lowered, and watched the destroyers churning around the three carriers in a protective screen. The submarine commander immediately alerted Heligoland, and from the island message after urgent message crackled out to the mainland. Soon two German airships and four planes were aloft and looking for game.

As Short 136 neared the coast, Childers strained to see familiar landmarks. He remembered how Cuxhaven looked, crouched low behind its great dyke. He remembered how the shore sharpened to a point like a claw, and how the innocent dyke became a long low fort bristling with guns. He remembered how, to the southward, the point dimmed out into dunes. . . .

Somewhere to the south of Cuxhaven lay the airship sheds, but exactly *where,* Intelligence had not been able to determine. They were of course new since his cruising days.

Now patches of mist seemed to drift toward them, making spotting hard. Kilner dropped down to 150 feet.

Maddeningly, the mist became a solid fog bank and it was each plane for itself in the dankness. Kilner's engine began to cough, then caught again.

Suddenly, miraculously, the fog parted. Directly below them in the roadstead lay battleships and cruisers of the *Hochseeflotte*. Childers counted six dreadnoughts, three cruisers, some smaller craft. He also noted great consternation aboard the ships. There was a sound like tearing calico around him, and he knew that bullets were going by. He tripped the wire releasing his three bombs, but the plane's momentum was such that they fell in open water.

Circling, Kilner buzzed the great ships again, at not much more than masthead height. His hardiness bought him a holed wing and some bullets through the fuselage, as both ships and shore batteries opened up.

Below, the consternation continued, and Childers saw that several of the closely-tethered cruisers were preparing to cast off.

It was time to go. To their relief the fog rolled over them again. Kilner's engine was sputtering as they headed for the coast. The fog lifted, just one corner of it, and Kilner swerved to avoid a church spire a few feet to port. As they swerved, Childers saw a dilapidated Prussian eagle on duty as the weathervane atop the spire. This martial glimpse seemed to stimulate the plane's engine to new efforts. Then, as they neared the coast, the sputter set in again.

Childers scribbled a note and passed it back to Kilner.

"Are you going to descend here?" the message ran. "If so, *don't*. It's very muddy."

Something, perhaps the warning note or the sea air, revived the engine, and they were able to cruise comfortably back to the new rendezvous. Two of the squadron had already been hoisted in. It was almost 1000.

In the meantime the German zeppelins and their escorting planes, as well as stalking U-Boats, had made contact with the task force. For nearly three hours, as Tyrwhitt's

136

ships steered west and then south to the rendezvous, they drove home their attacks. The two zeppelins were particularly tiresome. Dodging in and out of cloud cover, attacking from dead ahead and then from dead astern to offer as little target area as possible, they dropped bombs in what seemed like limitless supply.

Empress developed condenser trouble and began to lag behind. L.6, one of the German zeppelins, jumped her, and she became an intensive care unit of one for the airship's ministrations. She zigged and zagged, with great spouts of water to port and starboard marking her slalom course. Finally, *Undaunted,* firing her 6-inch guns from extreme range, managed to score a hit on L.6. With a wound that later proved mortal, the zeppelin wore away to the east and vanished behind a bank of cloud.

There ensued a short lull in the furious air-sea-under-water melee, a lull when everyone in the task force was wondering what next. Expectantly they watched as a signal was spelled out from Tyrwhitt on *Arethusa.* The message was cheerful and to-the-point like the man himself:

"I wish all ships a Merry Christmas."

Then a U-Boat's periscope was spotted, and the battle was on again. Thanks to dexterous shiphandling and the use of every gun and small-arm that could be brought to bear, the flotilla reached the rendezvous point unscathed. . . .

Commodore Keyes' *Lurcher,* mother ship to his widely-deployed submarines, was also under constant attack. One German seaplane came in low from dead astern—so low that *Lurcher's* after 4-Inch gun was able to get its sights on it. Keyes, who happened to be standing near the gunner, showed him how to give his gun a swing up as he fired, "as one does for a rocketing pheasant."

"The seaplane twisted and turned like a pigeon when the gun fired," Keyes notes wryly in his memoirs, "and like a pigeon flew away."

Three of the returning planes ran out of fuel before

137

reaching the appointed area. By the greatest good luck all three managed to splash down near *E*.11, one of Keyes' solicitous submarines. The crews were taken on board and the planes destroyed by *E*.11's deck gun.

The fourth pilot ditched near a Dutch trawler, who took him in tow. Before they crossed into neutral waters, he managed to sink his plane as ordered. Once ashore in Holland, he was treated as a shipwrecked mariner and sent back to England.

When it was clear that all planes were present or accounted for, Tyrwhitt shaped course for home. In deference to *Empress*, he set the speed at a decorous 16½ knots. The flotilla made home port with no further enemy attack.

Christmas Dinner, for all that it came on Boxing Day, was enjoyed by all hands, and the cooks.

Kilner and Childers had labored better than they knew. In her frantic attempt to get underway, the battle cruiser *Moltke* crashed into the battle cruiser *Von der Tann*, and both were so severely damaged that they were out of action for months.

Childers' precise report of what he saw in the roadstead, pieced out by the reports of the other observers, gave a much-needed picture of German naval strength in a vital area.

Although no bombs found the elusive airship sheds, several of the squadron's planes managed to bomb targets of opportunity in the Wilhelmshaven area, and some hits were scored.

There were two firsts. Leading Seaman Mills of *Undaunted* was the first man ever to shoot down a zeppelin, and received the Distinguished Service Medal for his skill.

More important historically, the Cuxhaven Raid was the first naval engagement in which there was no surface or ship-to-ship action. Whether because it was Christmas Day or because the Grand Fleet was known to be out in the North Sea in all its power, no single German ship emerged. Airships, planes and submarines were their only units to go into action.

Their Lordships of Admiralty were very pleased with the results, and conveyed their appreciation to the two Commodores.

Flight Commander Kilner was made a Companion of the Distinguished Service Order, and Observer Erskine Childers received a well-earned Mention in Dispatches.

In his memoirs, Admiral of the Fleet Lord Keyes of Zeebrugge and Dover recalls his impression of two of the participants:

"In the carrier squadron two people particularly impressed me, the Squadron Commander, C. Le Strange Malone, a young naval lieutenant who had been given the command over the heads of many seniors, and Lieut. Erskine Childers, R.N.V.R., an observer in one of the seaplanes. The latter was the author of the 'Riddle of the Sands,' and had devoted his leisure for some years to cruising in a small yacht in the German estuaries. His local knowledge was invaluable."

Praise from Lord Keyes was praise indeed.

The seaplane carrier, HMS "Ben-My-Chree", 1915

HMS "Ben-My-Chree" (right) at the Dardanelles in August, 1917. She was shelled by Turkish shore batteries and sank shortly afterwards.

photos courtesy Imperial War Museum

17.   Flights East and Firebrands West

On March 23, 1915, Lieutenant Childers was transferred to HMS *Ben-My-Chree,* another converted packet, built in 1908 in the Isle of Man. Capable of a flank speed of almost 25 knots, she was the fastest of the seaplane carriers. At 2,651 gross tons, she was bigger than *Engadine* and the other Channel steamers, and could comfortably house and service four planes. With the young Le Strange Malone as her resourceful captain and the seasoned Childers as one of her four observers, she continued the work of long-range reconnaissance so vital to the Grand Fleet.

By this time Molly and the boys had joined Childers at Felixstowe. The little family took up quarters at the Felix Hotel. Later Molly remembered how, when enemy airships came over, the hotel lights would flicker to summon the Navy pilots and observers. Then she and the boys would sit among the aspidistra in the lounge, along with the other wives and children, and listen. . . and listen. First they would count the number of seaplanes taking off to intercept the enemy. Then, after the raid was over, they checked off the planes coming in for a landing. If there were five take-offs, for example, and only four landings, they knew that something had happened to one of the crews. . . .

Later that spring *Ben-My-Chree* was ordered to the Dardanelles where she did good work photographing Turkish trenches and gun emplacements. Aerial shots of the anti-submarine nets across the Straits also proved a great help in assessing tidal currents.

On August 12, 1915, Flight Commander Charles H.K. Edmonds, on a one-man flight from *Ben-My-Chree* in Short 842, scored another historical first. He was hoisted out at dawn, carrying one 14" Mark X torpedo between his pontoons. Attacking a 5,000-ton Turkish steamer from a height of fifteen feet, with the sun dead astern of his plane to blind the enemy, he launched his torpedo from 300 yards. Striking amidships and exploding on impact, the torpedo sent a column of water and ship parts masthead high. The steamer settled on the sea-floor, with only her four masts and funnel showing.

After the collapse of the Dardanelles expedition, *Ben-My-Chree* returned to the North Sea area. But early in 1916 her services were again requested in the eastern Mediterranean, this time by the Royal Navy's East Indian and Egypt Station. The Station was lending support to General Sir Archibald Murray's Sinai offensive, designed to protect the approaches to the Suez Canal. The request made it clear that such alternate methods of gathering information as behind-the-lines agents were most unreliable. The use of naval gunfire to command the coastal road was another reason why the ex-packet was needed.

There is documentary evidence of at least one Palestinian reconnaissance by Childers off *Ben-My-Chree*. On March 7, 1916, Flight Commander Edmonds and he, in Short 846, were ordered to reconnoitre Beersheba, with especial reference to the bridge over the Wadi El Saba, and the garrison. They left the water at 0918 and by 0950 were over the coastal town of Gaza. At 1030 they raised Beersheba, 25 miles inland. Childers' notes were as usual neat and laconic:

"Bridge, 2 miles E. of town still incompleted. Two 6-arch viaducts spotted. Marked diminution in no. of Tents. Troops: numerous scattered groups in & around

142

town. Rifle and MG fire general. Several hits: no damage."

When Childers was detached from *Ben-My-Chree* at the end of March, 1916, Le Strange Malone paid him high tribute:

"This officer has served under me in *Engadine* and this ship since the outbreak of war and has carried out his duties as observer with renowned success both in spotting and reconnaissance work. . . ."

In due course Childers was awarded the Distinguished Service Cross, naval counterpart to the Military Cross. The citation, which appeared in the supplement to the *London Gazette* on April 21, 1917, read as follows:

"In recognition of his services with the Royal Auxiliary Naval Service for the period of January to May, 1916. During this time he acted as observer in many important air reconnaissances, showing remarkable aptitude for observing and for collecting the results of his observation."

The *Gazette* also noted that he had been promoted to Lieutenant Commander, as of December 31, 1916.

During those anxious early years of World War I, the prospects for Ireland's freedom seemed on the surface to have turned stone cold. Some 200,000 Irishmen were serving in the British armed forces. A bare 11,000 was about all that Eoin MacNeill's Volunteers could muster for troublemaking at home. Nor was MacNeill, a moderate at heart, inclined to favor any drastic military action.

Secretly, some of the more ardent members of the Republican movement were stoking the banked fires of freedom. Under the leadership of Padraic Pearse the poet and James Connolly of the Irish Transport Union, a nation-wide uprising was planned for Easter Day, which in 1916 came on April 23.

When he got wind of it, MacNeill tried to call off the

operation, and was able to do so in almost all the provinces. But in Dublin, on Easter Monday, the Irish Volunteers and the Irish Citizen Army (wings now of the Irish Republican Army) struck as one. They seized the Government Post Office and other key buildings, proclaimed the Irish Republic and broke out its banner over their Headquarters in the GPO.

From England, Field Marshal Lord French, the Home Forces commander, ordered artillery to be moved up, and sent reinforcements. On Friday, General Sir John Maxwell arrived to take over command, and made it clear that the city was not to be spared: "If necessary I shall not hesitate to destroy all buildings within area occupied by the rebels."

By Saturday, it was obvious that, despite bitter fighting and gallant holding operations, the insurrection was doomed. Pearse surrendered unconditionally that afternoon. The last of the local commanders to give up was the tall, gaunt Eamon de Valera, whose five companies had cut off a key British supply route.

Total casualties, including many civilians, were 1,351 persons dead or severely wounded. Appalled by the damage to Dublin and the inevitable looting, the Irish public was apathetic about the Rising. The general feeling was that it was ill-timed and mismanaged.

Then the British made a tactical mistake. In great haste, Sir John Maxwell tried and condemned fifteen of the leaders, sparing only the Countess Markievicz (Eva Gore-Booth) because she was a woman and De Valera because he was American-born. Beginning with Pearse, the men were shot in ones and twos and threes over a ten-day period from May 3 to 12. James Connolly, whose legs had been shattered in the fighting, was in the last batch. No one had thought that the British would execute a badly-wounded man. Incredibly, they strapped him to a chair in the Kilmainham jail-yard and shot him like the rest. He died, as they all died, with great courage and composure.

144

In his court-martial speech, Pearse had foreseen the future well: "If you strike us down now we shall rise again and renew the fight. You cannot conquer Ireland; you cannot extinguish the Irish passion for freedom; if our deed has not been sufficient to win freedom then our children will win it by a better deed."

Their deed in dying was enough. Irish opinion swung sharply around. The fifteen firebrands were martyrs now. Their cause and Ireland's flared anew. The Rising that had at first appeared so reckless was seen to be gallant, and glorious.

Yeats found the words to celebrate its deathless message:

> ". . .I write it out in a verse —
> MacDonagh and MacBride
> And Connolly and Pearse
> Now and in time to be,
> Wherever green is worn,
> Are changed, changed utterly:
> A terrible beauty is born."

The shifting mood of Dublin showed itself in the treatment of rebel prisoners as they marched through the streets on their way to British jails. Those who had been given life sentences, 65 in all, were handcuffed in pairs, and there were nearly 2,000 others who were being deported without trial. To their surprise, they were blessed and cheered by huge crowds and many women broke through the armed escort to stuff the prisoners' pockets with presents. "It was the first sign that had come to them of the turning of the tide," Dorothy Macardle notes in her history of the Irish Republic.

Prime Minister Asquith came to Ireland to see for himself what was happening. First he had a conference with Sir John Maxwell, and assured him that His Majesty's Government was firmly behind his stern policy of repression. Sir John soon to be known the length and breadth of Ireland as "Bloody Maxwell," was properly grateful.

To his credit, Mr. Asquith also talked to Home Rulers

145

and even to some Republican leaders. Without any question he sensed the shifting and crystallizing of Irish sentiment in favor of the objectives of the Rising.

Mr. Asquith had many grave matters on his mind. Verdun was taking its terrible toll of French manpower. The Russian front was causing great anxiety. German zeppelin and surface raids on the east coast of Britain were correctly believed to have been timed to coincide with the Rising, and it was well known that some German arms had actually been used in it.

Then, on May 31, came the Battle of Jutland. Even though the German High Sea Fleet withdrew, they battled the Grand Fleet ship-for-ship and gun-for-gun and inflicted greater casualties than they received.

Now as never before, the Allies needed American help and involvement. But public feeling in the United States was aroused against the British by the Rising, and by what the *New York World* called the "hurried vengeance of the military authorities."

There were memorial services and mass meetings of sympathy, and President Wilson made a lofty but unmistakably-aimed speech about the rights of small nations as well as large to choose their own sovereignty.

No member of the Coalition Cabinet appreciated the need for American armaments and manpower more than the vital and vigorous David Lloyd George, whose star was going up the sky as that of Mr. Asquith paled. In a private conversation that May he made a grim prophecy concerning the American elections coming in the fall: "The Irish-American vote will go over to the German side. They will break our blockade and force an ignominious peace on us, unless something is done, even provisionally, to satisfy America."

Lloyd George, who was Secretary of State for War, agreed to take on additional duties to find an Irish settlement that would "even provisionally" act as a sop to American opinion.

146

His new responsibility was made no easier by the fact that the British had not quite finished their judicial killing. Sir Roger Casement had been captured in Kerry trying to land German arms. Earlier, he had committed an equally galling offense by visiting Irishmen held in German prisoner-of-war camps and seeking to enlist them in the Irish cause.

In both endeavors he was remarkably inept, but a final payment was due. Ironically, the Crown Prosecutor at Casement's London trial was Sir Frederick E. Smith, the self-same "Galloper" Smith who had been such a close ally in helping Carson arm Ulster just before the war. He was now the Attorney-General of Great Britain.

Casement was condemned to death, and hanged on August 3.

His speech after sentencing reaffirmed the cause of Ireland's freedom "that has outlived the failure of all her hopes. . . ." The concluding words bore a simple eloquence: "If this be the cause I stand here today indicted for and convicted of sustaining, then I stand in goodly company and a right noble succession."

In death he joined the other fifteen leaders of the Rising, and his name is linked to theirs in the annals of Irish history.

Fed fresh fuel by Casement's trial and execution, quietly elated now by the Rising, the Republican movement—generally known as the Sinn Fein movement—spread and grew.

18.   Of Cosmetics and Conventions

Erskine Childers' reaction to the Rising is interesting if curiously detached. Writing to a cousin on May 23, 1916, he makes his own involvement seem far removed in time and space:

"My opinion about Ireland is indeed a very simple one. . . namely, that peoples denied freedom will rebel, the responsibility for the tragic results resting on those who deny the freedom. . . . There is no moment in history that I know of when it would not have been best both for England and Ireland that Ireland should govern itself."

Such indeed had been his view from 1908 on, when he became a Home Ruler. He goes on to give his opinion of the rebel leaders themselves:

"The typical rebel is often half-crazy and half-starved, a neurotic nourished on dreams. We shoot a decent number—again by a venerable convention, probably justified. . . the wisest then say, 'Yes, but we must now do something. . . .' "

He mentions Prime Minister Asquith's visit to Ireland, still for the purpose of setting up some form of Home Rule—and reminds his correspondent how bad Asquith's track record is on this subject, "a string of tactical surrenders to force from both sides."

Remembering how he and Molly were "wrapped up in Ireland when war broke out," Childers speaks of his misery and hers over the Rising, and says that they are both finding relief "in hard and unremitting work."

At a time when the Irish were becoming passionately aware of the legacy that was now theirs, Childers was still acting like a typical Ascendancy man. "*We* shoot a decent number" is a comment that aligns him with the British still. (It is interesting to note that Lieutenant Robert Barton, his cousin and comrade reacted quite differently. Although he was also in British uniform and guarding some of the Irishmen taken prisoner in the Rising, Barton was so moved and impressed by their spirit and discipline that he became then and there an all-out Republican.)

Cold as it is, Childers' letter is revealing. For it shows that intellectually he had almost given up on Home Rule, and was nearer than he perhaps realized himself to making the quantum leap into Republicanism. His reference to the typical rebel as a "neurotic nourished on dreams" is replete with irony, for rebellion was the direction in which he was tending.

Molly was back in London now, having taken a house at 13, Embankment Gardens in Chelsea. Her "hard and unremitting work" was for Belgian refugees and relief. Erskine's work continued to be naval duty in the North Sea area.

During the summer and fall of 1916 he served as Navigating and Intelligence officer in a squadron of 40-foot coastal motor boats operating off the Belgian coast. In April of 1917 he was sent to Eastchurch for a refresher course on observation and reconnaissance. Then, in July, Childers was detached from all naval duties and appointed one of the secretaries to the Irish Convention, summoned by Lloyd George to meet in Dublin to try to solve the question of Irish freedom.

When Gordon Shephard, a brigadier now and still flying on the Western Front, heard the news, he recorded his pleasure in his diary: "It is a very good thing that Erskine

Childers has now got the job for which he is most eminently suited and I imagine that the Convention will last for some time."

It lasted nine months.

The idea of a Convention in which Irishmen of many persuasions would meet in constructive spirit had been in the air for over half a year. Ever since the Welshman's elevation to the Prime Ministry in December of 1916, there was a growing hope that something really was going to be done at last. But the spring of 1917 was a most anxious time for the Allied cause. With the enemy's all-out submarine warfare at its height, Russia in revolution and military collapse, and the post-Verdun demands on British troops in France steadily growing, Ireland's problems simply had to wait their turn.

The United States declared war in April of 1917. The longed-for event actually increased rather than diminished pressure on Lloyd George concerning Ireland. Walter Hines Page, the American Ambassador in London, was an ardent Home Ruler and now, more than ever, he was in a position to press his own and America's wish for action.

Finally, on May 21, the Prime Minister told the House of Commons that the War Cabinet had decided "that Ireland should try her hand at hammering out an instrument of government for her own people."

From long experience, Erskine Childers was not over-sanguine about the Convention's prospects. For one thing there was Lloyd George's reputation for trickery as much as for energy. Making the Convention an all-Irish affair looked like a touch of Welsh wizardry: if it failed, the Prime Minister could say that he had tried his best and that even the Irish were unable to resolve their own difficulties.

Another cause for misgiving was the behind-the-scenes role of Sir Edward Carson, now a member of the War Cabinet. Purporting to be an enthusiastic supporter of the Convention, he was at the same time instructing the Northern Unionist delegation to hold themselves as aloof and detached

151

as possible. In particular, they were to avoid any solution that would commit Ulster to becoming part of a Republic or Dominion which included all Ireland.

Lloyd George left the composition of the Convention to the Irish, and the organizers agreed that 101 delegates should be invited as a fair cross-section. There were 95 acceptances. Of these 52 were nationalists under the fading leadership of John Redmond; 24 were Ulster Unionists, nine were Southern Unionists and there was a sprinkling of laborites and liberals. Although five members of Sinn Fein were invited, these more violent Republicans chose not to attend. Their feeling was that so small a group would misrepresent the growing power and influence of their movement.

Sinn Fein did have an interest in the Convention and wished to have a daily link with its proceedings. So a young publisher and farmer called Edward MacLysaght (who was Gaelic down to his Irish-made boots) while technically listed as a Nationalist delegate acted as their liaison officer as well.

Another Nationalist of an extreme stripe was George Russell (AE). But Russell came more as Sir Horace Plunkett's man, and like Sir Horace strove to remain detached from any narrow political bias during the sessions.

Of the delegates 32 were Chairmen of their County Councils, good solid businessmen and farmers who gave the Convention a measure of needed, down-to-earth reality.

Irish and Anglo-Irish peers attended in some profusion, representing various persuasions and their own wide holdings. These included the Duke of Abercorn, the young Marquess of Londonderry, four Earls—Desart, Dunraven, Granard and Mayo—Viscount Middleton and two barons, Lord McDonnell and Lord Oranmore and Brown. Three archibishops—of Armagh, Cashel and Dublin—and the Bishop of Raphoe were also present. There was a Catholic majority of ten among the delegates.

The Convention chose Trinity College, Dublin, as its meeting place, and the College offered a splendidly-proportioned room over the Front Gate as the actual Convention Hall, a room with beautiful plasterwork and indifferent acoustics.

A chairman was soon chosen: Sir Horace Curzon Plunkett. With on the one hand his excellent Anglo-Irish credentials (he was the son of the 13th Lord Dunsany) and on the other his splendid record in Agricultural reform, he seemed the perfect choice. Mildly inclined toward Home Rule, idealistic yet worldly, somewhat ironic under a charming manner, he had one surprising fault: a lack of skill as a speaker.

The main job of the secretariat was to prepare position papers on the myriad subjects under discussion.

Drawing on his Parliamentary training and powers of concentration, Childers was soon immersed in the kind of work he did so well. His own inclination was for a Dominion scheme, "that being the last faint chance of effecting a constitutional settlement."

For most of the nine months he and Molly stayed with Diarmuid Coffey, who had been a crew member on Conor O Brien's *Kelpie* in the old gun-running days. The Childers also saw a good deal of Edward MacLysaght. In an article on the Convention MacLysaght recalled Childers' mood: "I became very friendly with him. His outlook at the time was very moderate. Later on we differed but did not cease to be friendly."

Childers' mood was "moderate" because he became more and more discouraged with the progress of the Convention and was keeping his powder dry. As he saw clearly from the start, one near-fatal flaw lay in the original terms of reference. No one seemed to be quite clear what the delegates were being asked to do. To some, like the Northern Unionists, the purpose was simply to have exploratory talks. Others felt acutely the necessity of reaching a swift and definite agreement on some degree of Irish independence.

Lloyd George—nimble as ever, never quite showing his hand—promised the delegates that the government would

153

take all the needed legislative steps once "substantial agreement" was attained on the actual form of an Irish constitution.

To create a climate of good-will, the Prime Minister released the rebels serving life sentences, and the deportees, just before the Convention met—a gesture which most of the delegates accepted for what it was intended to be, but some took as an admission of weakness.

The Convention opened on July 25 in an atmosphere of hope and goodwill. As the first stage, Plunkett proposed a series of debates to identify the deep-seated problems and alternate solutions. It was also a time, he submitted, for regional delegates to learn first-hand about parts of Ireland they did not know.

Both proposals were accepted. There were endless debates, some brilliant, some boring. The Convention held sittings in Cork for the Ulstermen to see what the South was like, and in Belfast for the Southerners to discover the North. Nor, in the fostering of good-will, was entertainment lacking. Lord Iveagh, of the Guinness family, gave an enormous garden party and the Granards staged a magnificent soiree in their Dublin townhouse that made the war seem remote.

Underneath, cleavages were widening and hardening. The question of who would control the customs, under any form of constitution, kept cropping up like a King Charles' Head. The absence of Sinn Fein participation leant a note of unreality to the proceedings.

There were moments in December of 1917 and March of 1918 when the spirit of conciliation and compromise seemed to be taking over, with the Southern Unionists and the Nationalists making statesmanlike concessions. From behind the scenes, Lloyd George coached, cajoled, threw in brilliant improvisations. But always when the clutch came, the Northern Unionists dug in their heels and refused to change their previously-prepared position of non-involvement and delay.

John Redmond's death in March of 1918 came just at one

of the hopeful times. Out of respect for his long career and basic goodness, the Convention adjourned for what might have been a vital week, and lost steerageway thereby.

By late March, the Western Front was turning into a shambles. Between mid-March and the end of April, the British Army lost 300,000 men. Amiens, the linchpin of the defensive system, was in grave danger. Conscription for Ireland, where volunteering had almost disappeared since the Rising, became a distinct possibility and a smouldering issue.

Inevitably, Home Rule and conscription became linked. In the face of the military emergency, and the fierce resentment that the former aroused in the North (and the latter everywhere else in Ireland), both were shelved. The Convention died with hardly a whimper.

In forwarding the final report to the Prime Minister, Sir Horace let his frustration show at last: "We had," he wrote, "to find a way out of the most complex and anomalous political situation to be found in history—I might almost say in fiction." He went on to blame the failure to do so on two never-resolved difficulties: Ulster and customs.

Terence de Vere White, in his book *The Anglo-Irish*, sums up the North's basic reservation in succinct fashion:

> "Ulster was the only province that had flourished under the Union; it was natural that its beneficiaries were reluctant to put their fortunes to hazard for an ideal which they did not share."

To White, the cosmetic quality of the long Convention is particularly evident. It became "a pageant . . . a talk shop, with both extremists instructing the men in the middle."

With American involvement in the war growing apace, and vast pressures building up elsewhere on the Prime Minister's time, Lloyd George's feeling was predictably that the Convention *had* served a purpose, and proved a point that he had suspected all along: that which had been torn and divided by the centuries, no Irishmen could put together.

Near the end, Erskine Childers made a constructive suggestion. To reduce the resistance of the Ulstermen, he proposed to Sir Horace that British Labor bring its influence to bear on Ulster Labor. They would in effect say to their colleagues, "Your reactionary Unionism is a drag on the wheel." But in reality the solid bloc of Ulster Unionists, which held power in Parliament and influence at the Convention were capitalists and reactionaries not Laborites, and the interesting idea was stillborn.

Childers, with his disarming clarity, later recorded his own disillusionment and intent:

"The collapse of the whole Convention, and the attempt to enforce conscription, convinced me that Home Rule was dead, and that a revolution, founded on the rising of 1916, was inevitable and necessary, and I only waited till the end of the war, when I had faithfully fulfilled my contract with the British, to join in the movement myself."

Early in 1918 the Childers had taken a personal loss which was hard to bear: Gordon Shephard was killed in a flying accident in a routine patrol. Molly was in London when she heard the news. Her letter to Lady Shephard, Gordon's mother, is direct and touching: "I can't find words to tell you what this will mean to Erskine and myself. If Gordon had been our own son or brother, I don't think the blow could have struck closer."

From Dublin, Childers wrote in similar vein:

"I have just heard Gordon's death from Molly, and am full of sorrow for ourselves and deep sympathy for you and his father. . . . He is one of my heroes and always will be so. Molly and I loved him. We saw great things and lovable things in him from the very first, and the friendship has grown closer all the time. So proud you must feel of him in all your terrible sorrow."

Shephard's death severed another Establishment link in a chain that was coming under heavy strain now.

156

After the Convention broke up, Childers went back to his military duties. He undertook more coastal reconnaissance work of the kind that he knew so well. (By now he had logged over 200 hours flying time, a considerable achievement in itself.)

He helped plan a bombing raid on Germany that was to be the biggest yet attempted. Then the tide of battle swayed once again and for the last time. The Central Powers crumbled, the Armistice was signed—and the raid-that-never-was became just an historical footnote.

Erskine Childers was mustered out in March, 1919. With no undue delay, he travelled to Dublin and made his way to the Sinn Fein headquarters in Harcourt Street to offer his services to the Republican cause.

Now there was no turning back.

Mollie Childers and Mary Spring Rice aboard *Asgard*

19.   The Beginning of the Troubles

"My name is Childers, Erskine Childers. I have a note from Robert Barton for you."

To Robert Brennan, the small, spare man seemed prematurely aged. Only the eyes were young. Clear, kindly, alert —they were what Brennan remembered best when he recalled the meeting in his autobiography.

Brennan, working in the Propaganda Department of the Republican Government, was of course well aware of the man who stood before him, for Childers' novel, his gun-running and his recent role in the failed Convention were all well-known.

"I hope you are going to write something," he said politely after the usual courtesies had been exchanged.

"I want to tell you straightway," Childers answered, "that after a good deal of thought, I have decided that Sinn Fein is the right policy for Ireland. I have come over to give a hand any way I can help."

The room in the Sinn Fein Headquarters where they met looked out on Harcourt Street, with a glimpse of St. Stephen's Green. It seemed peaceful enough. But Dublin as a whole was taking on the appearance of an armed camp. Streets were cordoned off. Patrols complete with steel helmets and bayonetted rifles were much in evidence. Down on the docks, where the Liffey meets Dublin Bay, there were tanks and armored

159

cars and supply dumps by the acre, as if an expeditionary force were forming. The time was March, 1919, and the first phase of the Troubles was well underway.

Brennan asked Childers if he had ever met Arthur Griffith, the Minister of Home Affairs. Childers said he had not, but would very much like to do so. The ensuing meeting was cordial, and it was agreed that Childers should help to create the Irish *Bulletin* to tell Ireland's side of the rebellion.

"He's a good man to have," Griffith said to Brennan later with reference to Childers' assignment. "He has the ear of a big section of the English people."

A great deal had happened in the months since the Armistice.

In December, 1918, Lloyd George adjourned Parliament and called for a General Election to reaffirm England and Ireland's confidence in his Coalition Government, now that peace had come. The Irish saw the election as a chance to make real the rising power of Sinn Fein. It would serve as a national plebiscite as well as the choosing of a new Parliament.

When the votes were counted, 73 of the 105 Irish seats went to the Sinn Fein party. Of the remaining newly-elected members, there were 26 Ulster Unionists, as expected. The nationalists—the historic Home Rule party of Parnell and Redmond—managed to hold exactly six seats. Home Rule was a dead issue, for 70 percent of the people of Ireland now wanted a Republic. Their leaders moved resolutely and with speed to answer their spoken will.

They decided to make themselves into a separate unit in Dublin rather than journey to Westminister to serve as a small segment of the House of Commons. They called themselves the Dail Eireann or Irish Parliament.

The Dail Eireann met for the first time on January 21, 1919. It adopted a Constitution, issued a ringing Declaration of Independence and moved to form a Cabinet.

160

When the reading of the Declaration was finished, Cathal Brugha, who presided, reminded the Deputies what they were affirming: "You understand from what is asserted in this Declaration that we are done with England. Let the world know it and those who are concerned bear it in mind." It was the spirit of the Easter Rising that spoke, with the country behind the spirit now.

By April 1, when the Dail met again, of necessity in secret, De Valera had taken over as President, and there was a full Cabinet. Since the British still controlled revenues and taxation, a first loan of 250,000 pounds was organized under the leadership of the young and very able Michael Collins, whose work as Intelligence Chief would soon make him the most hunted of men.

Here was open defiance. Lloyd George's peacetime Coalition (which had been reelected but with a more Conservative tinge than it had once possessed) soon had to face up to the prospects of a full-scale war.

With Field Marshal Lord French as Viceroy of Ireland now, and troops pouring into Dublin, it was clear that the British had given up any pretense of governing Ireland except by the sword. The Royal Irish Constabulary, 10,000 strong, supplemented the growing Army of Occupation, and sought to control every Irish town and village from their well-fortified barracks.

As early as January, 1919, there were ambushes, raids and reprisals. The Irish Volunteers, soon to be known as the Irish Republican Army, had a great need for arms and ammunition, and they ranged and raided widely to obtain them.

Erskine Childers' decision to break with his fatherland and his English past seemed to him both logical and inevitable. He had paid his debt to England in two wars and much Parliamentary service. Step by step—and he was a man much given to intellectual phases—he had come to believe that

161

England was totally wrong about Ireland, understood nothing, would never let go unless forced to do so. Home Rule was no longer enough of an answer. Besides, Ulster would never permit it to happen. For Sir Edward Carson and his armed men were just as implacable and just as obtuse as their English brothers. Later, in self-justification, Childers referred to his "Dominion phase" as "something I passed through years before," something that was already pointing inevitably toward Republicanism:

> "I wrote and spoke much for Irish Home Rule in the years 1910–1914, and in 1911 published the 'Framework of Home Rule,' advocating and elaborating a Dominion Settlement, and stressing the vital importance of fiscal autonomy... But I set no limit to the national march. The keynote of the book was that Ireland should have what the Irish people wanted. As there was no Republican movement at the time and Sinn Fein was very weak, I naturally worked on Home Rule lines, though of the widest scope."

"Misled by the idea of a war for small nations," Childers realized that his World War I service was motivated by the same instincts that caused so many Irishmen to volunteer: awareness of the Hun as the common foe, and a wish not to be left out if there was a good fight going. (The fact that 49,000 Irish citizens gave their lives serving in an army that many of them would soon challenge was ironic and unfortunate.)

As Childers' misgivings grew and the Irish Convention, with its unreality and its face-saving, failed, it became merely a matter of time before he made the perilous leap.

Molly Childers was dead set against the move to Ireland and Sinn Fein. Erskine's decision to do so led to one of the rare quarrels in their near-idyllic relationship. Although her own latent hostility to the British surfaced from time to time, she was intelligent enough to know that Erskine would never be fully accepted by the Republican Irish. That Ascendancy, born-to-lead look, that accent that could not fail to sound supercilious—even though he was the least supercilious of men—these were barriers insuperable and she knew it.

"It was Erskine's sniff that got him shot," one of his Irish colleagues remarked after the searing events of the Civil War were over at last—and there is some truth in the devastating comment.

Molly was as loyal as she was intelligent. When Childers had run for the British Parliament she put heart and soul in his campaign—drafting speeches, speaking herself, encouraging him when he feared he was out of his element. She was ambitious for him (and his rejection by the British politicians was one more subliminal element in her anti-Britishness). She also was fully aware of the stubborn streak in his nature which simply followed the course that he knew was right and let the chips fall. Always and again, the iron string!

So when he decided, despite every argument she could muster, that the call of his motherland was the one he had to answer, she accepted his decision and went along with it. And like him she never once looked back.

What resulted was the most effective, the most creative and the most brilliant two years of their life together.

As Arthur Griffith knew well from his own days as a newspaper editor, the Irish version of the Troubles was not reaching the outside world in any recognizable form. British prestige was still at its immediate post-war high, and British propaganda hard to counter. For the most part the British press printed what they were told by the Viceroy and the Army: the feckless Irish, incapable of ruling themselves or even of agreeing among themselves how they could ever do so, were in rebellion once again. Military rule was the only answer, and there was no choice but to enforce it in county after lawless county. . . .

There were some in England and the United States who

163

were willing to listen to another side, if only the story could be made to reach them.

Brennan's immediate superior was the Minister of Propaganda, Desmond Fitzgerald, and it was to Fitzgerald that Childers himself reported. Fitzgerald, a romantic figure and a man of considerable charm, had been one of the founders of the Imagist Group of Poets in pre-war London. He also had a love of France, and a scholar's knowledge of French literature. He had spent so much time in France that he spoke Gaelic with a French accent. His contacts with the literary and newspaper community in London were still many. Now he made several trips to England to establish good lines of communication with the British liberal Press and the French bureau chiefs there.

In Fitzgerald's absence Childers went to work gathering material and planning the publication of the *Irish Bulletin,* which would first appear on November 11, 1919.

Late that spring he also carried out an assignment to Paris that convinced him all over again that total freedom was the only choice for Ireland.

One of the acts of the Dail in its historic first session had been to appoint three delegates to the Versailles Conference. It was considered of prime importance that Ireland's claims to independence receive a hearing at that vast assize of nations. The three appointed were De Valera, Arthur Griffith and the venerable Count Plunkett, Foreign Minister and father of one of the sixteen men executed after the Easter Rising.

An advance party had been sent to Paris to arrange a meeting with President Wilson, but was making little headway. Griffith instructed Childers to bring his sophistication and powers of persuasion to bear.

The Seine was in flood as never before. No one could remember a time when the stone Zouave guarding a stanchion of the Pont de l'Alma was submerged to the tip of his musket barrel by the swollen river.

164

It was a good omen, everyone said. For there was also at the moment a floodtide of hope in the affairs of mankind. Riding its crest was that near-deity, that symbol of hope incarnate, President Woodrow Wilson. . . .

The Irish mission was a failure. Too many other small nations were also waiting to see *Monsieur le Président Veelson* with prior claims, seemingly more pressing claims. There were Montenegrins and Serbs—Croats, Slovaks, Kurds—Silesians and Poles and Lebanese (both Christian and Moslems)—Lichtensteinians and Luxembourgeois and superb dark Arabs shepherded by the legendary Colonel Lawrence.

Worse still, the Big Four among the victors—England, France, the United States and Italy—controlled the agenda, and one single veto was enough to exclude an item. Lloyd George made very sure that the question of Ireland was never inscribed.

As for Mr. Wilson, he was fast learning the difference between being a prophet and a working statesman—and finding that the former role was the one he infinitely preferred. "He was able, as are all very religious men," writes Harold Nicholson, who was there, "to attribute unto God the things that were Caesar's. . . . Early in January he immersed himself within the Ark of the Covenant. No one thereafter, least of all Mr. Lansing [his Secretary of State] was able to get him out."

The noble principle of self-determination, which Mr. Wilson had proclaimed with such lofty idealism, crumbled under conflicting needs and claims. Cornered on his refusal to see the Sinn Fein delegates, Wilson said sadly, "You have touched the great metaphysical tragedy of today. When I gave utterance to those words I said them without the knowledge that nationalities existed which are coming to us day after day."

Childers had not expected that the Paris mission would accomplish much. Earlier in the year, when Wilson was in London on his way to Paris, he had glimpsed the triumphant President from the window of his club. Childers turned to

Basil Williams, who was also watching the city's tumultuous welcome, and said somberly, "It's a weak, vain face—he will do nothing."

Even though the Irish advance party failed, they did inhale the heady wine of freedom in Paris, which was there for all to breathe. With the rest of the world, the Irish watched King Feisal as he came in his white robes, and not as a suppliant, to demand his people's due. Nor did the boyish Lawrence go unnoticed at his side—by the Irish and by many —as the lines of his young-old face hardened into disappointment at promises unkept.

To the Irish, the lesson was obvious: don't place your trust in presidents and prime ministers. *If you want something, you must take it.*

Back in Dublin, Childers put his proven skills as a writer, his great powers of concentration, to the task in hand.

That first Armistice Day issue of the *Irish Bulletin* in 1919 consisted of a few sheets, of which 50 copies were mimeographed. It was distributed by hand to Dublin newspapers and to correspondents of the foreign press. For the next 20 months, daily for five days a week, without missing a copy, the *Bulletin* carried the Irish version of the Trouble to an increasing audience. Each Friday featured *The Weekly Summary of Acts of Aggression Committed in Ireland by the Military and Police of the Usurping English Government,* and this became a staple item to be compared with similar fact sheets issued by the "usurpers."

Within the year, the *Bulletin* had grown to 600 copies a day. Mailed to friends in Dublin and to the Irish Consuls in Paris and Rome, its news and opinions were widely quoted and reprinted.

Inevitably, the British tried hard to find the headquarters and the staff. There were in all eleven successive hideaways. Once, when the Auxiliary Police raided the press when they were in Molesworth Street, much of the equipment was cap-

166

tured—typewriters, mimeograph machines, spare copies, addresses. But the staff was not there at the time. . . .

By the fall of 1919, all the Childers had come to Dublin. Their house at 12 Bushy Park Road, where the family settled a year later, became a Republican rendezvous. It was—and still is—a pleasant row house with a half-timbered gable and a gravel front yard. Behind is a garden, with a low wall at the end of the garden, and open parkland beyond. It looks very much like its semi-detached twin, and not very different from the other houses in the block, and in the surrounding blocks. With its rather anomalous comforts, and good facilities for escape, it was in fact an excellent place to go to cover in.

Childers was almost on the run. His revealing articles appeared in the world press, some carrying his own by-line. His connection with the *Bulletin* was suspected by the British but never quite proved.

Although Molly was in constant pain now, she espoused the Republican cause with all her indomitable spirit. With her excellent French, she proved particularly useful in briefing—and bewitching—the foreign press. Henri Béraud, the French journalist, later recalled the roundabout ways by which he was brought to Bushy Park Road, and the pleasant conversation over the teacups, "of French literature, of Paris, of the Russian ballet" as well as of matters of more immediacy. Childers himself took little part, but from time to time Molly would translate for him and relay his answer. "He was very dark, very thin," Béraud remembered, "the temples turning gray, the expression kindly. The habit of meditation had furrowed his face; two long parentheses framed his mouth. . . ."

Among the men on the run who found refuge at Bushy Park Road was Robert Brennan. One night he was taking a bath when Childers knocked on the door.

"There's a lorry outside," Childers said through the door. "Do you think they're after you?"

"More likely you," Brennan answered.

167

"I don't think so. Would you think of slipping on some clothes and getting out through the back?"

"They'll have it covered."

A thundering knock on the front door ended speculation. Childers went down and opened it.

"What's the meaning of this?" he asked in his posh voice.

"Who are you?" a loud English voice countered.

"I'm Major Erskine Childers.* Who are you?"

"Can you tell us where we will find No. 8 Victoria Road?"

"I'm sorry I can't."

"You mean you won't."

"I mean I'm sorry I can't. Would you mind giving me your name and regiment. I intend making a complaint to the Commander-in-Chief about your conduct."

The officer, Brennan later recalled, "mumbled something, backed out and drove away."

So Childers' Englishness still stood him in good stead, and he was quite willing to use it as cover when the need arose. Once when a young lieutenant in another military search party dropped a cigarette on his best parlor rug, he wrote an indignant letter to the Press—and all Dublin laughed.

---

*Childers was mustered out with the Royal Air Force rank of major after the Navy's Air Service merged with the RAF.

20.   Battles of Gun and Pen

The war was hotting up. By the summer of 1920 the Black and Tans had come in force, adding an element of hatred that the regular army and the Royal Irish Constabulary had never induced. Mercenaries recruited into the Constabulary, they were combat veterans of a worthier cause. Their pay was ten shillings a day, and they drank most of it. In their green or khaki tunics, with black belts and dark police breeches (or dark tunics and tan breeches, whichever were available), they were a nondescript-looking lot with a developing taste for pincers and lighted matches under the toenails as ways of questioning prisoners.

That same autumn the Auxiliaries began to arrive, a more dangerous crew, also battled-hardened, working directly out of Dublin Castle and the civilian authority there.

Violence begat violence. On Bloody Sunday (November 21, 1920), Michael Collins' execution squad killed fourteen purported British Intelligence agents, some in their beds, several by mistake. That afternoon the Auxies, out of their anger and tension, fired into a Dublin crowd at a football match, killing fourteen and wounding 62.

In December, 1920, the Auxiliaries burned Cork City. Embarrassed, the British Government claimed that the fire had spread by accident from the main shopping area to the City Hall. There was a quarter of a mile and the river Lee between, which made the claim unconvincing to say the least. Besides, Company K of the Auxiliaries were proud of their work as arsonists, and wore burnt corks in their Glengarry bonnets to make sure that credit was given where due.

By early 1921 the ambushes and executions were increasing. There was even a set battle: at Rosscarbery, Tom Barry's flying column forced a thousand of the Essex and Hampshire regiment to break off an action, leaving 39 dead on the scene to Barry's three.

The irrepressible Lloyd George told Parliament during the spring that things were under control. "We have murder on the run," was the way he put it. The truth was that time was running out, and the tide of world opinion turning against him.

As early as December, 1919, Childers was given the task of answering Lloyd George, who had charged in Parliament that Ireland was trying to secede. "Any attempt at secession," said the Prime Minister," will be fought with the same determination, with the same resources, the same resolve as the Northern States of America put into the fight against the Southern States."

Childers' answer in the *Irish Bulletin* shows how well he tempered his steel in refuting a false analogy:

"The Irish answer to this declaration of war—this heroic defiance of the weak by the strong—is something like the following: We do not attempt secession. Nations cannot secede from a rule they have never accepted. We have never accepted yours and never will. Lincoln's reputation is safe from your comparison. He fought to abolish slavery, you fight to maintain it. As to 'resources,' yours to ours are infinity to zero. You own a third of the earth by conquest; you have great armies, a navy so powerful that it can starve a whole continent, and a superabundance of every instrument of destruction that science can devise. You wield the greatest aggregate of material force ever concentrated in the hands of one

170

power; and, while canting about your championship of small nations, you use it to crush out liberty in ours. We are a small people with a population dwindling without cessation under your rule. We have no armaments nor any prospect of obtaining them. Nevertheless, we accept your challenge and will fight you 'with the same determination, with the same resolve' as the American States, North and South, put into their fight for their freedom against your Empire. Ignoring transient issues, these are the permanent realities of the case."

From a propaganda point of view, the 74-day hunger strike of the Mayor of Cork, Terence MacSwiney, was an opportunity to dramatize the fortitude and resolution of the Irish, and the *Bulletin* played it to the hilt. When MacSwiney died in an English prison on October 26, 1920, Arthur Griffith telegraphed sentiments to his widow that the world echoed. "He has proved what he said—that victory in this struggle for Irish freedom is not to those who can inflict most, but to those who can endure."

In his work for the *Bulletin*, Childers had a trait that bothered Arthur Griffith. Every atrocity story, every crossroad incident or ambush, had to be meticulously checked and double-checked. Griffith recognized the necessity, in a time of inflammatory charges and counter-charges but sometimes Childers went too far, and finally Griffith's admiration for his colleague turned into sharp dislike.

Frank Gallagher, who worked directly under Childers, has left us a vivid glimpse of him at work at Bushy Park. It shows Childers' meticulousness in a more favorable light:

"Erskine was one of the most extraordinary workers I have ever met. . . he would often bring his work to the drawing room at night and write at the mahogany table as callers sat around the fire and put the world through their hands. He had developed in himself such powers of concentration that he would soon be writing there oblivious of all else. . . ."

171

"He decided to devote a *Bulletin* to answering criticism that Volunteers did not wear uniform. This the British made the excuse for executions as the Germans had made it in Belgium in the case of the *franc-tireurs*.

"The argument could best be used, he thought, in relation to the hanging a few days before of Thomas Traynor, father of ten children. An auxiliary Cadet fell in a long and hard-fought engagement in Brunswick Street, Dublin, in which the Volunteers had heavy losses. Thomas Traynor was captured, armed, near the scene of the battle. Tried by courtmartial and sentenced to death for 'murder,' he was hanged on 25th April.

" 'Give me about twenty minutes,' Erskine said three days afterwards, and then sat down by the fire staring into it without moving, still in his raincoat just as he had come in.

" 'I'm ready now,' he said suddenly, and he dictated without pausing for the better part of an hour. When I had finished taking him in shorthand he said: 'Go back to the third paragraph where I said *the names of the officers making up the court*, change it to *officers composing the court*.

" 'In the fifth paragraph change *certain requirements of Article I of the Hague Convention* to *certain requirements laid down by Article I*.' After that what he dictated was typed and no more alteration was necessary."

Among Childers' most widely discussed work was a series of articles requested by the editor of the London *Daily News* on "Military Rule in Ireland." The eight articles were later published in pamphlet form and distributed by the thousands in Europe and the United States. The purpose was simply to let the average English reader know what really was going on in Ireland at the time. Glimpses of sack and pillage, descriptions of arrest on testimony of people of "good position" who did not have to appear in court, a study of British use of propaganda to foment hatred (naturally put in sharp contrast to his own sober reporting), accounts of the climate of fear and suspicion that the Castle created—such are a few of the subjects covered. They alternate with perorations of considerable eloquence.

Here, for example, is a report of a search for a Sinn Fein official, based on a signed statement by the official's wife:

"Oaths, insults and threats are directed at the unfortunate lady, who is kept below shivering in night attire while the ground floor is searched. Her little boy begins to scream, but she is turned back with the bayonet from going to him. A mahogany door is wantonly smashed in. . . . Then to the living room, where even the children's beds are searched. Then to the skylight leading to the roof, where she is forced to remain while one officer hands a revolver to another, saying: 'If he's there use it on him.' At length away, leaving her exhausted and struggling to close the jammed hall-door. 'The woman can't close the _____ door now,' is the genial farewell as the lorry rattles away."

"All this in your name," Childers reminds the English reader.

It seems fairly tame now, but it was vastly effective at the time. One peroration must suffice to show Childers' awareness of the effect of a climate of violence on both sides, and on a cause however just:

"It is impossible for those who wage a war such as that in Ireland to make it respectable. It is disreputable and cowardly because it is waged by the strong against the weak for a base and selfish end. . . . It may be true that some wars have an ennobling effect on the conqueror; this kind of war has none. Even for the weaker side with all its heroisms it is impossible to escape from the subtle demoralisation which comes to people bludgeoned into silence by the law, driven underground to preserve

173

its national organization and forced under intolerable provocation into desperate reprisals. . . .

"The army incurs no risk here (two men killed among an average strength of 50,000) and it wins no glory—quite the reverse. Backed by the navy it could hold this land. But it cannot govern it."

In February of 1921 Desmond Fitzgerald was arrested and Erskine Childers became Director of Propaganda. In May he was elected to the Dail from Wicklow and Kildare, and that same month President de Valera appointed him Minister of Propaganda with full Cabinet rank.

In answer to a request by De Valera, Childers submitted a progress report on March 10 that has just come to light among the State Papers of the time. It shows another side of Childers—the crisp and proper bureaucrat, with the fires well banked:

"Since the last Report was submitted by this Department to a Session of Dail Eireann (January 18th 1921), the Director of the Department has been arrested.

"A new Director has been appointed and the work of the Department in all its services has been carried on as usual. The *Bulletin* is circulated daily to two hundred English newspapers and public men, and weekly to three hundred other persons including many Continental and Colonial newspapers and journalists. The Enemy Government have made repeated endeavors to prevent the circulation of the bulletin. They have been successful in a minority of instances. The *Bulletin,* however, still reaches the greater number of those for whom it is intended and is used with effect by many of its recipients.

"The Department assisted in the publication of the pamphlet *Who Burnt Cork City?* which has had an extensive sale in England.

"The interviewing of foreign journalists has been somewhat disorganized since the arrest of Mr. Desmond Fitzgerald, but it is hoped shortly to rectify this.

174

"Letter communication with foreign countries and the colonies is being arranged, and preparations have also been made to extend the work and the production of the Department.

"Steps have been taken to maintain closer touch with the Irish Press and to supply it, so far as can be safely done, with information of an authoritive character.

"This Department would suggest to all Members of the Dail to arrange in their constituencies for the collection of signed statements from the victims of enemy aggression, especially in the case of murders, floggings and attacks on women."

The report was not signed as the Cabinet was operating from cover.

Of all the Irish leaders who came to Bushy Park Road Michael Collins was the one most sought by the British. There was a 10,000-pound reward for him dead or alive. With his easy West Cork ways and countryman's grin (and a face not yet known to the enemy) he still managed to bicycle where he wished. Once a British raiding party found a cup of tea still hot on his desk in one hideaway. A swing up a skylight and a drop to the roof next door was all that saved him.

Collins dropped by often. The Childers, with their fine manners and good talk, fascinated him. He learned the forks, and they learned his vast warmth and power. Lying on a specially-designed couch in the drawing room, Molly would question him with that special skill of hers, that endless curiosity that was so intense and so flattering. He would tell her his ambitions and dreams for himself and for Ireland. In a more practical way, Collins also turned over vast sums raised by the National Loan for her to sequester and distribute.

As the truth of conditions in Ireland became known, opinion in England reacted more and more sharply to British

175

conduct there. "When is this going to end?" the *Nation and Athenaeum* asked after a particularly brutal brace of murders. Even Asquith denounced the "hellish policy of reprisals," and the Archbishop of Canterbury protested in the Lords with all his vast prestige. Officers of the British army, led by General Gough of Curragh Mutiny fame, made it clear that they felt the way things were being run in Ireland was a disgrace. Intellectuals like G.B. Shaw and H.G. Wells took up the cry and the cause, and the great newspapers like the *Times,* the *Manchester Guardian* and of course the *Daily News* never let up for long. World opinion, particularly American opinion, was not far behind in its growing sympathy for the Irish Republicans.

Molly Childers was lying on the couch in her red-silk dressing gown when the sharp knock came. Erskine was working at his desk nearby. Looking up at the sound, they both saw the Glengarry bonnets of several Auxiliaries in the bright garden below. Without extra motion, Erskine quietly took the papers he was working on and dropped them under a loose floorboard. Frank Gallagher, who was also there, noted how calm, almost indifferent, both he and Molly were.

Suddenly the room was full of troops. To reassure Molly, Childers went over and held her hand a moment. In so doing, he palmed off a small address book that he did not want found on his person if he were taken away.

A man with the face of a ferret seemed to be the leader. He showed Childers what he called a "seditious document" and asked whose the handwriting was.

"I cannot tell you that."

"We shall take you to the Castle. . . . You will know what to expect there."

The ferrety man turned to Molly with more questions, and she too said quietly that she could not answer them. He warned her that her silence might well mean that she would not see her husband again.

Then they questioned Gallagher, who said he was a free-lance writer come to interview Erskine Childers for the *Daily News*.

"Interviews about us, I suppose," said one of the officers sourly.

"Perhaps, but not necessarily."

More questioning. Suddenly the officer-in-charge said, "We're taking you."

"On what charge?" Gallagher asked.

"On no charge, we just think you're not what you pretend to be."

Childers and Gallagher were hustled into separate lorries. Each sat between the driver and an officer with a hand-gun at the ready. They were told they would be shot if there was any attempt to attack the convoy on the way to the Castle.

In brilliant sunlight they tore through the city. The convoy of two lorries and three smaller cars drew considerable attention. At the Dardanelles—where Wexford Street narrows into Aungier Street—Childers and Gallagher stiffened reflex-ively, knowing well that it was a place where attacks often occurred. To their relief they drew no fire. At last they swung into Dame Street and sprinted for the Castle gates. Now they steeled themselves against terrors unknown.

Childers was locked in a cell near the Lower Castle Gate. After a few hours, he was released by an official and told he was free to go. The official even carried his suitcase for him to the Gate, a fact that was later remembered.

What had happened was great good luck for Childers—and shortly for Gallagher. During that same day a letter had come to President De Valera from Lloyd George inviting him, and any colleagues he wished to bring, to a conference in London "to explore to the utmost the possibility of a settlement." In effect, the British Government had called for a Truce.

The Prime Minister had yielded at last.

177

Childers and his sons at the seaside resort of Worthing, 1919 —
photo courtesy of Radio Times, London

21.   A Flawed Treaty. . .

There had been Truce rumors in the air for some weeks. They were more prevalent in England than in Ireland, where the war was reaching a harsh crescendo. By now there were almost 80,000 British troops there. Winston Churchill, Chairman of the Cabinet Committee on Irish Affairs, and Field Marshal Sir Henry Wilson, the Chief of the Imperial General Staff, were coming to the sobering conclusion that it would take another 100,000 men, and Martial Law throughout the 26 counties of Southern Ireland, to stamp out the rebellion.

In his quicksilver way, Lloyd George now swung all the way from talk of small, eradicable murder gangs to a recognition that the vast majority of the Irish people favored a Republic.

So it was a crossroads time. On June 22, 1921, King George V made a speech at the opening of the Northern Parliament in Belfast which pointed the way to negotiation rather than all-out war: "I speak from a full heart when I pray that my coming to Ireland today may prove to be the first step toward the end of a strife among her people, whatever their race or creed. May this historical gathering be the prelude of the way in which the Irish people, North and South, under one Parliament or two as the Parliaments may themselves decide, shall work together in common love of Ireland. The future lies in the hands of my Irish people themselves. . . ."

Drafted with the help of Jan Christian Smuts and reluctantly cleared by the Cabinet, it was a courageous and groundbreaking speech. Just three days later came the letter from Lloyd George proposing the conference. At the end of the letter the Prime Minister expressed pious hopes about its success: "We wish that no endeavor should be lacking on our part to realize the King's prayer, and we ask you to meet us, as we will meet you, in the spirit of conciliation for which his Majesty appealed."

The actual terms of the truce were worked out in Dublin between Sir Nevil Macready, the General Officer Commanding the Army of Occupation, and two members of the Dail: Eamonn Duggan and Robert Barton, the latter having just been released from Portsmouth Prison (among many) as a gesture of conciliation.

The British undertook to send no more troops to Ireland and to call off all activity by secret agents there. Curfews were abolished. For their part, the Irish agreed to make no attacks on the forces of the Crown, to seize no Government property and to stage no provocative displays of force.

It was understood that, should Treaty negotiations break down, there would be a 72-hour interim before hostilities were resumed.

The next day De Valera arrived in London for preliminary talks with the Prime Minister. His company included Count Plunkett, Erskine Childers, Robert Barton and Austin Stack, who represented extreme, uncompromising Republicanism. By now the President had come to rely on Childers' judgment in many matters—considering him the greatest constitutional authority of the time. His admiration and affection, which would never falter, went far beyond that. Once De Valera put it into words, saying that if he had the choice he would "adopt the character of Childers as his model of men."

Like Childers, the President was only part Irish. His father was Spanish, which led Oliver St. John Gogarty to call him "the Spanish onion in the Irish stew." Gogarty was the wit among those who found De Valera's political subtlety hard to take. In another of his gibes he remarked, "Of course Dev's Irish. He's as Irish as those snakes on the cover of the Book of Kells."

Like Childers, De Valera had shown military talent and courage. They shared a steadfastness of purpose and a sense of history. Unlike Childers, the President was a master of the art of political maneuver—although he cloaked his skill by moving on a rather lofty plateau of statesmanship.

On July 14 De Valera was cordially received by Lloyd George at No. 10 Downing Street. They met alone.

"Come in, come in," Lloyd George said, perhaps not in those exact words for the story has grown with time. "I'm always happy to meet an Irishman, being a Celt myself."

The Prime Minister had noticed from the letterhead on De Valera's answering letter that the Republic called itself *Saorstat Eireann*; there ensued a discussion about the word *Saorstat*. The President explained that it meant, literally, Free State, and had been preferred by the linguists to *Phoblacht*, which was Gaelic for Republic. Lloyd George said this suited him very well, as indeed it did.

According to Lady Lloyd George, the Prime Minister had "had a big map of the Empire hung on the wall of the Cabinet room, with its great blotches of red all over it." The idea was to impress De Valera that there was no way for little Ireland to stop the march of Empire.

"I can put a soldier in Ireland for every man, woman and child there," Lloyd George said.

"Yes, but you must keep them there," De Valera countered.

In that first meeting, and in three following ones within the next eight days, there was a great deal of talk of history, with De Valera returning constantly to age-old Irish grievances. Lloyd George later told his son that the negotiations were similar to a merry-go-round on which he was one horse behind De Valera and never able to catch up.

181

Finally, on July 20, Lloyd George put down on paper some proposals. He offered Ireland Dominion status, but with no navy of her own, a limited army and the continued maintenance by the British of some bases in Ireland. The proposals also called for full recognition that the North would have to decide for itself whether it would join the Dominion or stay separate.

The rest of the summer and a good part of the fall were spent working out sufficient flexibility between these unacceptable terms and Irish Republican needs and hopes. De Valera's hand was strengthened by the full support of the Dail in whatever action he took. In recommending to his parliament that they reject the British exploratory proposals, the President was urged on by Childers, and the words he found to tell them so reflect the thinking of both De Valera and his Gray Eminence:

"There is no likelihood that we shall seek combination when it is simply combination with the enemy that has despoiled us most and would seek in the combination an opportunity of despoiling us still further. Still, an association that would be consistent with our right to see that we were the judges of what was our own interest, and that we were not compelled to leave the judgment of what were our own interests or not to others—a combination of that sort would, I believe, commend itself to the majority of my colleagues."

Here was the germ of the doctrine of "External Association," which would form the core of the Irish counter-proposals during the actual conference.

On August 23 the Dail with great firmness and unanimity turned down the British terms. For the next seven weeks there were many suggested alternatives, and several near-breakdowns of all communications. Sir James Craig, Carson's chief lieutenant and now Prime Minister of Northern Ireland, refused to take part in any talks, on the pretext that even

182

sitting down at a table would endanger the sovereignty of Ulster. But his intransigent presence and Carson's were almost palpable.

Although such key questions as whether Ireland should be Dominion or Republic and what her defense responsibilities should be—as well as that key question of one Ireland or two—were not resolved, enough understanding of each other's position was reached by Lloyd George and De Valera for the next step to be taken. The Conference was called for October 11.

Arthur Griffith and Michael Collins were named co-leaders of the Irish delegation. By now Griffith had succeeded Count Plunkett as Minister for Foreign Affairs. Collins was Minister for Finance and Director of Intelligence. The other three delegates were Eamonn Duggan, an able lawyer and very much a Collins man, Robert Barton, the Economic Minister by now, and George Gavan Duffy, also a lawyer. He had defended Roger Casement and was stylish, Francophile and very alert. All five delegates were members of the Dail.

The Chief Secretary was Erskine Childers, on President De Valera's insistence and over Arthur Griffith's misgivings.

The President overcame many urgings that he himself head the delegation. He wanted to keep a Republican, fall-back position in case the conference failed, and felt he could do so better if he were not totally involved. He also believed that the envoys' having to refer back to him in Dublin before taking any final decision or drastic step would keep them from being too impulsive. The tragic aftermath of President Wilson's long stay overseas at the Versailles Conference may well have influenced him to some degree.

In any event it was a most unfortunate decision.

Leaving for London, Erskine Childers was in high spirits. A lively girl called Kathleen McKenna, who was one of the secretaries in the delegation, later remembered him and Robert Barton rushing about the packet when they all first went on board, examining everything and calling to each other. Childers' mood continued for a while on the special

183

train from Holyhead to London. "For the first time since I met him," Miss McKenna wrote, "I saw Erskine Childers laughing, joking and carefree. He and his cousin Robert Barton were like two schoolboys exchanging tales of amusing adventures." Soon enough Childers was in a brown study again; then he turned to his endless drafting of "some vital document."

The delegation took up quarters in two rented houses, 22 Hans Place and 15 Cadogan Gardens. Office space and most of the living quarters were in the former; Michael Collins and his entourage settled in the latter.

The two delegations met that morning of October 11 in the famous Cabinet Room at No. 10 Downing Street. After being introduced to the Prime Minister, the five Irish envoys took their places across the broad conference table from their British counterparts. No one shook hands, as Lloyd George had foreseen, but thanks to his tactful stage management there was no awkwardness.

Facing the Irish was as formidable a delegation as Britain could muster. Pre-eminent among them was the Prime Minister himself—and the fact that Lloyd George managed to take part pointed up De Valera's absence. With his high coloring, white hair and mustache, and merry eye, he was a consummate actor. His great skill was to seem to be more impulsive, more impetuous than he really was. He was a master at probing for weakness and when he saw an opening he could move with the speed of light.

Then there was Winston Churchill, not much touched by Irish needs, a little bored with Ireland as roadblock to Imperial dreams; Lord Birkenhead, the Lord Chancellor of England, the dazzling pro-Ulster *arriviste* now fully arrived; Austen Chamberlain, Leader of the Commons and son of Joseph, a man so imbued with the grandeur of Empire that the idea of an Irish Republic was not to be contemplated. Sir Lionel Worthington-Evans, Secretary of State for War, and

Sir Hamar Greenwood, Chief Secretary for Ireland—both known to be bitter opponents of Sinn Fein—were the other two regular members.

For the next two months the delegations, in plenary sessions and in Committee work, sparred and jockeyed and sought some middle ground. Griffith and Collins, supported almost invariably by Duggan, were moving in the direction of compromise and the acceptance of Dominion status. Gavan Duffy and Robert Barton, vigorously backed by Childers as something more than Secretary, tended toward the De Valera-Childers formula of External Association, with a status "of equality with the sovereign partner States of the Commonwealth." The difference, not too apparent to the naked eye, lay in the actual wording of the Oath to the Monarch or Crown. Duffy and Barton's answer to the tricky problem of Irish defense was perpetual neutrality, guaranteed by the Commonwealth nations.

This growing rift in the Irish delegation added great tension to the sessions. "The other delegates," Winston Churchill noted, "were overshadowed by the two leaders. Mr. Duggan, however, was a sober-minded, resolute man. In the background Erskine Childers, though not a delegate, pressed for extreme measures."

Extreme measures to Churchill meant an Irish Republic slightly disguised as an External Associate. By contrast to Childers, Duggan was sober-minded and resolute because he made it clear he was willing to settle for less.

Life at Hans Place, cheerful enough at first, became grimmer as the tensions grew. Griffith, who liked to relax after the sessions, went to the theater often. *The Beggar's Opera* was the big hit that fall, and there was lots of Gilbert and Sullivan in repertory.

"Where's that fellow Childers?" Griffith would ask, still with a measure of geniality. "He's always writing those memoranda that aren't wanted and he can't be found to take the girls to the theater."

185

Matters grew worse as Childers marshalled every argument he could to save the idea of a Republic. Endless facts, figures and historical precedents were prepared by him for the delegates, to show that Dominion status, with British bases and naval rights—and in all likelihood a separate Ulster—would never work. Griffith became so exasperated that he could not be in the room with Childers. He was convinced that the Secretary was simply De Valera's spy, reporting every move to his master by courier or even telephone.

Finally, position papers drafted by Childers had to be signed by Barton, or Griffith simply would not read them.

Childers' work, and "the fierce, concentrated energy" it required—in Dorothy Macardle's phrase—was making serious inroads into his health. Those moments of hope and boyish enthusiasm on boat and train were a final upsurge, fast receding into the past as October soured into November. The years of combat during the war and of exhausting, never-ending propaganda work during the rebellion were telling on him at last. His failure to acknowledge the presence of his old friend Eddie Marsh at the conference table was one clue how far gone he was in misery now, for basically he was the most courteous of men.

Another clue came from Basil Williams, who had been shocked by his appearance when they dined together during the summer visit with De Valera after the Truce was announced:

"Physically he looked almost a wreck; thin and deadly pale and with quite white hair. His mind was as alert and bright as ever, but it seemed a hectic brightness, with almost all his old sense of humour and of proportion vanished, at least when he spoke of Ireland. I say almost, for when we got him for a few odd moments to talk of old loved things, or of joys we had shared in former days, then the old Erskine seemed to flash out with that dear smile of his. But it was not for long, for he could not keep

186

off Ireland for many minutes, and when he spoke of her, he would accept no compromise and could not for a moment see that the substance, for example, of Dominion status might mean all and perhaps more than all that the name of a republic would give. And when it came to means of achieving his end, he had become almost ferocious and pitiless. Not that he did not love England still; that love he never lost, but he felt that, even in her interests, uncompromising sternness was the only possible policy."

Williams himself never saw Childers again, for he was in Canada that fall when the Treaty making was in process. But one day Erskine telephoned Williams' wife and asked to come to supper. According to Mrs. Williams, when he came he was "as worn and emaciated as when we had seen him in the summer, and his smile was more wan. He spoke mostly about Ireland, and the treaty in progress, and asked, 'how do you like the title, Irish Free State?' He smiled only once, at an allusion to an immortal poem of his childhood, a poem about 'Hooky Beak, the Raven, and his disconnected tail'."

Further evidence of a near-breakdown is furnished by his performance in the Joint Sub-Committee on Naval and Air Defence. Childers had presented a memorandum insisting that naval defense should rest in Dublin, and the British turned it down. The next day, in a confrontation with Winston Churchill and an admiral, Childers made so rambling a rebuttal that Michael Collins, embarrassed but still caring for his friend, took over very gently from him. In a similar discussion with another naval officer, Collins noted sadly that Childers was a "total loss."

Collins himself was in many ways the star of the Irish team. He had come reluctantly and only as a soldier doing what he was told. Now all London had a look at the most celebrated rebel of them all, and liked what it saw. Here was no cut-throat gunman but a splendid leader of men. Churchill and Birkenhead, swashbucklers themselves, came to admire

187

and respect his judgment. Often they dined and talked and enjoyed each other into the small hours after the arduous sessions—usually at the house of Sir John Lavery, the painter, and his beautiful wife.

When urged, Collins would bellow out his favorite ditty which began:

> "So here's to the *Maine*
> and we're sorry for Spain,
> Said Kelly and Burke and Shea."

(Mr. Churchill continued to maintain a rather ambivalent attitude toward the Treaty-making itself. Robert Barton told the present writer that at one plenary session he occupied himself, with a studied indifference bordering on insolence, cutting out of a long screed of paper dolls.)

There was another song, that fall of 1921, which everyone in England was singing. It began, "There's a hole in the pot, dear Henry, dear Henry," and it drove poor exhausted Erskine Childers wild. The girls at Hans Place hummed it as they worked, and its jangling jingle floated in from the streets. Erskine Childers would clench his jaw and drive himself endlessly on. . . .

"There had been a terrible change in Childers," Michael McInerney tells us in his paperback, *The Riddle of Erskine Childers* (1970). "He had worked himself to the point where he seemed to be suffering from some severe illness."

In one of his position papers Childers was still able to do effective and useful work. Reverting to his long-held theory of the difference between Dominion status for far-off Canada and for an Ireland lying in England's lee, he put up a paper which showed how independent Canada had become in usage and fact, while paying lip-service to the Crown. This in turn, as forcefully presented by Griffith, had a considerable effect on the thinking of the British delegation.

The unfolding story of the treaty-making, leading up to

188

the great drama of the final hours, has been told in full and vivid detail by Lord Longford in *Peace by Ordeal* and in a brilliant chapter of Winston Churchill's *The Aftermath*.

Only its highlights can be touched on here. Griffith seems to have allowed himself to be mesmerized in private by Lloyd George. He even put in writing his willingness to sign a treaty whose terms granted less than the minimum which De Valera's instructions called for.

Chiefly to avoid the baleful presence of Childers, Lloyd George suggested that Griffith and Collins meet with the British alone in plenary sessions, and this was agreed on. It was a development deeply resented by Gavan Duffy and Barton as well as Childers.

In the matter of Ulster, the British came up with an ingenious idea that had a promising look about it: the creation of a Boundary Commission which would arrange a Plebiscite to delimit Protestant territory. The underlying idea was that the three-man Commission—a British member, a Free State member, and an Ulsterman—would with the aid of the Plebiscite and their own built-in two-to-one majority be able to so reduce the Northern boundaries that Ulster would have no choice economically but to align itself with the new Dominion of Ireland. . . .

Journeying back to Dublin after nearly eight weeks of argument and debate, the Irish delegation presented the new British terms to the Cabinet. They were found unacceptable. Counter proposals, including some language for a workable Oath to the Crown, and a re-drafting of External Association, were worked out, and the envoys told to return to London.

Indication of how badly the delegation was riven now was the fact that its members travelled back to London in two groups. Barton, Duffy and Childers sailed in a packet from Dublin's North Wall. Griffith, Collins and Duggan took the night boat from Dun Laoghaire. It was a far cry from that first merry and sanguine departure two months before.

189

They met with the British again on Monday, December 5 and this was to prove the fateful day. In full plenary session that afternoon, Lloyd George laid down an ultimatum to the Irish: *sign now, with no more concessions, or face instant and terrible war.* The Churchillian account of what followed is the best we have:

"The Irishmen gulped down the ultimatum phlegmatically. Mr. Griffith said, speaking in his soft voice and with his modest manner, 'I will give the answer of the Irish Delegates at nine to-night; but, Mr. Prime Minister, I personally will sign this agreement and will recommend it to my countrymen.' 'Do I understand, Mr. Griffith,' said Mr. Lloyd George, 'that though everyone else refuses you will nevertheless agree to sign?' 'Yes, this is so, Mr. Prime Minister,' replied this quiet little man of great heart and great purpose."

Lloyd George then said that all the Irish must sign in order to make the Treaty valid.

The Irishmen went off to make their final decision. Collins and Duffy lined up with Griffith in his willingness to sign. "This is not the Republic: it is the stepping-stone to the Republic," Griffith endlessly maintained. Michael Collins put it even more succinctly, "This is peace to obtain peace."

Barton and Duffy, urged on by Childers, thought that it was a case of perfidious Albion all over again, with Lloyd George bluffing—and fully aware that the British public would not tolerate a new war. Childers, ever the parliamentarian, held that what they were confronted with now was not a treaty but a British dictation of terms from on high. A treaty, he reminded his colleagues with feverish intensity, was an agreement between sovereign states, not an ultimatum laid down by one to the other.

There was no suggestion of telephoning De Valera for guidance. All during the weeks of treaty-making, the Irish had sent almost daily couriers, believing that every wire was tapped. "None of us even thought of using the phone to try to resolve the difficulty," Robert Barton told McInerney in 1970.

The pressure brought to bear on Barton and Duffy as the evening wore on was very great. At one point Collins turned to Barton and said, "You will be hanged from a lamp post in the streets of Dublin if your refusal to sign causes a new war in Ireland."

Robert Barton had demonstrated many times that he was not a man who frightened easily. But the prediction from Collins, who was placing his own life in hazard to the extreme Republicans by his own act of signing, carried great weight. Barton did not wish to bear by himself the awesome burden of starting another war—and it was clear that Duffy was already about to capitulate.

Finally Barton made up his mind to sign, and Duffy quickly joined him.

It was well after midnight when the envoys returned to Downing Street. Winston Churchill remembers how calm and quiet the Irish were. The pause before Arthur Griffith spoke seemed long.

At last he said, "Mr. Prime Minister, the delegation is willing to sign the agreements."

There were a few minor details of wording to be straightened out, Griffith went on. But the indelible step had been taken.

The two delegations settled the technicalities with a new sense of shared purpose. Then they all signed the Treaty which created an Irish Free State within the British family of nations.

Mr. Churchill rings down the curtain on the historic scene:

> "As the Irishmen rose to leave, the British Ministers upon a strong impulse walked round and for the first time shook hands. . . . This was the moment, not soon to be forgotten, when the waters were parted and the streams of destiny began to flow down new valleys toward new seas."

191

Erskine Childers in 1920—*photo courtesy of Radio Times, London*

22. . . . and a Bitter Debate

Leaving the Cabinet room after the signing, Lloyd George ran into Erskine Childers and later described what he saw. Childers, the Prime Minister noted, was "sullen with disappointment. . . a man incapable of compromise."

Childers' own most vivid recollection was of a triumphant Winston Churchill surging out of the room, "with a big cigar, looking like the bowsprit of a ship."

The Prime Minister's comment on that inability to compromise points up the irony of Childers' whole performance. For of all the men there, Childers knew best, from his long parliamentary years, that politics is the art of compromise. His actions clearly show how far gone he was in illness and despair. In his exhausted frame there was no give left, and no take.

Winston Churchill's streams of destiny quickly turned into troubled waters. When De Valera heard that the Treaty had been signed he naturally concluded that Irish counter-proposals had been accepted. He first saw a rough text of the Treaty in the newspapers, and this in itself was upsetting. *No Republic, no satisfactory solution of the Ulster problem, oath to the Monarch still, and British bases*—such seemed to be the gist of what had been signed. When Eamonn Duggan arrived with the exact text, his worst fears were confirmed. De

Valera's statement to the press left no doubt about his reaction:

"You have seen in the public press the text of the proposed Treaty with Great Britain. The terms of the agreement are in violent conflict with the wishes of the majority of the nation as expressed freely in successive elections in the last three years. I feel it my duty to inform you immediately that I cannot recommend the acceptance of the Treaty either by the Dail Eireann or to the country."

He summoned the Dail to meet on December 14 on this grave issue, saying that "there was a definite constitutional way to resolve our difference." Many thought that the President's pronouncement was so weighted against the Treaty—especially in claiming that it was in conflict with majority wishes—that the constitutional way was already being bent to his strong will.

The Council Chamber of University College was chosen as the place for the Dail to hold its public sessions on the Treaty. The great debate would last from December 14 to January 7, with the official report running to some 300,000 words. Before two days were over the news came from London that the House of Commons had overwhelmingly ratified the Treaty and that the Lords had quickly followed suit.

On opening day the public and press sections of the big hall were jammed. There was an expectant hush as Arthur Griffith rose to present the motion approving the Treaty which he had done so much to bring into being.

No orator, he read from typewritten slips, picking them up and laying them down as he went along. But his sincerity made the words impressive:

"We have brought back the flag; we have brought back the evacuation of Ireland after 700 years by British troops and the formation of an Irish army. . . I signed the Treaty not as an ideal thing, but fully believing, as I believe now, it is a Treaty honourable to Ireland, and safeguards the vital interests of Ireland."

He called the Treaty one of "equality" and the alternate device of External Association a "quibble of words" not worth the life of one single Irishman.

When De Valera rose to present the opposite view, he looked pale and ill. Although the overcrowded hall was hot, he wore an overcoat. But Padraic Colum for one was "dazzled and profoundly moved" by his words:

"I am against this Treaty because it does not reconcile Irish national aspirations with association with the British Government. I am against this Treaty, not because I am a man of war, but a man of peace. I am against this Treaty because it will not end the centuries of conflict between the two nations. . . ."

When he sat down there was long applause.

Michael Collins in his turn said he was going to speak plainly and he did. But his splendid presence and the way he tossed his black hair with his hands lent drama to the words: "In my opinion it gives us freedom, not the ultimate freedom that all nations desire and develop to, but the freedom to achieve it."

Collins also made an effective point about the British. Their military strength was, he said, their only hold on Ireland. "I maintain that the disappearance of that military strength gives us the chief proof that our national liberties are established." The maturity of his reasoning and the statesmanlike way he spoke had powerful appeal. WHAT ABOUT ULSTER?

During his comings and goings to the Dail sittings, Erskine Childers seemed a pale ghost now. Elizabeth Lazenby, a young American friend of the Childers, noted that about him "hung disillusionment, complete, ashen, as of all time." He walked with his head bent and his eyes on the ground, "paying not the slightest heed to anything going on about him."

y 1998 Republican Sinn 195 Fein voted unanimously accept the partitionist state, in the interests of peace, y Adams see's the agreement as a stepping stone to a ed Ireland. He grows closer to Micheal Collins' position !!

When he came to speak, some of the old vigor and clarity came back. One reporter noted how "reflective" he was, "in that pale, rather white and keenly cold way of his."

The thrust of his words was that the members of the Irish delegation had been urging honorable terms until "that last terrible hour." The proposals they themselves put forward were basically those of an External Association—a voluntary joining up with Britain after an interval of total independence.

Speaking calmly and with all the authority of his career as clerk to a great Parliament, he explained why the Treaty brought something less than Dominion status:

"If you place under a foreign power responsibility for the defense of the coasts of Ireland, inevitably and naturally you place responsibility for the defence of the whole island on that foreign government. How can you separate the coast defences of an island from its internal defence?"

He showed how easy it would be for England to re-possess Ireland in the event of some emergency of her own choosing, some crisis or war with another power. The fact that they had retained some bases was all the foothold needed.

Toward the end, he made a reversal of the Parnellite dictum about there being no boundary to the forward march of a nation. "This Treaty is a step backward, and I, for my part, would be inclined to say he would be a bold man who would dare set a boundary to the backward march of a nation which of its own free will had deliberately relinquished its own independence."

It was brilliant, if a little too cold and clever, and it was coldly received. In closing, Childers predicted that the assemblage would "inflexibly refuse" to take the backward step of endorsing the Treaty.

Childers was followed by Kevin O'Higgins, who less than a year later would relentlessly hunt him down. O'Higgins, then only 30, was beginning his remarkable rise. "Magisterial in manner," as his biographer Terence de Vere White tells us,

196

he addressed his audience "as it were from a height." (Later O'Higgins would find favor with Churchill, who found apt words to describe him: "A figure from antiquity cast in bronze.")

His argument in favor of the Treaty made Childers' strictures seem fussy and dated:

"I hardly hope that within this Treaty there lies the fulfillment of Ireland's destiny, but I do hope and believe that with the disappearance of old passions and distrusts. . . what remains may be won by agreement and peaceful evolution. In that spirit I stand for the ratification of this Treaty—in that spirit I ask you to endorse it."

It was another of those ultimate ironies that the English-born Childers, the former civil servant in the mother of Parliaments, should be entreating the Dail not to trust England's word while the all-Irish O'Higgins, who had served in the Volunteers against England, urged trust in her and mutual good faith.

Robert Barton's speech was brief and manly. He simply told what happened on the fateful day when the Treaty was signed. Here is the heart of his remarks, and indeed the heart of the matter:

"Speaking for himself and his colleagues, the English Prime Minister with all the solemnity and power of conviction that he alone, of all men I met, can impart by word and gesture—the vehicles by which the mind of one man oppresses and impresses the mind of another—declared that the signature and recommendation of every member of our delegation was necessary or war would follow immediately."

In effect, Barton was explaining that he had signed under double duress since there was extreme pressure both from Lloyd George and later from his own fellow envoys. He did not repudiate his signature. He simply recommended the Treaty, in a perfunctory and final act of support, because he had no choice but to sign it.

197

In the days that followed, the debates were with some exceptions of a fast-diminishing quality. There was great activity behind the scenes as votes were counted and positions taken. In his feverish way Erskine Childers worked to prepare the celebrated Document Number Two. This was a re-drafting and refining of the doctrine of External Association for presentation to the Dail by De Valera. It was also to serve as a way of reopening negotiations with the British once Document Number One (the Treaty itself) was rejected by the assembly.

Mary MacSwiney spoke with a passionate logic that had a certain power. In her two-hour peroration, the sister of the self-martyred mayor of Cork explained why she considered the Treaty a turning-back. "Half measures," she said, "are no longer possible, because on the 21st of January, 1919, this assembly declared by the will of the people the Republican form of Government as the best for Ireland, and cast off forever their allegiance to any foreigner."

General Mulcahy, the Chief of Staff of the Irish Republican Army, reminded his hearers of the I.R.A.'s weakness. With his scholar's brow, thin lips and ascetic look of a military monk, his words were convincing to many: "We have not been able to drive the enemy from anything but a fairly good-sized police barracks," he said in all candor. "How could we drive them from our ports?" He saw no alternative to accepting the Treaty.

On December 22 the Dail adjourned for the holidays, assembling again on January 2. Both sides agreed to no speech-making in the interval. The result was a net gain for the pro-Treaty faction, for the Press played up the dangers of a new war. "Ratification or Ruin," one headline screamed, while less sensational arguments *against* the compromise Treaty went largely unreported.

There were five more days of debate. A young Army Commandant called Liam Mellows impressed as he attacked the pro-Treaty slant in the Press. "The people are being stampeded," he said. Against the belief that terrible war was

198

the only alternative to signing he hit hard: "that is not the will of the people; that is the fear of the people."

At long last it was Arthur Griffith's turn to sum up. Although to some he showed a deep bitterness now, his plea for the Treaty was a reasonable one, and consistent with what he had been saying all along:

"It does not forever bind us not to ask for any more. England is going beyond where she is at present. . . and in the meantime we can move on in comfort and peace to the ultimate goal."

There were 122 Deputies present. In order to vote on the motion of appeal of the Treaty their Roll was called and each spoke up in turn.

The vote was 64 in favor, 57 against.

The Irish had settled for half a loaf of the good bread of freedom.

what in jaysus name is ½ freedom?
its called democracy.

MERRY WIDOW'S SECOND HUSBAND: COURT STORY

DAILY SKETCH.

No. 4,272. | Telephone { London—Holborn 8846 / Manchester—City 6861. | LONDON, SATURDAY, NOVEMBER 25, 1922. | (Registered as a Newspaper) | ONE PENNY.

ERSKINE CHILDERS EXECUTED IN DUBLIN

Mrs. Erskine Childers is an American with strong Irish sympathies. An invalid for many years, she collapsed on receiving news of her husband's execution.

Erskine Childers (left) was executed in Kilmainham Gaol, Dublin, yesterday. The Irish Master of the Rolls had refused to grant a writ of habeas corpus applied for on his behalf. Childers is here photographed with Mr. E. J. Duggan (right) when in London at the time of the Irish Treaty negotiations.—(Daily Sketch.)

Erskine Childers first became famous as author of "The Riddle of the Sands." Latterly he was De Valera's right hand.

Erskine Childers had a distinguished war record. He served in the R.N.A.S., and was awarded the D.S.C.

Erskine Childers's son daily visited the courts to hear the pleas made for his father's life.

The news of the execution of Erskine Childers, after a four days' legal fight for his life, was officially announced by the Free State yesterday. Childers was captured in Co. Wicklow and charged with "having possession of an automatic pistol without proper authority."

Mr. Patrick Lynch, K.C. (left), appeared for Erskine Childers before the Military Court, in Dublin, by whom Childers was tried and sentenced to death. Counsel also applied to the Master of the Rolls for a writ of habeas corpus.

23.   A Sad and Sour Spring

De Valera and Erskine Childers had misjudged the predominant mood of Ireland. As a whole, the country was sick of war and wanted to get on with its destiny as a nation, even if the freedom achieved still had a few strings attached. The mood of the majority had clearly been reflected in the Dail referendum, close as it was.

After the vote, De Valera resigned his Presidency and led his supporters out of the Dail. As they left the hall, Collins, in a highly emotional state after the strains of the debate, roared after them, "Deserters! Deserters all to the Irish cause in her hour of trial!"

(At an earlier, private session of the Dail in the Mansion House, it had already become clear to Collins that his thinking and Childers' were too far apart ever to be reconciled. Robert Barton remembers Childers and Collins arguing in a corridor at the moment when the younger man gave up.

"Does this mean we're going to part?" said Collins.

"I'm afraid so."

Collins' strong temperament was beginning to break through the iron discipline that had supported him in the years of strain and danger. He crushed his fists into his eyes, tossed his head in misery and rushed off with a roar of pain.)

Although he had resigned, De Valera decided to test Arthur Griffith's victory once more. The pro-Treaty members of the Dail had promptly nominated Griffith to be President of the Republic for the interim period until the public had a chance to vote on the Treaty. De Valera agreed to run against him.

This time the margin was even closer: Griffith received 60 votes to De Valera's 58.

The British forces started to go home. Symbolically the initial ceremony was held in Dublin Castle, with Lord Fitz-Alan, the last Lord-Lieutenant, turning that collection of buildings of many centuries and one grim association over to Michael Collins on January 16, 1922.

As one of the British troopships was sailing from the North Wall a crowd of Irishmen watched the ship stand out into the river.

"Goodbye and good riddance," one of them called. "Now we can fight our own battles in peace." without 3rd party, interference - o STUPID YANK

His Irish illogic was only too accurate. All spring, Arthur Griffith and Michael Collins and their colleagues worked to build a new government out of the surviving elements of the old. Griffith as President of the vestigial Republic presided over the Dail. Collins was made head of a Provisional Government created to operate during the transition until a plebiscite on the Treaty was held. Collins doubled as Finance Minister in Griffith's Cabinet. It was in effect an interlocking directorate. Outside it, the unregenerate, firebrand Republicans like Cathal Brugha, Austin Stack, Mary MacSwiney and Liam Mellows closed ranks with more doctrinaire diehards like De Valera and Childers to make every kind of trouble they could.

There was a sad scene in the Dail that January when Childers and Arthur Griffith, who was in a state of near-exhaustion after his long ordeal, had a head-on collision. The Republican opposition was baiting Griffith about his equivocal position as President of the Republic. For it was a time when he was putting all his remaining strength into rallying support for a Treaty that would end the Republic's life.

202

Childers' gadfly questioning stung him out of his usual calm:

Griffith: "I will not reply to any Englishman in this Dail."
Childers: "My nationality is a matter for myself and for the constituents who sent me here."
Griffith: "Your constituents did not know what your nationality was."
Childers: "They have known me since my boyhood days."
Griffith: "I will not reply to any damned Englishman in this Assembly."

At another session Griffith resumed his attack with the charge that Childers had "spent his life in England's Secret Service." He thumped on the desk as he made the wild charge.

"Withdraw! Withdraw that at once!" Childers rose and shouted.

"I will give you your records, Childers." (But Griffith never did).

Cathal Brugha, most dedicated of all the Republicans, made a motion of censure against Griffith. Later, before a packed assembly, Childers presented his own case. In so doing he showed his more chivalrous side, never far absent.

"I do not want to impart bitterness into this debate." He went on to say that he was not an Englishman in any true sense, although he could quite understand Griffith's point of view that he did seem to be an interloper. Obviously, Griffith regarded Childers, in his opposition to the Treaty, as someone thwarting his life work.

"But we are all faithful and true to Ireland. . . all united on the simple basis that we are loyal to our country." Such was the note Childers closed on, and it was the essence of the man that spoke.

Starting in January, Childers took up his Republican

203

propaganda work again. His medium now was *An Phoblacht,* the official journal of the party. He published it once or twice a week and in it sought to counter the slanted press by bringing home the bad features of the Treaty. By the same token, the advantages of Document Number Two were juxtaposed paragraph by paragraph for all to see.

Childers' argument was strengthened when, a few weeks later, Winston Churchill denied in the Commons that Ireland had received Dominion status. He was also reinforced and buoyed by the backing of Robert Barton, who had predictably repudiated his support of the Treaty and come over to the Republican cause lock, stock and barrel.

Childers himself worked in bursts of febrile energy. In her book, *Ireland—a Catspaw,* Elizabeth Lazenby remembers her first meeting with him at Bushy Park Road: "The photographs I have seen of Erskine Childers have little prepared me for the shock. . . . Thin almost to the point of emaciation, and looks ill and unhappy almost to the point of death. I can only liken his face to a mask, to which the eyes alone give life. Restless they show him, and haunted, as if he is driven by an inner soul-consuming fire. However courteous, he is aloof. . . . One emotion only lightens the intensity of his eyes—his very real devotion to his wife."

The Childers family was together again at Bushy Park Road. Molly's strong hand began to show more and more, both in *An Phoblacht* and in her influence on those who came to the pleasant, book-lined drawing room where she lay on her couch and a fire was always burning.

Many still came. Elizabeth Lazenby remembers how well Molly overcame her lameness: "Certainly no trace of it was evident in her indomitable spirit. The blue silk shawl thrown over her, and the blue Chinese jacket she wore, set off the rich gold of her hair, and matched the vivid blue of her eyes."

By now Molly had completely adopted her husband's thinking and added a few strong convictions of her own: the Treaty had been signed under duress. . . the delegates should

204

never have done so without checking Dublin and De Valera first. . . and how could Ireland be called a Dominion with six of her Northern counties lopped off?

She put her faith in those who were faithful to their oath to the Republic.

"There is the Army to reckon with," she reminded Elizabeth, her eyes flashing, for it was a time when the I.R.A. was beginning to desert the Free State in droves. "The Free Staters are the rebels!"

Molly was never one to do anything by halves.

"Collins," she explained to Elizabeth, who was preparing some articles for the American press, "is the king-pin of the situation. Ultimately he must choose between the British and the Republicans; and the Republicans are the youth of the country determined to see the thing through no matter the cost. *Glorious youth* to whom the Republic is a question of honour! The only alternative to civil war is a period of quiescence, during which matters must be so handled that a Republic will slip in through the keyhole."

It was very fierce, very Molly, but it did also mirror the mood and the delaying tactics of De Valera and Childers.

According to Elizabeth Lazenby, who was as highly-charged as Molly and like her not always accurate, the Republican high council had developed three alternatives for handling Michael Collins: a) bring him around to their way of thinking and launch him as popular hero; b) discredit him; c) shoot him. This had been filtered through to her by Molly Childers at her wildest and most indiscreet, and must be accepted with some reservations.

In one of her many talks with Lazenby, Molly showed her true colors, all green now, with no red showing. There was a new tone of defiance in the charming voice as she unfurled them, and she snapped her fingers as she spoke:

"Curiously enough, Ireland is the keystone in the arch of the predatory system. What happens here will happen in other parts of the Empire. Britain has no right to hold all these

205

people by force! Egypt and India—why should they be kept under an alien hand? It is not for Ireland alone we are struggling. I do not care that"—again she snapped her fingers—"for the independence of Ireland; *it is simply if Ireland goes the whole structure will fall.*"

This was an astonishing outburst, and again some grains of salt must be sprinkled over it. It is an emotional replay of Erskine's memorable message to the British in the *Military Rule in Ireland* series two years before: "This Irish war, small as it may seem now, if it is persisted in, will corrupt and eventually ruin not only your Army, but your nation and your Empire as well."

Only, Molly Childers transcended her husband. He was making a prediction. She is willing something to happen.

It was a sad and sour spring as the rifts in Ireland widened and the lines of battle began to form. The very able Kevin O'Higgins, Minister for Economics now, described the climate of the country in a prose that has sinew and logic like the man himself: *at self government. It is the RUSSIANS who had a Revolution (1917)*

NO, just a weak attempt

    "It is necessary to remember that the country had come through a <u>revolution</u> and to remember that a weird composite of idealism, neurosis, megalomania and criminality is apt to be thrown to the surface in even the best-regulated revolution. It was a situation precipitated by men who had not cleared the blood from their eyes and reinforced by the waywardness of a people with whom, by dint of historical circumstances, a negative attitude had tended to become traditional. With many it was the reaction from a great fear. With others it was fanaticism pure and simple. With others still it was something that was neither pure nor simple, an ebullition of the savage, primitive passion to wreck and loot and level when an opportunity seemed to offer to do so with impunity."

In March of 1922 open warfare was narrowly averted in

206

Limerick when I.R.A. Irregulars (as the anti-Treaty forces were now called) tried to take over the city barracks from the retiring British.

Also in March the Irregulars captured a British naval tug at Cobh with almost suspicious ease. The tug was on its way to England carrying machine guns and ammunition from evacuated barracks.

On April 14, the Irregulars seized the Four Courts and turned that magnificent shallow-domed building on the Liffey into their Dublin headquarters.

On May 1, they acquired some 275,000 pounds for their war chest by robbing various branches of the Bank of Ireland.

All spring, as counterpoint, there was persecution of Catholics in the Northern counties, and the continued arming of the Ulster Volunteers in case Southern violence spilled over into the North or a takeover was tried. The Boundary Commission, having served as a useful exigency during the treaty-making, pretty much died a-borning.

Finally, on June 16, the General Election took place, with 128 seats in a new Dail to be chosen. The pro-Treaty faction collected 58 seats; 35 went to the Republicans and, surprisingly, 35 went to members with "other interests." It was more a vote for coalition than anything else, but Michael Collins, rampaging now, took it as a mandate for the Treaty and the Free State.

Under heavy pressure from the British, particularly from Winston Churchill, the newly-elected Government delivered an ultimatum to the Irregulars holding the Four Courts.

At 4 o'clock in the morning of Wednesday, June 28 the ultimatum expired, with the Irregulars under Liam Mellows and Rory O'Connor still in open defiance. Using three 18-pounders borrowed from the British, and of necessity British gunners as well, the Army of the Free State Government opened fire. *we thought the BRITS HAD LEFT BY 1922* ?

Dubliners awoke to the deep *buh-loom buh-loom* of the guns, a sound they had not heard since the Rising.

President Erskine Hamilton Childers in front of a portrait of
Eamon De Valera, at Aras an Uachtarain, Dublin, 1973

208

24. "The Women and Childers War"

The Civil War that everyone knew was bound to come had come at last. Erskine Childers' reaction as a military man and veteran of active service in three wars was instinctive. During the long day when the 18-pounders were hammering away at the Four Courts, he vanished from Bushy Park Road. Not long after he reported to the Southern Brigade of the I.R.A., having received an appointment as Staff-Captain. His orders: to set up a weekly edition of *An Phoblacht* there for distribution to the Irregulars in Cork and Kerry and adjoining counties and to other interested parties. In Phase One of the Troubles this had been the official publication of the Republican Army; now it also took over the propaganda work of the *Irish Bulletin*.

Putting out *An Phoblacht* was hard and lonely work. Even finding the paper to print it on was difficult now. Moving with the Brigade—often under fire and usually on the run—Childers carried a little hand press and other portable equipment with him.

Distribution of the newssheet, once printed, was not the least of the problems. The I.R.A. columns read it, and were heartened in their fight. Reaching them was fairly easy. Mysteriously, *An Phoblacht* found its way to I.R.A. prisoners in Free State jails, and they too took heart. As the *Bulletin* had in less disparate times, *An Phoblacht* also reached the foreign press, European embassies in Dublin, friends in England and America. . . .

Childers' arguments did not come through quite as clearly now, the message was a little muted. But still, for all to read on the little handprinted sheet, was the reminder that Ireland could be no real Dominion with six of her Northern counties in British hands. Another point that was forever stressed was the reminder that the oath to the Republic was true and binding, for life or in death. . . .

For the rest, there were occasional hit-and-run successes of the Irregulars to be reported. Sean Hendrick, one of his assistants, has given us a glimpse of Childers standing on a five-barred gate and calmly making notes half-way between Irregular and Free State forces as the bullets went whipping past in both directions. In such moments as these the joy of battle was on him again, and he could forget for a little his weakness and his woes.

The bombardment of the Four Courts, which also housed the National Archives, lasted 48 hours. Then it burned and blew up. Charred fragments—priceless shreads of the heritage of Ireland—rained down on Dublin.

With the Four Courts blazing like a torch, the surviving defenders finally came out. Last of all, from one of the outposts, there appeared a blackened figure with a revolver in each hand. Refusing pleas to surrender from both friend and foe, he was gunned down by a burst from a Lewis gun—and Cathal Brugha—born Charles Burgess, a man as English as Childers, and as Irish—died as he had lived. TOTALLY INCORRECT

The Dublin fighting lasted eight days. When the tide turned against the Irregulars, Eamon De Valera, who had been fighting in their ranks as a private, simply walked away. The onetime President of the Republic was on the run again.

His anti-Treaty cause fared badly from the first, with the Free State army moving quickly to take over principal cities and towns. The Catholic church withdrew its support from the Republicans, so that in many counties the people were indifferent or openly hostile. Being unable to rely on the natives to hide and feed them, the guerrillas were denied the vital base that they had enjoyed against the British in the first phase.

They took to burning the houses of prominent Free State figures. Sir Horace Plunkett's house (and art collection) was destroyed. So was George Moore's, and Sir Thomas Grattan Esmonde's. Sometimes, if they liked the victim, he was given fair warning. In the case of Sir John Keane of Cappoquin the arsonists waited upon him, said they were sorry and set a date far enough ahead so that he could remove his furniture and pictures, and even make full measurements for future reconstruction. Then they gutted his fine house for him.

The Free State army reacted to ambush and arson in much the same way that the British once had. There were by midsummer of 1922 over 60,000 men in their ranks. Well-supplied by the British, they blasted their way into cities and towns, until West Cork and Kerry, where the populace supported the diehards, were the only areas where the Irregulars were still able to put up a reasonable show of opposition.

There was brutality on both sides, for it is a fact that a war of brothers is often the cruelest of all wars. The Government side of the story was fully told in the British and Irish press, but the Irregulars' version of the bitter war only reached the world in a trickle through the various editions of *An Phoblacht*.

One atrocity that shocked the world took place at Tralee. Free State troops took nine Republican prisoners from the jail there and carried them by lorry to a place where there was a tree across the road and a land mine placed beside it. They tied the men with their backs to the tree by an electric wire, and then blew the mine. Miraculously, one of the prisoners, a man called Stephen Fuller, was blown clear, into a ditch, and somehow managed to survive to tell the terrible story.

Erskine Childers, during this last summer of his life, confined himself entirely to his propaganda work. But Arthur Griffith, more exhausted than he himself realized, and Kevin O'Higgins, with growing hatred, assigned to Childers a much larger role, as saboteur and night rider. They saw his lethal hand in every ambush and blown bridge. This was in part because they wanted to do so and in part because of Childers'

211

record in three wars and his reputation as a military writer. Such books as *War and the Arme Blanche* are full of technical observations on irregular warfare in general, on the correct use of the element of surprise and of shock action.

One wag called this Phase Two of the Troubles. "The Women and Childers War," helping to perpetuate the legend of Childers as night rider and saboteur. The first part of the label stems from the fact that all eight women in the Dail had voted against the Treaty, and several of them like Mary Mac-Swiney and the Countess Markievicz were in full and vociferous action on the side of the Irregulars.

As the summer wore on, Michael Collins became a man possessed of some grim spirit. Hating to fight his old comrades-in-arms, he nevertheless took over command of the Government forces. The frequent shifts in loyalty, the growing role of the informer and the climate of fear and suspicion that came into being depressed his usually-exuberant outlook. He missed the black-and-white certainties of fighting the Black and Tans.

In the blight of the spirit that had overtaken him, Collins even turned completely away from Childers, his onetime mentor and friend. During the Treaty-making he had begun to criticize, writing to a friend that "the advice and inspiration of C. is like farmland underwater—dead." But some affection for the man had remained. Now that too was gone.

On August 12, 1922, Arthur Griffith had a massive stroke while under observation in a nursing home. He died within minutes. It was as if a block of granite had been removed from the foundations of Ireland. Michael Collins marched at the head of the funeral procession. For the first time the stricken nation saw him in full regalia as commander-in-chief, felt his vigor and knew that its fate was still in firm hands.

The basic goodness and chivalry of Childers shows through in the tribute that he wrote on Griffith for his propaganda sheet. "Death can hush the bitterest controversy that ever rent a nation," the obituary notice ran, "and it is in that

212

spirit that we endeavor to write these few lines. Deep and impassable as is the gulf that in recent months has divided us from Arthur Griffith, we join in mourning the death of a great Irishman." Very gently, Childers makes some partisan points: "For even if the Republic were, as he thought, an unrealistic symbol, to which allegiance could be justly discarded, or, as we hold, a living state, to which our sworn devotion never can be violated, all at any rate must agree that in our generation Griffith was the greatest intellectual force stimulating the tremendous national revival. . . ."

Just ten days after Griffith's death, Michael Collins went on an inspection trip in his home county of Cork. Many believe he was hoping to meet some of the key anti-Treaty leaders and persuade them that their cause was a lost one.

Toward dusk, at a place called Beal Na mBlath, there was a partial roadblock. Collins' convoy made the mistake of coming to a halt. There was a brisk fire fight for some minutes. Then men were seen running for the hills.

"There they are," yelled Collins, sprinting up the road in pursuit, rifle in hand. Dropping to a prone position, he kept up a steady fire for a while and then there was no more firing but only a still figure and a terrible, gaping wound in his head. He died as one of his party whispered the words of the Act of Contrition. Sadly, the little convoy wove its way back to Cork in the growing dark, with Major General Dalton cradling the body of his lost leader.

Sean Hendrick and Frank O'Connor, who by now were both helping Erskine Childers, remember how they rejoiced when they heard of Collins' death, and how their pleasure turned to self-questioning when they saw the moving tribute that Childers wrote.

First he noted the circumstances of the ambush and then commented on them: "Like a gallant soldier he took the risk of that perilous passage through hostile country—and like a gallant soldier, he fell on the field of action."

Collins' great qualities received full recognition. "His buoyant energy, his organising powers, immense industry, acute and subtle intelligence. . . . charm and gift of oratory. . . . he flung without stint into the Republican cause for five years."

Then, very delicately, Childers applied the cutting edge of the propagandist's scalpel: "What was his dominant motive? There may have been a bias due to ambition—the glamour of a career like that of Jan Smuts—but standing now at his grave few will be ungenerous enough to doubt that his ruling motive and sincere belief was that the Treaty was a necessary halting-place on the road to a recognized Republic, that it gave us freedom to achieve a freedom which was beyond the power of Ireland now to wrest from her mighty enemy."

Now colder, second-growth men took over—steady men, able men—rather like the realists in the business world who pick up where the great inventors, half-dreamers, half-doers, leave off.

William T. Cosgrave became President in Griffith's place. Kevin O'Higgins moved up to be Minister for Home Affairs. General Richard Mulcahy replaced Collins as Commander-in-Chief and also kept his own portfolio of Minister for Defense. *Move Over Mick, Make Way for Dick* was a slogan scrawled on Dublin walls, half in grief, half in assurance that the war would go on.

With the death of Griffith and Collins, the Civil War became still more brutal and bitter. The Free State Army asked the Parliament for emergency powers, including the right to inflict the death penalty for the possession of arms, for looting and arson and for aiding and abetting attacks on the National Forces.

In supporting the Resolution, O'Higgins made a most remarkable speech, aimed directly and in a most sinister way at Erskine Childers:

". . .I do know that the able Englishman who is leading those who are opposed to this Government has his eye quite definitely on one objective, and that is the complete breakdown of the economic and social fabric, so that this

214

thing that is trying so hard to become an Irish nation will go down in chaos, anarchy and futility. . . . He has no constructive programme and so he keeps steadily, callously and ghoulishly at his career of striking at the heart of the Nation. . . ."

A fellow Deputy interrupted O'Higgins: "On a point of information, may I ask to whom you are referring?"

O'Higgins: "I am now referring to the Englishman, Erskine Childers. I trust the Deputy did not think my words were capable of being applied to anyone else."

The Army received their emergency powers. And notice had been served that Erskine Childers was the man the Government wanted most.

Childers meanwhile was publishing his newssheet from Cork City. It was there that Frank O'Connor, who would one day become one of the greatest of Irish writers, met him for the first time. Childers was staying at the Victoria Hotel, and came down the stairs to meet his new assistant. Here is how O'Connor describes him in his autobiography, *An Only Child:*

". . .a small, slight, grey-haired man in tweeds with a tweed cap pulled over his eyes, wearing a light mackintosh stuffed with papers and carrying another coat over his arm. Apart from his accent, which would have identified him anywhere, there was something peculiarly English about him; something that nowadays reminds me of some old parson or public-school teacher I have known, conscientious to a fault and overburdened with minor cares. His thin, grey face, shrunk almost to its mould of bone, had a coldness as though life had contracted behind it to its narrowest span; the brows were puckered in a triangle of obsessive thought like pain, and the eyes were clear, pale and tragic."

Cork was a dangerous city to be in, that summer of 1922. It was an open city of sorts, with both sides coming and going, but with Irregulars taking the greater risk as the side on the run now. Its only advantage was that, as the second Free State city, it was big enough to get lost in.

215

Childers couldn't remember whether he had registered in his own name at the Victoria. O'Connor checked for him and found that he was logged in as "Mr. Smith."

A day or so later O'Connor and Sean Hendrick of Childers' small staff watched their chief wandering rather aimlessly down King Street. They noticed that he was being shadowed, his window-gazing matched by a man who was obviously an enemy agent.

O'Connor and Hendrick sprinted ahead of Childers and his shadower. They confronted Childers, told him he was under scrutiny and asked if he had a gun on him. Childers produced a small .22 automatic clipped to his suspenders by a safety pin. It was, O'Connor remembers, the kind of gun "a middle-aged lady of timid disposition might carry in her handbag."

O'Connor and Hendrick told Childers he must turn over the gun to them for his own safety. With great reluctance he unclipped the automatic and handed it over.

Later, in the secrecy of their office, they gave it back. "When we returned the gun to Childers," O'Connor writes, "he looked happy for the first time since we had met him. He had not worried himself about being shadowed but was concerned for the loss of his gun. . . . He pinned it back on his braces as if it was a flower he was pinning to his buttonhole and told us in the dry tone that Englishmen reserve for intimate revelations that it was a present from a friend. Someone told me later that the friend was Michael Collins. . . ."

When the Southern Brigade took up Headquarters at Fremoy north by east of Cork, O'Connor and another Irregular shared a room with Childers. After rigging his light so that it would not shine in their eyes and keep them awake, the older man read *Twenty Years After* and *The Deerslayer* until far into the night. He also did his best to smother a persistent cough. . . .

Molly Childers was worried. The Republican fortunes of war were on the wane, and the brutality on the rise. In a letter that has disappeared but that the Childers family is sure she did write, she begged her husband to flee the country while the going was good.

An old friend of Childers called David Robinson, Ascendancy figure and Wicklow neighbor, was also serving with the Irregulars. As alarmed as Molly, and even more aware of the implications of O'Higgins' hatred, Robinson explored the idea of having Childers escape to France by fishing boat. But one of Childers' immediate superiors cut him off with a curt phrase:

"Staff-Captain Childers is under my command," he snapped, and that was the end of that.

Like Childers, Robinson had been a British officer in World War I. One of his tasks had been to walk ahead of French tanks and show them the way through enemy barbed wire. Despite his casual bravery—with a swagger stick as his only weapon—the tanks did not always follow. In one such episode he had been badly wounded in the legs. He had also lost an eye and was known irreverently to the Irregulars as "Dead-eye Dave."

Both he and Childers found the casual discipline of the anti-Treaty forces hard to fathom. They rarely if ever posted sentries, bedded down wherever anyone would risk having them, and in general made a travesty of regular military procedure.

"I'll never understand this country," Childers remarked to Frank O'Connor with a wintry glimpse of his old charm. "I thought I was going off to a bloody combat, and instead I found myself in Mick Sullivan's feather bed in Kilnamartyr."

Robinson once worked out a plan to attack a Free State outpost at dawn, with two Irregulars disguised as tinkerwomen approaching from the front while others crept up from behind. Linen sheets hung out by a Republican sympathizer next door were to serve as cover.

The tinkerwomen would kill the lone early-morning sentry at the door, the main body would lob incendiaries into the blockhouse and shoot the men of the garrison as they came running out. It was bold, as David Robinson was. Sean

O'Faolain, who was a member of Robinson's company, was one of exactly four soldiers who turned up on time. The others had a late breakfast and strolled over at their ease, far too late for any surprise to be maintained. They were, notes O'Faolain in *Vive Moi!*, "too devious or too polite to tell him what they thought." As experienced soldiers, Robinson's methods were simply too unorthodox to appeal to them.

In another version of this aborted plan, one of the soldiers, after listening to Robinson's crisp and cutting remarks on their dereliction, said, "Ah, now, sor, it's easy enough for you to get up early. You don't need as much sleep as we do, with only the one eye."

This kind of gallows humor was offset by many brave and often doomed actions in which Irregulars unnecessarily lost their lives.

After Cork City was evacuated on August 12, 1922, Erskine Childers set up his little press in various small villages and secret valleys of West Cork. At Ballymakeera, near Macroom, his printing shop was a deserted barracks. Later, near Ballyvourney, it was an empty two-room cottage.

Sometimes, on the move, when he was not too ill and depressed, Childers could momentarily be his old self. In *Allegiance*, Robert Brennan remembers one such time in a most revealing way. They were traveling together in a military lorry through a pleasant countryside in Cork.

Brennan observed how ironic it was that Arthur Griffith, for so long the advocate of peaceful change, should be making war against his own countrymen. Childers, still the Englishman in good part, answered on what seemed a tangent.

"You people have always underestimated the British."

"What has that got to do with it?"

"Griffith was deceived by Lloyd George."

"I can see that, but I still can't understand what bearing that has on the Civil War."

Childers was very patient:

"The British can sign, and find a way to repudiate their signatures. They've done it over and over again. You need not go back to the Treaty of Limerick. You have Malta and Egypt, for instance. They can always find high moral reasons for such repudiation. They are opportunists. Griffith, however, having given his word, would stick to it whatever the consequences, even though it meant the disaster of a civil war. They knew that."

"You've no hard feelings against him?"

"No, not at all," Childers said. "He was unfair, but I can see his point of view."

"I wish I could achieve your detachment," Robert Brennan said.

While on one of the sudden moves, Childers lost part of his printing press in a bog. Even more discouraging, he kept finding unopened packages of his newssheets in out-of-the way places and cobwebbed corners. Once he found a batch of them in a rainswept barn where he took refuge in a sudden storm.

Even his strong spirit began to waver. Realizing that the propaganda jig was nearly up, he asked for re-assignment. At Headquarters, his superior officers showed great reluctance to take him on, for they knew very well he had a price on his head. In effect they said, "We'd have no peace night or day if the Free Staters knew you were with us." The remark reveals a lot about their own wish to be let alone to wage their own brand of fairly non-belligerent warfare.

His English-ness was hurting him now. No one seemed concerned about his safety, only their own. Nor were his talents in warfare rather than propaganda recognized. He seemed to be someone who bothered too much over petty detail. Pieras Beaslai's judgment that he had "the mind, outlook and ability of a capable British civil servant" but gave an "impression of fussy, feverish futility" was made the year before, but it seemed more relevant than ever.

One of his superiors, Connie Neenan, now living in New York, remembers Childers as having the qualifications of "a good adjutant", qualifications which the most-wanted label more than cancelled out.

Then, suddenly, in late October there came a summons to Childers from Eamon de Valera, who was in hiding in the Dublin area. There was, it seemed, a great need to re-define and re-constitute the Republican Government. During all that swirling summer and early fall, the I.R.A. had functioned almost as a law unto itself. De Valera himself had been leader in name only, more bystander than participant. Now the I.R.A. was calling for more guidance, and a measure of civilian control.

As a start, De Valera created a Council of State to help him, with such old Republican hands as Austin Stack, Robert Barton and Mary MacSwiney among the members.

Erskine Childers' known skills as historian and parliamentarian were greatly needed as Secretary to the government in transition. He was to come at once.

With David Robinson as companion, he set out for Dublin by way of the counties of Waterford, Wexford and his own Wicklow, all held by pro-Treaty troops. A careful plan was developed by which they would be driven over backroads from friendly house to house. But nothing worked out quite as planned. Travel in the event was mostly on foot or by farm cart—when they could persuade some suspicious countryman to help, and ask no questions. They slept under the stars, or in strange houses.

On November 10 they dropped down—through one of the gaps in the Wicklow hills—to the valley of the Avonmore. On the high, bare slopes the streams were falling like downward smoke, but they were so tired and hungry they hardly noticed the beauty around them. By nightfall they reached Annamoe and slipped across the home fields to Glan.

Such was Childers' homecoming. His last free hours on earth would be spent at the house where he had been happy once.

25.   The Hunter and the Hunted

Glan sits on a raised terrace. Beneath the dining room in its southeast corner, there is a dark, cellar-like space. The only access is a sliding panel in the floor—under the sideboard and invisible to the naked eye.

The master of Glan was not there that November night when Erskine Childers and David Robinson arrived in the dusk. Robert Barton had been captured by the Free State forces and was once again in prison. He had, however, left certain specific instructions; one of them was that if his cousin Erskine ever took refuge at Glan he was to be hidden in that dark cellarage.

Childers was so tired that all he craved was the narrow bed in his old room off the long second-floor gallery. Despite the urgings of the staff and the misgivings of Robinson, he made his way there and literally tumbled in. Shaking his head, Robinson went off to a hiding place of his own.

No one knows to this day who it was that tipped off the Free State authorities in the area that Childers had come home. Some think that it was a disgruntled member of the household, others that it was a former employee on the estate with a grudge.

In the small hours, two squads of soldiers surrounded the house. Some sixth sense aroused Childers. He came out of his room revolver in hand to find soldiers in the long gallery. At the exact moment, as he lifted his arm to fire and they raised their rifles, two of the old family servants came running. One of them threw herself in front of him crying, "You'll not shoot Mr. Childers."

Childers shifted his gun to a free hand. Before he could fire, three men pinioned him from behind, and one of them twisted the little gun from his grasp.

So Erskine Childers was captured at last. Guarded by six soldiers—one of them cradling a Thompson sub-machine gun —he ate a last breakfast at Glan. Then he was driven by cart to Wicklow town and the jail there, and shortly thereafter by car to Portobello Barracks in Dublin.

Mr. Churchill, campaigning for his political life in Dundee (Lloyd George had called a General Election), could hardly restrain his glee: *"Such as he is may all who hate us be."*

And Kevin O'Higgins, Mr. Churchill's man cast in bronze, went into swift and deadly action—proving that his feet at least were of clay, and rooted in the grim soil of reality.

On November 17, O'Higgins, as Minister of Home Affairs, ordered the immediate execution of four young Irregulars who had been caught carrying revolvers. Although the emergency act had been in operation for a month, no death penalty had been exacted up to that time. The same night, after the sentences had been carried out, O'Higgins came under sharp questioning from fellow Deputies in the Dail. His explanation was full of an ominous foreboding:

"If they took, as their first case, a man who was outstandingly active and outstandingly wicked in his activities, the unfortunate dupes throughout the country might say that he was killed because he was a leader, because he was an Englishman, or because he combined with others to commit rape."

That same morning, Childers—unmistakably the Englishman in question—had gone on trial at Portobello Barracks. The case against him was no wide range of wicked activities as O'Higgins sought to imply. He was simply accused of committing an offense "in that he, on the 10th day of November, 1922, without proper authority, was in possession of an automatic pistol when apprehended by a party of National forces."

The Military Court, which met in secret, consisted of two high-ranking officers and a legal adviser. Three lawyers acted as Counsel. One of them was Michael Comyn, K.C., in whose house Childers had several times taken cover. (Comyn's sister had described Childers' involvement in Irish quarrels as being "like a child in a blizzard".) Admiring him greatly, realizing how much he needed help, Comyn had volunteered his very able services.

During the seven days leading up to the trial, O'Higgins saw to it that the most elaborate precautions were taken to prevent the escape of his prize prisoner, or any rescue from outside. Childers was moved constantly from prison and barrack—including Portobello, Beggar's Bush, Mountjoy and Kilmainham—for safe-keeping. A sergeant, a corporal and six enlisted men were always with him. They were hand-picked men, and they were told that Childers must be "kept alive at any price." In this instance O'Higgins wanted no equivocal "killed-while-trying-to-escape" formula. This was the reason that the first move, from Portobello Barracks, was made. As one of the surviving guards told the writer, "The officer commanding there would shoot his own grandmother."

In the detention room where they were planning Childers' defense, Comyn gave his client his own mug of tea.

"You know, Comyn," said Childers sipping it gratefully, "there is no defense in fact. I did have a gun."

"That may be," Comyn answered. "But you are too famous a figure to be condemned without due form and solemnity."

The fact was that Childers was not the kind of man to go down without a struggle, whatever the evidence. He told Comyn that he refused to recognize the jurisdiction of the Military Court. He was, he said, an officer of the Republican

223

Army taken in war and deserved treatment as such under the rules of the International Red Cross. All men serving in the Irregular forces had been instructed to make this plea if captured.

Around this refusal, Counsel decided to build the defense. At the opening of the trial, a written statement was submitted: "Captain Childers does not recognize the legality of the Provisional Government, and consequently does not recognize the legality of the Court. . . . He is an officer of the Irish Republican Army and he claims that if he be detained at all, by an Army whose legality he repudiates, he should receive the treatment of a Prisoner of War."

Then Childers proceeded to make a presentation of his life and work. In its cool precision, it is quite a remarkable statement, and it also shows how little Childers understood the Irish.

Here are some of the highlights:

"I have constantly been called an Englishman who, having betrayed his own country, came to Ireland to betray and destroy Ireland, a double traitor. Alternatively, I have suffered the vile charge or innuendo that instead of betraying England I have been acting as a spy or agent provocateur in England's interest."

Vigorously denying the charges as having "no particle of proof," he went on to say. "I am by birth, domicile and deliberate choice of citizenship an Irishman." Then he gave a resume of his transition from "Unionist and Imperialist" to Liberal working and writing in the cause of Irish freedom.

He spoke modestly of his Boer War service, of the arms-running to Howth and his work in World War I, in which he, like so many Irishmen, was misled "by the idea of a war for small nations." He hit hard against the British-agent myth by showing how the kind of Intelligence and Reconnaissance work he did in the North Sea and elsewhere contributed to it. He told, much as this biography has related, of his work in the Irish Convention, his disillusionment and his wish to join the

Republican movement as soon as his military duties for the British were fulfilled.

The last paragraphs of the speech give the essence of the man:

"I took a strong line from the first against the British Dominion scheme and in so doing came for the first time in three years into conflict with Republican colleagues and comrades. Until then not a shadow of a cloud has disturbed the absolute harmony of our relationship. For myself I had passed through the Dominion phase years before, discarded it and sworn allegiance to the established Republic.

"The slow growth of moral and intellectual conviction had brought me to where I stood, and it was and is impossible and unthinkable to go back. I was bound by honour, conscience and principle to oppose the Treaty by speech, writing and action, both in peace, and when it came to the disastrous point, in war. . ."

In the final peroration, the fanaticism shows through, buttressed by the convert's zeal for the principle that he finally came totally to believe:

"I have fought and worked for a sacred principle, the loyalty of a nation to its declared Independence and repudiation of any voluntary surrender to conquest and inclusion in the British Empire. That is the faith of my comrades, my leaders and myself. Some day we shall be justified when the Nation forgets its weakness and reverts to the ancient and holy tradition which we are preserving in our struggle, and may God hasten the day of reunion amongst us all under the honoured flag of the Republic."

It is in its way a fine and manly statement, even a moving one, and it moved the Court not one jot. His service in the British cause held no special appeal, his course from Imperialist to Republican appeared at best labyrinthine and wilful to realistic men who had opted for the middle course. The preoccupation with the Republican form of government, the full loaf of freedom, seemed obsession only.

225

Nevertheless, the two high-ranking officers and their legal adviser listened with great courtesy. They had their instructions. Childers, the renegade Englishman who had wandered into a family quarrel, was to be given a fairly fair trial and then shot. It did no harm to do what had to be done with some decorum.

The Court sat all that day and the next but no verdict was handed down in the presence of the prisoner.

Meanwhile there was activity on the part of the Free State Cabinet which shows how closely they guided the developing drama. The minutes of these Cabinet meetings were declassified in March of 1976, along with many other State Papers of the period, and they are terse and business-like, with much left out and much to be read between their lines.

For instance, on November 18, 1922, the Cabinet of what was still known as the Provisional Government, with President Cosgrave presiding, addressed itself to the plea of various relatives of executed men that the bodies be handed over:

> "It was decided that the request could not be granted, and that the relatives should be informed that the bodies will be coffined and buried in consecrated ground."

Four days later, the President, O'Higgins and the others took up a request by a number of the Dail that relatives be informed before an execution:

> "It was decided that this could not be granted but that it would be arranged in future that the parents or nearest relatives, when known, would be advised immediately after the execution."

Also on November 22, the Cabinet turned its attention to the request by another Deputy that Military Court proceedings be published "where persons are sentenced to death."

> "It was decided that this could not be done but that

in future the statement of the charge could be supplemented by a brief resume of the circumstances."

At this same Cabinet meeting, the Minister of External Affairs (Desmond Fitzgerald, Childers' onetime comrade in propaganda work) was instructed "to arrange for the publication of the directions given to the Irregulars by their self-styled Chief of Staff on the 1st of November not to recognize either Civil or Military Courts, even when such recognition might save them from the death penalty."

There were, of course, many other matters afoot. Mary MacSwiney was in prison now, and on a hunger strike that was receiving wide publicity. Should she be released as an embarrassment? Might the island of St. Helena be used as a place to send political prisoners? Should Pieras Beaslai be given a subsidy to write the official life of Michael Collins? Was 5500 pounds a fair price to pay per trawler for the purchase of armed trawlers from the British?

But setting the scene and preparing the public for Childers' execution were in the forefront, as these sparse and carefully-circumscribed entries show. His name was never mentioned but his presence was there nonetheless, among his former comrades and his enemies.

As the days passed, the outside world became concerned about Childers' chances of survival. Among the recently-declassified papers are scores of letters and telegrams, some laconic and many eloquent.

Douglas Hyde, the great Gaelic scholar who later became President of Ireland, wrote to President Cosgrave: "If Mr. Childers is sentenced I would most respectfully beg that his great services to Ireland during the Black-and-Tan terror be remembered. I had the opportunity of observing how very much his writings at that time impressed the British people. I hope very much that owing to his past services the extreme penalty may not be enacted."

From Foynes, Lord Monteagle, Mary Spring-Rice's father, made an interesting point in his second communication to the President: "I beg to renew my appeal on behalf of Childers. General Collins told me three days before his death that Childers being an Englishman might well be deported, and having regard for his past services to Ireland especially in propaganda venture to urge commutation."

Mrs. Fiske Warren, Molly's sister Gretchen, cabled Sir Horace Plunkett, who it so happened was abroad at the time: "CAN YOU INTERVENE MAKING SENTENCE DEPORTATION FISKE OFFERS HOUSE IN ANDORRA SPAIN" (where Warren was making one of his single-tax experiments). An anxious Mary Spring-Rice found the cable at Plunkett House in Dublin and forwarded it to President Cosgrave for "special consideration."

Jack Yeats, the painter and brother of the poet, sent a short, strong note to Cosgrave: "I write you to urge you to hold your hand and not execute Erskine Childers. I write to you in the name of humanity and in the name of sober judgment." (Across the letter a Cosgrave assistant had scrawled: *The man you plead for had neither Humanity nor Sober Judgment.*")

From California the Delegates to the Annual Convention for the Recognition of the Irish Republic sent a terse cable: "WE WOULD LOOK UPON THE KILLING OF ERSKINE CHILDERS OR ANY OTHER REPUBLICAN PRISONER OF WAR AS MURDER AND HOLD YOUR FREE STATE JUNTA RESPONSIBLE."

Desmond O'Neil, who had fought in Phase One of the Trouble and later settled in England, wrote: "Don't copy English methods. . . . You are doing to the Irregulars just what the British did to us. We claimed treatment as POW's and got the rope and the bullet."

Again and again the theme of magnaminity was stressed. Professor C.H. Oldham, writing from Dublin, struck it well. After first expressing his respect for the President, he went on: "It depends on you and Mulcahy to lift us all up at the present time. It is not the ethics of a dog-fight that Ireland expects from true spirits like yours, like Mulcahy's. We expect. . . .

the touch of magnaminity that is able to transform a whole people."

De Valera issued a press statement in the form of a message to the people of Ireland, few of whom ever saw it. He hinted at reprisals if Childers were executed. He blamed England for urging Ireland to kill "a man whose crime was that he had worn himself out in the service of Ireland and that he had remained incorruptible when many became corrupt."

To all these and many more, President Cosgrave made no reply himself, simply acknowledging their receipt through an aide's perfunctory answer.

On the afternoon of Saturday, November 18, the second day of the trial, Childers reversed himself about the legality of the tribunal by allowing Counsel to enter a plea of *Habeas Corpus*. The reason he did so does him credit. There were at the time eight other prisoners also on trial on a similar charge of the unlawful possession of arms. The Provisional Government had taken the odd measure of withholding their names. Only by a parallel case, and one in which the name of the defendant was known, could their lives be spared.

For the sake of protecting the eight men, Childers told Michael Comyn to proceed with the application in his name. It was formally delivered to the Master of the Rolls, Sir Charles O'Connor, on November 20.

Meanwhile Childers, skilled at propaganda and at placing propaganda, smuggled out of prison a written statement for his friends which showed that he was not going down without a fight. The November 19 statement is a strong indictment of O'Higgins' explanation of why the four ordinary prisoners were shot "before any leader" and of Winston Churchill's remarks in Dundee. Their attempts to influence a case that was actually *sub judice*, their thinly-veiled appeals for his execution, O'Higgins' failure to enumerate any "outstandingly wicked activities" and Churchill's calling him a "mischievous and murderous renegade" all aroused his eloquence and his righteous ire.

He ends on a brave clear note:

229

"I do not say this in the desire to shirk any penalty. If it is to be so, I will gladly and happily suffer the lot of the four lads executed on the 17th on the same charge as mine. But I have to consider others and the true interests of our country. Holding the policy of executions wrong and disastrous, I regard the averting of any execution as a public advantage and as a means possibly of averting others. . . . For myself as I said at my trial, my chief feeling is of pain at the load of ignominy which had been heaped upon the cause, the slander against me which I have no public means of refuting, and when these are repeated and scattered broadside by eminent men at the very time when I was awaiting and undergoing trial in camera I feel that a solemn protest is necessary."

On the same day that the writ of *Habeas Corpus* was applied for, which was in effect a delaying action requiring the Court to produce the persons of Childers and the other eight in his name, Erskine Childers was informed that the Military Court had finished their deliberations.

The recommendation was death by firing squad. He had come to realize its inevitability. On hearing it, he wrote to Molly a last letter of which this is a passage:

"I have been told that I am to be shot to-morrow at seven. I am fully prepared. I think it is best so, viewing it from the biggest standpoint. To have followed those other brave lads is a great thing for a great cause. I have a belief in a beneficient shaping of our destiny, and I believe God means this for the best; for us, Ireland and humanity. . . It is such a simple thing too, a soldier's death; what millions risk and incur, what so many in our cause face and suffer daily."

At 10 p.m., on that same night of November 20, the execution was postponed. The Master of the Rolls was still holding hearings in the High Court of Dublin concerning the application for a writ of *Habeas Corpus*, and this was the reason for the Government's delay.

November 21 was "another day of waiting and meditation."

That night he gave some of his few possessions to the guards, including a little essay-like book called *Smoking Flax* which he had been reading and which he signed in a firm hand:

Erskine Childers
Nov. 21. 1922.

_____

November 22 was still another day. In his letter to Molly reporting this further postponement, Childers told his wife:

"In case I should forget, I wish to say that my treatment here has been very considerate and courteous— Commandant, officers and men of the guard and all, nothing to complain of, on the contrary. Within the range of things allowed, food, writing material, papers and so forth, I have been given whatever I asked for. It has made a vast difference. Everything that bridges this ghastly gulf between the armies is good, and I hope to God nothing has been conceded to me which is not to others."

On November 23, the Master of the Rolls made his ruling to the Dublin High Court. He refused the application for an order of *Habeas Corpus* on the ground that a state of war existed, and that his Court could not, "for any purpose, or under any circumstances, control the military authority."

This ruling was embarrassing to the Government, which was maintaining that it was dealing with a revolt, not a war, and that captured insurgents were therefore not prisoners of war.

In refusing to take jurisdiction, the Master paid high tribute to Childers' lawyers for their zeal and professional skill. (Michael Comyn had at one point addressed the High Court for five hours, ending in a state of near-collapse.)

Counsel for Childers promptly filed notice of appeal against the Order of refusal. But the Military Authorities did not wish to wait any longer for the result of any such appeal, or take the risk that the Master's ruling might be reversed. Moreover it was rumored that efforts to rescue Childers were underway.

At ten that evening of Thursday, November 23, Childers was told that the sentence of execution would be carried out the next morning. He made several requests. One was to be alone that last night, another that he be allowed to see a last sunrise. The Commandant, who had his specific orders, turned down the first and granted the second.

He was told that he could see his older son. The boy, who was just under seventeen at the time, would never forget the farewell scene, and it colored his whole career.

"Promise me," Erskine senior said after they had talked

for a while in the cell, "that you will shake hands with each person who figured in my death."

Almost overcome, Erskine junior promised to do so.

"And, son, promise that you will never use my name to any political advantage." This too the boy promised.

After his son had gone, Childers began a last letter to Molly:

"The guard was relieved at eight, and the men going off all said good-bye and God bless you, and I to them. They wanted souvenirs, but I have very few, some books and some signatures. It will be the same with the present lot—in case I am unable to record it—all friendly and infinitely considerate. So we, 'Children of the Universal Mother,' touch hands, and go our ways in the very midst of the horror of this war of brothers. . ."

Another request of Childers' was to see Father Albert, a Catholic priest who was a friend. Instead, he was offered a choice between Dr. Browne of Maynooth and the Reverend Edward Waller, the Anglican Dean of Kildare, whom he had known as a young man. He chose the latter.

In after years Dean Waller never wished to talk about those last hours he spent with Erskine Childers. The writer did interview one of the guards, who was still alive in 1972. The guard had also been a member of the firing squad. He remembered how calm Childers was, and how he talked in a most normal way and with no trace of vindictiveness. One topic touched on was the Abbey theater and its great achievements, and Childers said he would have liked to have written a play himself.

(On one of the earlier days, Childers was taken off in an armored car for a brief appearance in Court. He was back within the hour. "Home again," said the prisoner cheerfully, "and glad to be.")

My 1972 witness also recalled that Father Waller was "a big, clean-shaven, gray-haired man" and that it was obvious he was a great comfort to Childers.

233

Early the last morning, he wrote a few more lines to Molly:

"It is 6 a.m. You will be pleased to see how imperturbable I have been this night and am. It all seems perfectly simple and inevitable, like lying down after a long day's work."

He was taken to the courtyard of Beggar's Bush Barracks, then as now a fortress-like building with long battlements of stone and turrets at the corners. As the party reached the court, Childers said to Waller, "I am at peace with the world. I bear no grudge against anyone and trust no one bears any against me." He was not a practising churchgoer, either Protestant or Catholic, but his were the words of a most Christian man.

He shook hands with each member of the firing squad, several of whom showed that they were under great strain. Then the Officer-in-Charge marched him to the wall, saluted, and left him there.

The squad took up their positions across the prison yard.

"Come closer, boys," Childers called to them. "It will be easier for you."

The squad had been carefully instructed. One man had been issued a blank cartridge, but which man it was no one knew. The officer-in-charge would hold a white cloth vertically above his head. When he lowered the cloth to a horizontal position the men were to exert first pressure on their triggers. When he dropped the cloth, they were to fire.

Not blindfolded, not trussed, Childers stood with perfect composure against the wall.

At the agreed signal, the volley crashed out with military precision. Now all that was left was a small crumpled heap on the bare ground and a stillness which seemed to spread over the barracks, over the city itself.

Erskine Childers, who had tested himself all his life in storm and battle and council chamber, had been true to himself in the supreme and final test.

234

Aftermath

Molly Childers knew by intuition that her husband was dead. Just after eight that morning she told her older son that he had been shot. The official news came at 9:45 a.m., in accordance with the Government ruling that next of kin were to be promptly informed.

The press announcement from Army Headquarters in Dublin gave the barest details:

"Erskine Childers was tried by Military Court at Portobello Barracks, Dublin, on November 19, 1922, charged with having possession, without proper authority, of an automatic pistol when apprehended by a party of National forces, on November 10, at Annamoe, Co. Wicklow. Accused was found guilty and sentenced to death. The finding and sentence were duly confirmed, and the execution was carried out this morning at seven o'clock."

The time was not quite correct but the laconic spirit mirrored Government intent.

After some moments of near-collapse, Molly Childers pulled herself together and managed to do the things that had to be done. She cabled to the Fiske Warrens: "Erskine died as he had lived, heroically." A similar message went to Basil Williams and his wife in London: "He sent you both his love, was serene, contented, fulfilled." She managed a statement for the press: "His sacrifice is as much a gift to me as it is to his comrades who serve Ireland's cause."

The press reaction was one of banner headlines and predictable comment along party lines.

The *Irish Times,* reflecting Free State policy, tried hard to be objective: "Of all the many men who have met their deaths in the Irish political arena, none was a more remarkable type. . . . Brilliantly clever, he might have attained success in almost any walk of life. History will not excuse him for the part which he has played in the hurly-burly of Irish politics during the past twelvemonth. . . . Erskine Childers never compromised. Right or wrong he had made up his mind, and nothing would change it."

The Irish paper also made much of his physical deterioration and pointed out that all that sustained him toward the end "was the ardour of fanaticism."

The British press ran the gamut from temperate to extreme. The *Times* called Childers "a good man gone wrong" and felt that the Free State authorities had no choice but to do what they did: "In renouncing his own country Childers took his life in his hands, and with a personal courage beyond cavil faced the consequences of his action. He challenged the only constituted authority in his adopted country, and has met his doom. . . The Free State Government have made their choice with a courage certainly not inferior to that of their adversaries and with a responsibility far greater."

Some of the reporting was less sober. The *Daily Sketch* played up the mystery, and the influence of Molly: "With Childers passes, if not one of the most remarkable, certainly one of the most mysterious figures in Irish political history." His birth, education and distinguished career in British service did nothing "to predispose him toward any rebel cause." Nevertheless, "he became one of the most embittered of all Sinn Feiners. Why he should have done so is a mystery, but many have attributed it to the influence of his wife. . . Of her, an invalid, it has been written that she espoused the Irish cause in much the same way as one might take up Spiritualism."

236

"SOLDIER, WRITER AND TRAITOR" the *Morning Post* cried, and fell back on the old Imperial position: "He is only one of many thousands of victims that have had to be sacrificed in order to prove to the Irish that they are unfit to govern themselves, that only stark force will ever reduce their country to prosperous and peaceful conditions."

Several London papers touched on the theory that he was in fact a British secret agent, and one hauled out the old canard about the British official at Dublin Castle carrying his suitcase for him when, in 1921, he was released after what must have been a false arrest. The non-politically-biased *Referee* made a decent attempt at impartiality in a lead editorial: "Many will regret the necessity of his execution; few will be found to dispute it. It is most sad that such a life, once so full of promise, should have had such an end."

In the United States a sense of horror predominated. The *Boston Post* called the execution a "tragic blunder". The London correspondent of the New York *Tribune* foresaw that the death of De Valera's right hand man might lead to "a new and even darker chapter in Irish history." The *Nation* (on December 6, 1922) captioned their article "The Free State Gone Mad", and denied that the execution was necessary: "It seems as if the new Irish Free State government in taking over Dublin Castle took over the spirit as well of the men who occupied it for so many centuries."

There were bitter scenes in the Dail, Gavan Duffy, Childers' old ally of treaty-making days, could not believe that the Government could shoot a man while his appeal was pending, particularly since he was "one of the noblest men I have ever known. . . . a great Irishman in fact and in law." The next day he resumed the attack, saying that it was neither law nor justice "to try a man for one thing and execute him for another."

Defending the Government's action, O'Higgins made one of his tigerish statements. Childers, the Englishman, had come to Ireland "on the last emotional wave." The country, O'Higgins said, was entitled "to act on its own intuitions of

237

self-preservation," and the Government "will see that any people coming in here for adventure will get it."

(O'Higgins himself was fated to die by an assasins' bullet less than five years later. He was gunned down on his way home from church, and his killers were never apprehended.)

Very soon, Molly Childers took up Childers' work of propaganda for the waning Republican cause. Sean O'Faolain, who at 23 became one of her assistants, remembers her drive and her fierce courage. "A madonna with a bomb" is the way he described her when I interviewed him 52 years later. He respected her, and feared her too. Looking back, the celebrated Irish novelist and short story writer said she was "something more than human and less than human." He remembered how she put fresh flowers under Childers' photograph every morning—and the way she "gored" him, as he had never been gored before, when his copy was late.

On May 24, 1923, Eamon de Valera issued a pronouncement telling the exhausted Irregulars to "cease fire" and "dump arms". For a long time it had been obvious that the unequal contest was drawing to a close. Now a semblance of peace came at last, although for months there was a good deal of lawlessness.

That December, Molly Childers arranged for a service in Dublin in memory of Erskine and the four young Irregulars who were shot, just before he was, for the same crime of carrying arms. In the program, she linked her husband "in loving comradeship" with these first victims, who "died forgiving their slayers." The Irish band opened with a march called "Cavalry of the Clouds." Mr. James Rawle, a bass, sang "Messmates o' Mine"; there was a selection from *The Gondoliers*, and Miss Mary Morissey, a soprano, sang "The Battle Hymn of the Republic."

In April, 1931, Molly contributed an introduction to a new edition of *The Riddle of the Sands*. It shows how fully she had now become the spokesman for her husband. Her theme, in a

238

few short paragraphs, is that Childers, once the strong advocate of preparedness as the best preventive to war had later swung far away from that concept:

"His profound study of military history, of politics, and of the Great War convinced him that preparedness induced war,. . . led to international armament rivalries and bred in the minds of the nations concerned fears, antagonisms, and ambitions, that were destructive to peace. Whatever the views held by readers upon this question, the book remains the cherished companion of those who love the sea and who put forth in great or small sailing ships in search of adventure and the magical contentment to be won by strenuous endeavour."

Molly often spoke of Childers as being still with her, as indeed he was. "I love working side by side with my husband", she told Helen Richardson, an American cousin, in 1954.

Her gift for friendship, and that outgoing quality of endless interest in others, flourished even though she was always in pain and often in bed. Joan Comstock, who saw her often when she visited in America, remembers her lying under a scarlet coverlet, with several radios and a tray of sharpened pencils ready to hand. There was no aura of the sickroom about her ever, nor any trace of self-pity. "You've come!" she would exclaim to Mrs. Comstock. "Now tell me. . . ."

Molly's mother, Mrs. Osgood, lived with her at Bushy Park Road until her death in 1934. With Molly's help, Mrs. Osgood published a fine anthology of religious and philosophical poetry, put out in London by Jonathan Cape. In it there is a translation from a Latin prayer, *Veni Sancte Spiritu,* by Erskine Childers which is like a clear echo of the man himself:

> "Cleanse what is sordid,
> Water what is arid,
> Bend what is rigid,
> Warm what is cold,
> Guide what is straying,

239

> Give to Thy Faithful,
> Trusting in Thee,
> The sacred Seven-fold Gifts."

Molly, who was loved for her fierce sense of commitment as well as feared, took great pride in her two sons. To Robert Alden Childers, her second son, the fierceness was really a form of passionate protectiveness for all she most cared about (although he remembers ruefully that she beat him harder than his father ever did).

Robert had a successful career in the business and labor-relations end of newspaper publishing, retiring as a Director and Vice President of the London *Daily Mail*. From 1939–1945 he served in the Irish Army, for much of the time as adjutant and aide to General McKenna, the Chief of Staff in a time of anxious neutrality.

Erskine Hamilton Childers, the older son, spent most of his life in politics. He was a member of the Dail for 35 years, and held many Cabinet posts. He was the ablest Minister of Health that Eire has had, and was also Deputy Prime Minister. In 1973, at the age of 68, he was elected President, defeating Tom O'Higgins, the nephew of the man who hunted down his father, by 636,167 votes to 587,577. He died in office on November 17, 1974.

During his mother's lifetime he had already become Minister of Transport and Power, with his gifts of administration and his political flair already firmly established. Like his grandfather the lexicographer and his father before him, he had enormous powers of concentration.

Molly Childers died on January 1, 1964, 61 years almost to the day from the date of her marriage. In a special story cabled from Dublin, the *New York Times* gave a full account of her role in the search for Irish freedom and added that "many political writers of the time agreed that the real power behind the De Valera revolutionary movement was Erskine Childers and that the power behind Mr. Childers was his wife."

240

Helen Landreth's privately-printed memoir, *The Mind and Heart of Mary Childers (1965)* catches the essence of her personality in warmer terms. Commenting on the *Times* obituary, Landreth writes: "The impression it gives is distorted to that of an almost sinister propagandist, exerting her charm and intelligence with ruthless determination. . . . She was predominantly a creature of love and good will. In her presence, in her letters, the quality of perfect love is always there, warming and blessing."

Above else, in those long years in Dublin and later at Glan, her pride was in the recognition of Erskine Childers, and the way it grew and spread. For death had over Childers but brief dominion. Within less than two years his body was removed from Beggar's Bush, where it had been hastily buried, and laid to final rest at Glasnevin Cemetery among Ireland's heroes.

We have seen how, as early as 1929, Winston Churchill reversed himself by his tribute in *The Aftermath*.

In 1936, Frank Pakenham, later the Earl of Longford, published his definitive study of the Tready-making, *Peace by Ordeal*. Because the book quickly became and has remained the standard work on the subject, the author's comment on Childers is significant:

"The figure of Erskine Childers seems certain to stand out always more clearly as we move onward. . . . For, with all his wanderings, his was a continuing journey, governed by no passing influences, guided by no ephemeral ends. He lived and labored and fought and died, under the shadow of the eternal."

In *The King's Grace,* John Buchan's biography of George V, written for The King's Jubilee in 1935, the writer-statesman refers to Childers as a man "than whom no revolution ever produced a nobler or purer spirit," an encomium Childers himself would have liked, coming from someone he had read and admired.

Enduring Irish respect and appreciation were more un-

241

even, for it took a long time for the fires of the early 1920s to burn low. Eamon de Valera, who became Prime Minister in 1932 and was in office for many years, never failed to record his affection and admiration. As President of Ireland, and as family friend, he was the chief mourner at Molly's funeral.

When in 1967, *Asgard* was declared a national shrine at a colorful ceremony, De Valera presided and found the words to celebrate both the occasion and the man.

Although Robert Barton, who died in 1975 at the age of 93, never did write his own autobiography, he talked often about Erskine Childers and helped to keep his memory green. To him the request by Childers to the execution squad to move closer was an act of reconciliation and reassurance. It was, he felt, the noble essence of his cousin and dearest friend.

The last word belongs to Basil Williams, who knew Childers longer and better than any friend outside the family:

"We may think him wrong-headed and a fanatic, we may think of him as 'nourished on dreams', to quote a phrase of his own. . ., but of one thing all those who knew him well are convinced, that there was no particle of meanness or treachery in his nature; and that whatever course of action he adopted—however we may deplore the judgment—it was based on the prompting of a conscience and sense of honour as sensitive and true as one may meet. He is at rest now, that eager, loving soul, but the love he inspired remains as an abiding treasure to those he loved."

Erskine Childers' life is the story of a man who went too far. Because of his mixed heritage and blood, he felt that some excess of zeal was necessary. This zeal of the convert manifested itself most particularly in his obsession with the Irish Republic, and the oath to the Republic.

In a religious sense, the convert is someone who tends to put great store by the ritual of the faith he espouses, a matter which the average worshipper performs almost by rote. Childers, who was neither a practising Protestant nor, as is

242

sometimes suggested, a near-convert to Catholicism, made Republicanism his cult and his religion.

The tragedy is that there was so much that was gifted and good in him before the stubborn streak and the iron self-reliance froze into fanaticism.

Erskine Hamilton Childers, the political son, never could face his father's failure. His emotional involvement was so great that the facts and the hallowed memory could never be aligned. Robert Alden Childers, younger, less involved at the time of the execution, came to the conclusion some time ago that his father was mistaken in his uncompromising stand on the Treaty. He also feels that Erskine Childers, senior, was, in his quiet and self-contained way, an adventurer who sought the bright face of danger all his life.

There is no riddle of Erskine Childers. The final mystery is that there is no mystery, For he was neither a devious nor a complicated man. The legends that have swirled about his name arose because his simplicity, his directness, taxed belief. In one of those last letters to Molly from his cell, he wrote, "I die loving England and passionately praying that she may change completely and finally towards Ireland." He meant exactly that, although many people cite it to prove that he was a British spy all along, or at least that he was bewilderingly double-faced.

To a man of his self-reliance, each step of his seemingly-contradictory course was absolutely logical. "No one dies for Home Rule," he wrote Alfred Ollivant in 1919, when he saw that the Dominion plan was doomed. "Freedom is the thing men die for, and it is not a thing that can be disguised under phrases or whittled by imagination."

Could anything be clearer? Each phase was totally absorbing, and the earlier commitment sealed-up and forgotten, with no backward glance.

Gretchen Warren is said to have accused her sister Molly of driving Childers to his death. But this Molly did not do. He had already gone far beyond her in his lonely convert's zeal.

243

For reasons of her own, she tore up many of the letters which he wrote during those last months before his capture—letters which showed how extreme he had become. There is no question but that Molly was strong, but she also recognized the steel that was in Erskine, the iron string he vibrated to. She was loyal unto death, and beyond. But he made his own decisions.

Did he seek his own death? The whole matter of carrying around that little, almost useless automatic makes us wonder. In one of those last letters, to Molly, he speaks of his execution as being "best for us and for Ireland". Strange words indeed! He certainly went half-way to meet a death that was an end to ill-health and failure. His words still rang clear and true now, but the "spoonbowl metal was old and worn", the sword had almost outworn the sheath.

Molly accepted his harsh fate as a gift, and this too sounds strange. But it was a gift that put his whole life in a gallant, a memorable frame.

How wrong was he in his fanatical Republicanism? He was about as wrong as a man and parliamentarian can be. In 1926 the leader he influenced so profoundly reversed himself: Eamon de Valera discovered that the oath to the King was not such a terrible thing after all. He took it, founded the Fianna Fail party and went on to contest the next national election.

By 1949 Ireland had peacefully and tranquilly left the British Commonwealth of Nations and become a full Republic. The pro-Treaty moderates had been right, and Ireland had the full loaf at last.

So, in Erskine Childers there was this one great, tragic flaw. Because of it he failed, and seemed to be quite willing to pull Ireland down with him. But he paid his debt for failing with such courage that the failure became a kind of triumph.

Acknowledgments

The late Joan Comstock encouraged the author to embark on this biography nine years ago, and recreated Molly Childers as she knew her in her later years. The late Sir John Wheeler-Bennett encouraged me in many ways, believing an uninvolved American best suited to unravel the controversial Childers story.

Sir Frank Cooper, Permanent Under Secretary in the British Ministry of Defense, briefed the author on Ulster yesterday and today. Barbara Tuchman and Barbara de Keller have given the project welcome support.

Members and relatives of the Childers family have answered many questions. These include Robert and Christabel Childers of Glendalough House, the late Robert Barton, and Diana Childers Stewart. Margaret Pearmain Welch, a favorite cousin of Molly Childers, was particularly helpful over the Boston chapter and connections. Ruth Ballard gave useful glimpses of the Fiske Warrens and of Harvard, Massachusetts.

My thanks for interest and help also go to: Father F.X. Martin, O.S.A., of University College, Dublin; Sean O'Faolain (for verbal sketches of Erskine and Molly Childers, and other insights); and His Excellency John Molloy, the present Irish Ambassador in Washington. The late William Fay, Irish Ambassador to the United States in the 1960s, drew on his wide learning for me, and imparted his enthusiasm.

Breandan MacGiolla Choille, Keeper of the State Papers in Dublin, broke out many documents I could not have uncovered alone. Frank Corr and Miss Byrne of his staff also helped most competently in the quest. Oliver Snoddy of the National Museum in Dublin gave of his time and knowledge of recent Irish history.

245

My witness who had been a member of the Beggar's Bush firing squad particularly requested that his identity not be revealed. "Memories are long in Ireland," he said.

In London, F.J. Willis of the Imperial War Museum, A.F. Lambert of the Public Record Office, and F. Bailey of the Ministry of Defence Naval Library could not have been more professionally helpful.

In County Waterford, Robert and Phyllis Lee, Eo Merrill and the late Frederick Merrill, and Phyllis Mitchell made the author feel at home on location. In Washington Louise Dickey Davison, Deborah Groberg and Julia Kelly Brown did skillful research, and gave editorial assistance.

Courts Oulahan let me study his vivid and useful book on Michael Collins, now in preparation. Michael McInerney of the *Irish Times* allowed me to reproduce photographs from *The Riddle of Erskine Childers*, which grew out of a profile of Childers written in 1970 on his centenary. The book itself was most useful as basic reference.

The principle works of Erskine Childers are:

In the Ranks of the C.I.V. London; Smith, Elder & Co., 1900.

The Riddle of the Sands. London: Smith, Elder & Co., 1903.

The H.A.C. in South Africa. London: Smith, Elder, & Co., 1903.

War and the Arme Blanche. London: Edward Arnold, 1910.

German Influence on British Cavalry. London: Edward Arnold, 1911.

The Framework of Home Rule. London: Edward Arnold, 1911.

Military Rule in Ireland. Dublin: The Talbot Press Limited, 1920.

Bibliography

Aspinall-Oglander, Cecil. *Roger Keyes*. London: The Hogarth Press, 1951.

Beaslai, Pieras. *Michael Collins and the Making of a New Ireland*. Dublin: Phoenix Publishing Co., 1926.

Bell, J. Bowyer. *The Secret Army. A History of the I.R.A., 1916–1970*. London: Anthony Blond, Ltd., 1970.

Bowle, John. *The Imperial Achievement*. Boston: Little, Brown and Company, 1975.

Brennan, Robert. *Allegiance*. Dublin: Browne & Nolan, Ltd., 1950.

Carr, W.G. *Brass Hats and Bell-Bottomed Trousers*. London: Constable & Co., Ltd., 1933.

Churchill, Winston, *The Aftermath*. London: The Macmillan Company, 1929.

Colum, Padraic. *Ourselves Alone: A Biography of Arthur Griffith*. New York: Crown Publishers, Inc., 1959.

Cox, Tom. *Damned Englishman*. Hicksville: Exposition Press, Inc., 1975.

Dangerfield, George. *The Strange Death of Liberal England, 1910–1914*. London: MacGibbon & Kee, Ltd., 1966 (re-issue).

Davis, Richard P. *Arthur Griffith and Non-Violent Sinn Fein*. Dublin: Anvil Books, 1974.

Farwell, Byron. *The Great Anglo-Boer War*. New York: Harper & Row, 1976.

Figgis, Darrell. *Recollections of the Irish War*. London: Ernest Benn, Ltd., 1927.

Gallagher, Frank. *The Four Glorious Years*. Dublin: Irish Press Publishers, 1953.

Hassall, Christopher. *A Biography of Edward Marsh*. New York: Harcourt, Brace and Company, 1959.

247

Holmes-Pollock Letters (2 vols.). *The Correspondence of Mr. Justice Holmes and Sir Frederick Pollock (1874–1932)*. Boston: The Harvard University Press, 1941.

Keyes, Admiral Lord. *The Naval Memoirs of Admiral of the Fleet Sir Roger Keyes, 1910–1915*. London: Thornton Butterworth, 1934.

Killen, John. *A History of Marine Aviation, 1911–68*. London: Frederick Miller. ND.

Lazenby, Elizabeth. *Ireland—A Catspaw*. New York: Charter Publishing Co.,

Leslie, Shane. *Long Shadows*. London: John Murray, 1966.

Longford, the Earl of and O'Neill, Thomas P. *Eamon De Valera*. Dublin: Gill and MacMillan (in association with Hutchinson of London), 1970.

Macardle, Dorothy. *The Irish Republic*. New York: Farrar, Straus & Giroux, 1965. (Revised from British edition, first published in 1937).

Marsh, Sir Edward. *A Number of People. A Book of Reminiscences*. London: William Heinemann, Ltd. (in association with Hamish Hamilton).

Martin, F.X., O.S.A. *The Howth Gun-Running*. Dublin: Browne & Nolan, Ltd., 1964.

McDowell, R.B. *The Irish Convention (1917–18)*. Toronto: University of Toronto Press, 1970.

McInerney, Michael. *The Riddle of Erskine Childers*. Dublin: E. & T. O'Brien, 1971.

Nicolson, Harold. *King George V, The Life and Reign*. London: Constable & Co., Ltd., 1952.

Nicholson, Harold, *Peacemaking, 1919*, London: Constable & Co., Ltd.

O'Connor, Frank. *An Only Child*. London: MacMillan & Co., Ltd., 1961.

O'Connor, Frank. *The Big Fellow—Michael Collins and the Irish Revolution*. Dublin: Clonmore & Reynolds, Ltd., 1965.

O'Faolain, Sean. *Vive Moi!* Boston: Little Brown & Co., 1964.

Pakenham, Frank (later Lord Longford). *Peace by Ordeal*. London: Geoffrey Chapman, 1962 (re-issue).

Ryan, Desmond. *Remembering Sion*. London: Arthur Barker, Ltd., 1934.

Shephard, Gordon. *Memoirs of Brigadier General Gordon Shephard, DSO, MC.* Edited by Shane Leslie. Privately printed, 1924.

Stevenson, Frances (Countess Lloyd George). *Lloyd George, A Diary.* Edited by A.J.P. Taylor. New York: Harper & Row, 1971.

Ussher, Arland. *The Face and Mind of Ireland.* New York: The Devin-Adair Company, 1950.

Vansittart, Lord. *The Mist Procession.* Hutchinson of London, 1958.

White, Terence deVere. *Kevin O'Higgins.* London: Methuen & Co., 1948.

Woollard, Claude L.A., Commander, RN. *With the Harwich Naval Forces, 1914-1918,* Antwerp: G. Kohler, 1931.

Younger, Calton. *Ireland's Civil War.* New York: Taplinger Publishing Co., 1969.

Magazine articles, newspaper features, privately-printed memoirs and official publications that served as source material include:

Bailey, Anthony. "Profiles—Son and Father." *The New Yorker,* Jan. 27, 1975.

Barton, Rachel. "My Memories of Aunt Molly Childers." *Privately printed. ND.*

Béraud, Henry. "Erskine Childers." *The Living Age,* Mar. 3, 1923.

Clarke, I.F. "The Shape of Wars to Come." *History Today,* Feb., 1965.

Landreth, Helen. "The Mind and Heart of Mary Childers." Privately printed. 1965.

McInerney, Michael. "You will be Hanged from a Lamp-post in Dublin." *The Irish Times,* 12 Aug., 1975.

McKenna, Kathleen. "In London with the Treaty Delegates." *The Capuchin Annual,* 1971.

McKenna, Kathleen. "The Irish Bulletin." *The Capuchin Annual,* 1970.

Ollivant, Alfred. "The Shears of Destiny." *The Atlantic Monthly,* Feb., 1923.

Scott-James, R.A. "Erskine Childers." *The Nineteenth Century,* Jan., 1923.

Welch, Margaret Pearmain. "One Girl's Boston." Privately printed. ND.

Young, John N. "The Death of Erskine Childers." *The Sunday Press* (Ireland), Nov. 19, 1972.

(Also, unsigned; "The Free State Gone Mad." *The Nation,* Dec. 6, 1922.)

"Home Waters," from the Naval Staff Monographs (Vol. XII, Part III). Monograph No. 28 printed by the Director of Training, Admiralty in May, 1925, covers actions from November, 1914 through January, 1915.

The State Papers in Dublin Castle, with supporting documentation, were used extensively, particularly for the period of October-November, 1922.

Index

251

253